# KNOW YOURSELF, LOVE YOURSELF, EXPRESS YOURSELF

an inspiring guide for intentional living

## SHAHAN SHAMMAS

WORTHWHILE PUBLICATIONS

ISBN-13: 9780966202830

Printed in the United States of America

*To my wife Barbara, and my daughters Olivia and Emily, and their husbands Ben and Antony. To our grandchildren Dylan and Chloe. To anyone ready to know, love and express themselves.*

# CONTENTS

Title Page

Copyright

Dedication

Introduction     1

Part I     7

A Guide for Living     8

Does Life Have a Purpose?     19

Why Are We Born, Live and Die?     30

We Are in a Theater     38

We Are on a Journey     42

We Are a Work in Progress     47

We Are Not Perfect     49

We Are Connected     58

The Nature of Earthly Experiences     66

Part II     73

Levels of Knowing     74

Trinity     82

We Are a Trinity     89

The Physical     95

The Astral     106

The Spiritual     125

I Am   140

Knowing Our Source   143

We Are in the Image of Our Source   149

We Have Three Names   153

The Three Names of God   162

How Can We Know for Certain?   173

Part III   179

Concepts of Self   180

Accept Yourself   189

Forgive Yourself   195

Love Yourself   202

Love Others   207

The Nature of Love   211

The Quest for Happiness   217

Part IV   221

Be Prepared, Always   222

Be Fearless   226

Highlight Your Uniqueness   230

Sharpen Your Toolset   235

Express Yourself   248

Part V   255

The Secret of Christianity   256

Secret of the Mustard Seed   275

Secret of Prayer   280

Secret of Sleep and Dreams   290

Secret of the Breath   297

Secret of the Alchemists   301

Secret of the Millennium   305

Conclusion                                             309

Acknowledgement                                        315

About The Author                                       317

Books By This Author                                   319

Books By This Author                                   321

Books By This Author                                   323

# INTRODUCTION

Being human is not easy. Animals have it easier. They instinctively know how to live the moment they are born. They do not question the meaning of their existence. They do not wonder where they came from or where they will be going after they die. Animals know what to eat, where to sleep and how to fit in. They do not fuss over what to wear and what they look like. They live in harmony with nature.

Humans, on the other hand, are complicated. We have to figure out where to live, how to earn a living and pay our bills. We are prone to worry, can have sleep, emotional and psychological issues. If we get sick, we need a doctor; if we get sued, we need a lawyer. We can grow up normal or saddled with traumas. We can have comparatively easy lives or harsh ones. Yet, no human would prefer to be an animal. What we want is, not only to be human, but to also live happy, healthy and content lives. We want to have poise, confidence, be assertive, but not domineering. We want to be ourself, unafraid and spontaneous. We want to know how to deal with negativity, confront adversity, handle difficult situations, and feel good about ourself afterwards. However, for many these qualities are illusive and unattainable. Many are shy, lack confidence and feel victimized. Others are hesitant and gripped with fear. Why are we so different from one another? Is the answer environment, circumstance and inheritance or is there more to it?

Born in Aleppo, Syria to practically illiterate parents, in a staunchly traditional Christian community, my future looked bleak. What was certain was that I would go to school for a few years, but after that, there was only one option: to get a job and to survive. Serving in the Syrian military was obligatory. There was no escaping it. If I had served in the Syrian military, most likely, I would have been killed in one of the wars. Adults in industrial countries can have freedom of choice, but what choices do children have born and living in third-world countries? Hardly any. Unless something radically changed, I was not going to escape my fate; I was trapped. Tragically, my mother passed away at the age of 36 leaving behind 6 children. This was a wild card that forced drastic changes upon us. My father, unable to care for us, placed the three youngest in orphanages, asked the oldest to leave, kept my younger brother at home and gave me to the church to study and become a member of the clergy. Fortunately, the clergy are exempt from serving in the Syrian military.

I left Aleppo to go to Lebanon where I entered a monastery. It was there that I discovered I had freedom of choice. I could do what is expected of me, become a monk and serve the church or I could leave and pursue a life of my choosing. If I stayed, I must follow and obey. If I left, life would be uncertain, but I would be free to determine my own fate. As a youngster, I followed traditions and obeyed blindly. I had no personal power because I was not encouraged to think on my own. In the monastery, I felt free of my childhood trappings and began to think for myself for the first time.

After two years in the monastery, I quit and went to high school and through incredible fortune and against all odds, I went to and graduated from the American University of Beirut (AUB). Fortunately, my siblings and I were granted visas to immigrate to the US. Soon after, I joined the US Army and worked as an Electron Microscopist at Ft. Meade, MD and

Walter Reed Army Medical Center in Washington, DC.

For the first time in my life, I was independent. I was on my own, working and earning a living. I could decide what to do with my life. I began reading extensively, continuously educating myself and decided on a spiritual path.

Soon I realized that the vast majority of people do not exercise their freedom of choice in important matters. They simply follow the path of least resistance. In reality, not exercising freedom of choice is the same as not having any. Perhaps, as many as 90% of people fall into this category. They follow without questioning, pursue wealth and material goods as the most appropriate means to happiness. This is the road most travelled and its byways are well paved.

Then there are the truly spiritual. These people rarely need to exercise their freedom of choice since their choices are always known. They choose the good, the positive and the empowering. Perhaps, about 5% of people fall into this category. Christ would be the best example here. He never chose or needed to, for His actions were always for the good.

This leaves us with about 5% who actually use their freedom of choice. They reflect, think, evaluate, compare and contrast and then decide. They imagine, visualize, contemplate and listen to The Voice Within. They would be our innovators, philosophers, scientists, artists and engineers.

I am not the same person I was in Aleppo or Lebanon. I have been transformed and reborn into a new being. Even though each individual's path is unique, my transformation is based on continuous education, fearless questioning and regular introspection. I accept and am responsible for my thoughts, beliefs and decisions. Fortunately, we live in an age where, in many countries, knowledge is accessible, censorship and reprisals are at a minimum and opportunities are abundant to learn and to make wise decisions.

Reading books by audacious thinkers and committing to an active spiritual life helped open my eyes, heart and mind. I was no longer afraid to think freely. I refused to accept that I was born in sin or even that I was a sinner. In my heart, I knew that I was worthy. I did not require mediation between myself and God. Instead of accepting other people's interpretations of "scripture", I took it upon myself to study, think things through, analyze, question and investigate. I began to gain my personal power.

I joined an organization that emphasizes individuality and the unfoldment of spiritual values. Here, questioning is encouraged and the expression of personal insights is welcomed. The path I chose was the road less traveled. I was happy and content.

I concluded that what I needed to live a full, valuable and productive life was an excellent education, mental tools and techniques, and an understanding of my true nature. With these I could chart my own course to a future of my choosing.

I started examining my beliefs carefully before I accepted them and then lived accordingly. I was no longer fooled by source, authority or title. I questioned, reflected, listened to my intuition and The Voice Within. Only by their teachings did I distinguish one system from another. Those that empowered me, I nurtured and those that took away my power, I shunned.

Everyone must make their own bed to sleep in. We are responsible for our actions and the results we experience. Where we end up on the ladder of life is mostly up to us. The quality of our life is in our hands. If our lives are not what we want them to be, we can change them. We must acquire the proper knowledge and take the necessary actions to ensure the results we want.

Obviously, we are limited in how much we can do. We have

genes, heredity and environment to contend with. Yet, we are not powerless. We can influence our genes, compensate for our heredity and manipulate our environment. The more of an active role we take in our lives, the more we can shape our future.

Being proactive not only affects the quality of our life but it is also the intelligent way to live. By taking positive steps to redirect the course of our lives, we become empowered. Focusing on our positive attributes strengthens them. These attributes are fruit emanating from the tree of knowing **ourself.** We can live the life we want if we know ourself intimately, accept and love ourself unconditionally and express ourself fearlessly. Once we eat of the fruit of this tree, we will know peace, contentment and happiness. Knowing, loving and expressing ourselves is a worthwhile pursuit because once we do, we will live a content life and contribute our best to the advancement of humanity.

Each human being is a reflection of the Creative Cosmic Intelligence and deserves a life of high self-esteem, abundant confidence, and unshakeable personal power stemming from an intimate knowledge of self. Yet, no one can give us these attributes; this book points the way. Each individual must make their own choices, walk the path, and take the necessary steps. If it is to be, it is up to each of us to make it so. Once on the path of self-discovery, we can ask for help and guidance. We have a Higher Self ready and happy to assist us.

There are three simple steps to grow and blossom, to contribute to society and to live up to our potential:

1. First, we must know ourself intimately – our true self;
2. Next, we must accept and love ourself unconditionally;
3. Finally, we must express ourself fearlessly.

That's it, three simple but not easy steps. By knowing, loving and expressing ourself, we live up to our potential and we contribute to the well-being of others. These three steps are not separate. They are intertwined and must be considered together, for we cannot intimately know ourself without accepting and loving ourself. If we accept and love ourself, we will confidently and fearlessly express ourself. Even though the steps are three, they are in fact one and the same. If we focus on the first step and master it, then the other two will follow automatically.

# PART I

## The Nature of Life

1. A Guide for Living
2. Does Life have a Purpose?
3. Why Are We Born, Live and Die?
4. We Are in a Theater
5. We Are on a Journey
6. We Are A Work in Progress
7. We Are not Perfect
8. We Are Connected
9. The Nature of Earthly Experiences

# A GUIDE FOR LIVING

*Ideals are like stars; you will not succeed in touching them with your hands. But like the seafaring man on the desert of waters, you choose them as your guides, and following them you will reach your destiny.*
— *Carl Schurz*

When my job transferred from Ft. Meade, MD to Walter Reed Army Medical Center in Washington, DC., I discovered that they had a Standard Operating Procedure (SOP). This SOP, not only made my job easy, it also ensured consistency, one-stop shopping for operations and an easy way to update changes to procedures. It would have been nice if we were born with an SOP on what it means to be human, but we are not. What we need instead is a guide for living – what to expect as a human. The sooner we equip ourselves with this knowledge, the better prepared we will be to face our challenges, grow steadily and contribute our best. Our modus operandi is on the job training. We mostly learn through trial and error, but there is a better way – an SOP or a guide for living.

As homo sapiens, we share a great deal with our closest primates. Yet, we are a distinct species endowed with faculties that no other species has. Among them is freedom of choice. We can reason, compare and contrast, and then decide. This distinctive quality, freedom of choice is our most precious asset. It can diminish or it can enhance the quality of our lives.

Unlike animals who are born with an instinct to survive, we need help. We depend on our parents, not for a few months or a couple of years, but for many years. Even our parents are often at a loss as to how to best prepare their children for life. A basic guide for living with practical knowledge of how to face challenges, confront obstacles, and sail smoothly through life would be of enormous value.

What would be in this guide for living?

1. Basic facts about life such as what it means to be human, how the body changes over time, intricacies of relationships, what marriage entails, parenting and responsibilities of citizenship;
2. The nature of competition and the benefits of cooperation;
3. Facts about the body, mind, emotions, spirit and soul, and how to best care for them;
4. How to live a productive and purposeful life;
5. Examples of humanity's best and worst individuals, what to emulate, and what to shun;
6. What to expect in the various stages of our lives;
7. Mental tools and how to best use them.

This book is a rudimentary attempt to contribute toward such a goal. It explains what living is about. It provides a basic understanding of the purpose of life. It describes why difficulties are an important part of life, what we can learn from them and how to manage them.

## *On Being Human*

Now that we are born as a human, what is in store for us? Obviously, each person will have a unique set of experiences. Yet, there is a lot we have in common.

## A. Challenges

1. Living is not meant to be easy. Challenges, obstacles and difficulties are a normal aspect of the human experience. It is how we learn and grow and should be viewed as the tests and trials that we must face. They are opportunities to learn from, to contribute and to demonstrate mastery. This does not excuse abuse. Those who have been abused must seek professional help, learn to release and determine to succeed in spite of the abuse. The world is not perfect. There are many sick, traumatized and immature people who are violent and abusive. It is important that each succeeding generation has less violence, abuse and neglect. We must be agents of change and contribute to progress.

2. We will know ability and disability. At times, we will feel invincible and at other times, we won't be able to do the simplest of things. When we are sick and incapacitated, we are at our low point. When we are healthy and vibrant, we are at our peak. Mostly, we are in between. Because we get sick, we must value our health and do what we can to stay healthy as long as possible.

3. We should expect ups and downs in our lives. It should not be a surprise when we experience them. Pain, suffering, pleasure, joy, triumph and defeat are a normal part of life. During the course of living, we will know exhilaration and disappointment. We will be healthy and we will be sick. We will live normal lives and we will have exceptional moments. Accidents, unexpected outcomes and highs and lows are in our future. We should accept this and be

prepared. What we cannot control, we must learn to deal with. Whenever we can, we should prevent and lessen the frequency and duration of negative events.

4. Learning to manage time, fame and wealth are among our greatest challenges.

5. Resisting change is futile. By welcoming change, we can take advantage of new opportunities. Over time, we can adapt to any environment.

## B. Relationships

1. Relationships are vital, yet they are difficult because each individual is in their own world. Moving out of our comfort zone is not easy, yet it is necessary if we want to shed our skin and grow. It requires intention and takes effort. Intimate relationships are vital for our wellbeing. The more touch, affection and love we experience, the healthier we are. Improving our ability to relate is a worthwhile endeavor. It starts when we stop being selfish, focused only on ourselves.

2. It is inevitable that we will make mistakes. Most mistakes are minor with temporary consequences. A few are major with lasting impact. While some learn from one mistake, others require several repetitions before they learn. If the mistake is against another, we should apologize and remedy the situation. If the mistake is against us, we forgive. We can be more tolerant of each other's foibles. We all have our shortcomings.

3. Each of us has a unique world view. We create a comfort zone and abide in it like a cocoon. This makes us feel safe. It is normal to measure others by our own standards. We tend to judge others to be like

us when they are not. Some are more sensitive than others. Some are more compassionate than others. Some are good listeners while others will not hear a word. Some are naïve, others are sophisticated. Some are childish, others are mature. Each is in a different class in the school of life.

4. Except for babies and some children, no one is perfect. Imperfections make us human. Yet, we should strive to be the best version of ourselves. We have strengths and weaknesses. We have vices and virtues. We always have something we can work on and improve. We are on Earth in a physical body to experience, learn, improve and contribute. Each of us has issues to deal with. Hopefully, as we learn and improve, these will be fewer and fewer.

5. We are never fully independent. As members of a society, we have rights, freedoms and responsibilities. Depending on others for our necessities keeps us connected. We are a community. By cultivating strong relationships, we stay healthy, vibrant and everyone benefits.

6. We do not live only for ourselves. Whatever we do impacts those to whom we are connected – parents, siblings, spouse, children, friends and acquaintances, even our communities, country and the world. Remembering this, we should act responsibly.

## C. Decisions

1. We must decide what makes us happy – the simple pleasures of life or the more complex. We can demand a great deal to be satisfied, or we can savor the little that is afforded us. We can train ourselves to be content with the simple pleasures of life. Most

importantly, we must be thankful for all that we currently have.

2. We have the ability to sculpt ourselves into what we choose within limitations. We can define, shape and live the way we see fit. We are on a journey of becoming. This can be random or directed through intention and the choices we make. Our lives are ours to do with as we see fit. Accepting responsibility for our lives is a sign of maturity. It is up to us to direct our course to a future of our own choosing.

3. It is more important for our life to have meaning than for life in general to be meaningful. Deciding on a purpose for our life makes it easier to deal with adversity. It helps us make the most of our allotted time instead of wasting it on trivia. Life does not have to have a meaning, but our life must. We do not have to accept others interpretations of what life is about. We can formulate our own philosophy of life.

4. We are susceptible to influence and prone to mimic. It is how we learn as children. This can be a strength or a weakness. It is best to imitate the ones we want to emulate and avoid the ones with negative inclinations.

5. Our freedom of choice is influenced by our subconscious mind based on the experiences we have had and the memories we have formed. Most of what goes into our subconscious is beyond our awareness. Living in a society, we cannot help but be influenced by others. We observe and we imitate. Periodically, we should examine our thoughts, beliefs and expectations.

6. We can learn from our failures and from our successes. Even better, we can learn from others

successes and failures. We can progressively get better, make fewer mistakes and be happier. We can be happy by being content and thankful. We can be grateful and continue to improve. We can be satisfied and reach for more knowledge, understanding, intimacy and love.

7. Our experiences are what we make of them. We can ignore them or learn from them. Two individuals sharing the same experience can have completely different interpretations. Our education, culture and the expectations we have play a major role in how we view events. We should examine what we read or hear before we accept them as true.

## D. Our Nature

1. Our origin is the female egg and the male sperm. We are the synthesis of male and female qualities. Our guides are the brain and the heart. Our brains have two hemispheres, left and right. Some favor one aspect over the other. Some become artists while others end up as scientists. Some predominantly use reason, others intuition. The left and right hemisphere attributes are complementary and must work together. It is joyless to be all brain and no heart. Similarly, it is ineffective to be all heart and no brains. We must employ reason and intuition, gentleness and firmness, justice and compassion, male and female qualities. Femininity and masculinity are complementary and must coexist in the same individual, be integrated and expressed appropriately.

Sex is biological. Femininity and masculinity are cultural. We are often indoctrinated as to what our genders mean. Since we started life from the joining of the sperm with the egg, we have both qualities within us to varying degrees. We are both masculine and feminine. We must integrate these qualities and master their appropriate use.

2. We are born into a culture. This culture has a great influence on who and what we become. We inherit our language, religion, customs and traditions including biases. We are born into a country that has its own ethos. We go to school, make friends, get an education and start a career. We are more bound by our culture than we realize. This is a double-edged sword. It can be an advantage or a hindrance. We can adopt the beneficial aspects and let go of the rest.

3. Some of our traits are the result of forces beyond our control – genes and heredity. Even the microbes that dwell within us influence our moods and how we feel and act. Yet, through awareness and intelligent action, we can have the upper hand. We can adjust our environment, manage our microbes by eating healthy real (unprocessed) food and we can use intention to influence our genes.

4. We are the only species with art, science, religion, philosophy, politics, judicial systems and governments. We are the only species that makes an art of cooking, merriment and traveling. We are the only species with rituals for birth, marriage and death. We are the only species that laughs heartily, seeks a purpose for living and a meaning to existence. We chronicle our progress through artistic creations and scientific discoveries. Let us celebrate our uniqueness by taking full advantage of what sets us apart as a species.

## E. Circumstances

1. Some are born into fortunate circumstances while the majority are not. Some are born into well-to-do families while many are born into poverty. Some are welcomed with joy and celebration into families ready to receive and nurture them. Others are born to single parents who find raising a child challenging. Many are born into poverty, neglect and abuse. While many have normal childhoods, others endure traumas and hardships. Some face challenges early in life, while others confront them later on. Some are born in industrialized nations while others are born in third-world countries. Some inherit fortunes while most must earn their keep. Each is an occasion to face unique personal opportunities and challenges. These are the tests and trials we need to find out how we will deal with them. How we handle our challenges and opportunities determines our future.

What connects us is our humanity. Foremost, we are human beings before we are Christians, Jews, Moslems, Hindus or even black, white, male or female. Just as we have common features shared by all, we have distinctive qualities that set us apart from each other. Many identify with what sets them apart. "I am an American female of Italian descent." "I am a 43-year-old doctor living in Philadelphia." We should also appreciate what we all share which is far more than that which sets us apart.

2. Uncertainty is the norm. We will oscillate between fortune and misfortune, health and disease, pain

and pleasure. By detaching, observing, reflecting and living in the now, we can make the most of what is at hand. Sunshine and storm are both necessary and are in our future.

3. Unlike animals, instinct plays a minor role in our lives. We are born to experiment, discover, learn and improve. Intuition, on the other hand, is an important asset to cultivate.

4. Under certain conditions, we can easily lose our humanity. Placing someone in a unique environment such as the military and by giving them a uniform and authority, can drastically alter their personality. Torturing and inflicting unimaginable pain and suffering on fellow humans becomes acceptable. We should be aware of these circumstances and avoid them.

5. We are surrounded by mysteries. Our entry onto the stage of life is mysterious. So is our exit. We have a role to play and a contribution to make. We can use our passions and synchronicities to guide our way.

6. Our days are numbered and our lives are unpredictable. Because life is short, we should be patient, compassionate, and forgiving with each other. We should value each day as a precious gift.

7. There are only a handful of circumstances when we reflect on our mortality such as during a funeral, fatal accidents or calamities. Yet, death is a fact of life. It is our lifelong companion. Ignoring it, we live as if we are physically immortal. Death and dying are not part of our education system. We are never adequately prepared for them. We react to them with surprise as if they are not normal and a necessary part of the human experience. Yet, death

is our constant companion. We need to accept our mortality and live as if we could die today. Accepting that we could die at any moment should compel us to make the most of our short stay. Similarly, a loved one could depart unexpectedly. We should cherish each other while we can. Instead of heaping praise on the deceased in eulogies, let us offer it to them while they are alive.

# DOES LIFE HAVE A PURPOSE?

*You are not here merely to make a living. You are here in order to enable the world to live more amply, with greater vision, with a finer spirit of hope and achievement. You are here to enrich the world, and you impoverish yourself if you forget the errand.   – Woodrow Wilson*

I f life were a game, then learning the rules and winning would be the purpose of life.
If life were a stage, then rendering our best performance would be the purpose of life.
If life were a journey, then arriving at our destination safely and enjoying the process would be the purpose of life.

Life is a game in that we should not take it too seriously.
Life is a stage in that each of us is an actor with a role to play.
Life is a journey with a destination. However, there are numerous ways to get there.

At first glance, the immediate, external and obvious purpose of life is survival and propagation. We have an inner urge to survive and to propagate, yet we do not know for what purpose. To survive and to propagate is ingrained in all life forms. There must be a reason why this is in our genes. It is easy to understand why survival is essential, but why the urge to procreate?

Life is not stationary; neither are our lives. We are on a journey of becoming. We began as a single fertilized egg just as life on Earth began as a single-celled microorganism. Everything evolved. We are not done yet. Our growth and maturation continues. To ask, "what is the purpose of a newborn?" is meaningless. We must wait until the newborn is fully grown and mature. So it is with the purpose of life and the meaning of our existence.

We do not know the ultimate end of the progression of life on Earth. We can only surmise what humanity will become and be able to accomplish once fully mature. What we do know is that we can direct the course of our life and assign a meaning to our existence. We can decide on a purpose for our lives and thus render it meaningful.

There are three options as to how we view the meaning of our existence:

1. We are here by pure chance. Our existence is a random, meaningless occurrence;
2. We were created and placed here by design;
3. We are here by choice. Our existence is purposeful.

Science postulates that we are the result of random forces of nature. We have evolved based on natural selection and survival of the fittest. Religion contends that we were created by God, placed here to toil and gain our redemption. Even though these two options are the prevailing beliefs of the majority of people, the third option is the only one consistent with having freedom of choice. If we have freedom of choice, which we do, then we cannot be here against our will or the result of random forces.

Is it possible that we are here because we chose to be here?
Is it possible that prior to our birth, we decided to be born and undergo our earthly experiences, but forgot this soon after we were born?
Is it possible that we are the major players in determining our fate?

In our hearts we know that our lives are not random and meaningless. At our core we know that we matter and that our experiences amount to something. We know that we are progressing toward something, perhaps a full awakening, maturity and enlightenment. Intuitively, we know that we are more than a body, that we have a soul and that death is not the end of it all.

There is no denying that natural selection and survival of the fittest played major roles in our evolution. That is true of our physical bodies. We, however, are more than physical bodies. We have a spirit and a soul within us that is the core of our humanity. Without these, we are mere beasts.

The answer to the mystery of our existence is obvious. All we need to do is to shed our blinders, open our eyes and see clearly. Life is eternal. Existence is cyclic. Value and meaning are at the core of existence. Why else would we crave to make a meaningful contribution, to relate, to belong, to be accepted, loved and valued?

The purpose of life is not the pursuit of pleasure. Pleasures are temporary, impossible to hold onto for long and require constant effort. The purpose of life is not the accumulation of riches. Wealth does not guarantee happiness or mean much once we have enough to live a comfortable life. In fact, it is meaningless to accumulate and hoard. This is because our lives are unpredictable. We could die at any moment. The purpose of life is not comfort, for we cannot escape pain and suffering. Pain, suffering and misery will find us wherever we are.

The purpose of life is not simply to enjoy ourselves, be merry, or even be successful. If it was, those who have them would be fulfilled and content. They are not. They know there is more to life. They too seek value and meaning. The purpose of life is not even to worship and to please God. God never needs anything from us mortals.

The purpose of life must explain all that we experience – pain and suffering, pleasure and joy, the nature of our individual circumstances, our experiences, why we are here, where did we come from and where do we go after we die.

The purpose of life is obvious. It is what we have been doing since our conception – **growth**. We live to grow. To grow, we must experience so we may mature. To mature, we must toil, face adversity, overcome difficulties, confront challenges and solve mysteries.

Growth is the only common denominator in all that we experience, for we can learn and grow from any situation including pain and suffering, misery and disaster, pleasure and joy, abundance and scarcity. By digging deep into our experiences, we can find gems buried within, especially our painful ones.

We are more than our physical bodies. We have a Higher Self and The Voice Within that have been guiding us through promptings and synchronicities. While our physical growth is on autopilot, our emotional, mental and spiritual growth are not. These require effort and nurturing. How fast we grow depends on what we make of our experiences, how quickly we learn and how effectively we incorporate lessons learned into our character and personality.

Growth alone, however, is not the sole purpose of existence. As babies, we cannot survive on our own. Our parents provide us nutrients, love and nurturing. Their contributions are vital to our existence. Because we require the contributions of others to survive, the purpose of life has to be dual – to grow ourselves and to contribute toward the growth and maturation of others, just as our parents did for us.

Since our growth is not only physical, we must grow emotionally, mentally and spiritually and we must contribute to the welfare of others in a similar fashion. When we do, we discover the purpose of our lives and the meaning of our existence becomes clear.

Our growth and contributions to the welfare of others does not make much sense if it ends with everyone's death. Unless our growth distills into our character and personality, it is lost with our bodily death. When we eat food, we extract valuable nutrients and incorporate them into ourselves. Similarly, when we learn important lessons, they are distilled into our makeup, as our character and personality.

It is evident that human nature is evolving. Each generation is better off than the previous one. Our knowledge is massive because it is the accumulated knowledge of humankind. We are standing on the shoulders of those who preceded us. The next generation will benefit from our discoveries. Each of us is a link in the vast chain of humanity. We are beginning to realize how inter-connected we are. Hence, no contribution is ever wasted. No growth is ever without impact. Growth and contributions persist.

Earth is an ideal garden that provides us the best environment to experience a diversity of situations through which we learn, grow and contribute. To fully realize the purpose of life, we must remain engaged for that is the best way to grow and to contribute. We gain little by living isolated lives. We must immerse ourselves in life, participate, and maintain an open mind.

If we accept the purpose of life as growth and service, then the answers to the two most perplexing questions of why we are here and where do we go after we die, become evident. If our purpose is to learn, to grow and to contribute, then that is what we are here for. It explains why no one is perfect for if we were, we would not need to be here on earth. As to where we go after we die, it depends on how much we have learned and contributed. Obviously, once we complete our earthly lessons, mature and gain mastery, we no longer need to come back here for another life.

Furthermore, if we accept the purpose of life as growth and service, then evil, pain and suffering can be explained. Evil is perpetrated by immature people. It is our opportunity to confront it, stop it and transmute it. Pain and suffering are often the only way we develop empathy for what many people go through. Through pain and suffering we grow emotionally and spiritually. If we do not live wise and preventive lives, pain and suffering give us the pause we need to evaluate, adjust and change course. We are far more emotional than logical beings. We seldom learn from our mistakes or the mistakes of others. We require pain and suffering to wake up and change our ways. Pain and suffering make us more humane and better able to relate to others in similar situations. Yet, pain and suffering can be minimized through intelligent living.

The best way to make sense of our experiences, especially the painful ones, is to evaluate them against the dual purposes of life.

1. What can we learn from this experience?
2. Is this experience an opportunity to contribute to the well-being of others?

How much we learn, grow and contribute in each lifetime varies from one individual to the next. Each has their own lessons to learn and contributions to make. The best way to live our purpose is to pursue our passions and do what we find most meaningful. Honoring our inner promptings and trusting our gut feelings are sure ways to growth, joy and contentment. Pursuing our passions is the best means to confront our challenges, overcome any setbacks and be content.

Growth is not a simple accumulation of memories and experiences. These must be integrated, distilled and incorporated into our character and personality. Each "lesson learned" is a credit in our bank account. When a critical amount is accumulated, we experience a shift, a jump into a higher quantum, a shedding of our old skin and a rebirth into a new being. How many of these shifts we go through in a lifetime, if any, is based on our individual effort.

Our growth is a march from infancy, to childhood, to adolescence, to adulthood and finally to maturity. The ultimate goal of our growth is the full realization of our potential– physical, mental, emotional and spiritual.

I have often wondered about the symbology of the serpent in ancient cultures. It is the most widely known animal symbol with the greatest number of associated values. One of the most significant features of a serpent is its ability to shed its skin and emerge, renewed and reborn. I never forgot the first time I saw a complete serpent skin in the wild in Aleppo, Syria. I was with my cousins looking for hedgehogs. The sight of an intact serpent skin puzzled and alarmed me. Later, I learned that serpents shed their skins regularly so they can continue to grow.

The serpent can easily be our personal symbol, the story of our lives. As we live and experience, we are confronted with temptations, challenges and decisions. If we choose wisely, we grow and accumulate life-lessons. When we amass sufficient knowledge, we reach a turning point. We shed our old skin and we are reborn.

In the Garden of Eden, Adam and Eve were told that if they give in to temptation, they will gain knowledge, wisdom, and their eyes will open making them like gods knowing good and evil. The serpent, representing desire, acted as the tempter. We, too, will face many temptations in life. The object of the temptation will look appealing to sight and desirable to experience. Temptation is a necessary force to impel us to use our freedom of choice and act appropriately. We must evaluate consequences before we act. We will not learn or grow and our eyes will not open until we experience. To experience, we must act.

The purpose of life as growth and service make perfect sense. All the pieces of the puzzle fall into place and a clear picture emerges. We are here to experience, to learn, to grow and to contribute. Gradually our eyes will open. We will know. When we **know** who we are, we will discover and live our purpose. We will seize every opportunity as a means for learning, growing and contributing. Gradually, we will mature and gain mastery.

Living a purposeful life is a very good way to live. Having a purpose gives us a focus, energy and something to aim for. We live a more content and satisfied life.

◆ ◆ ◆

## The March to Maturity

We are an ecological system marching toward maturity. This march is evident everywhere. We see it in our relationships, in our sciences and in our technologies. We mature slowly and gradually through our experiences. The progression of life is to ever greater interdependence, efficiency and effectiveness. In other words, it is a progression to perfection.

Maturity implies the incorporation of the following traits:

### 1. **Confidence**

Confidence comes from experience. Having been there, done that. Faced with innumerable challenges, the mature person is self-aware, decisive, confident and knows exactly what to do and when to do it. Being mature is being ready to handle what life brings our way. It is being prepared, ready and confident that we can manage any given situation. A confident person has a decisive, assertive and magnetic character and personality.

### 2. **Being at Ease**

The mature person does not worry, fret or stress over what is beyond one's control. Maturity brings a sense of calm, poise and peace that envelops the person. A mature person acts with intent and purpose. A mature person hopes for the best outcome, but accepts and deals with whatever the outcome is.

### 3. Knowing What is Important

Knowing how to separate the trivial from the important is a sign of maturity. Most events have no lasting impact and should be ignored. What is important is that which contributes to growth, well-being, health and happiness especially in the long run.

Doing the important things first and without delay is a sign of maturity. Allocating time to cultivate the mind, emotions and spiritual values is paramount. Pursuing the critical 20% and ignoring the trivial 80% is a sign of wisdom. So is living an unencumbered, simple and balanced life.

### 4. Having Vision (Seeing the Big Picture)

Mature individuals have vision and do not get mired in dramas and problems. They rise above, detach and see the bigger picture. Mature individuals are in the world but not of the world. They do not contribute to conflict and become part of the problem. They know how to assist without creating dependencies. They are excellent observers and listeners. They know how to stay clear of other people's dramas.

### 5. Being Unselfish, Considerate and Empathetic

Mature individuals are unselfish. It is not all about "them". Others are equally important. In fact, with mature people the focus is often on the other, for it is by serving and enriching the lives of others that they are happy and content.

### 6. Accepting Facts and Reality for What They are – Living in the Now

Mature people do not live in a fantasy world. They see and accept reality as it is. They do not expect that everything will always be rosy. There has to be some ups and downs. There has to be some rain to enjoy the sunshine later. And while they are enjoying the sunshine, they prepare for the rain. And while they are facing hardships, they keep in mind that "this, too, shall pass." By facing difficulties and overcoming challenges, they grow and blossom.

While immature people fight, bully, intimidate and push their way, mature people focus on the good in people, emphasize commonality and create win-win situations. When a mistake is made, a mature person immediately acknowledges the mistake and makes amends.

While individuals can be mature or immature, so can nations. Any nation that looks at another nation as an enemy, schemes and plots and goes to war to solve problems, is immature. Mature nations cooperate, respect others, create partnerships and undertake joint ventures.

## 7. Loving and Serving

Mature individuals radiate love and a desire for service. They serve to empower. They love others because they can see exactly where these people are. They do not judge because they know that everyone is doing the best they know under the circumstances. They see others as themselves for they have been there.

To love others in a mature way is to want the best for them. It is to help them without interfering in their personal choices. It is to allow others the freedom to be themselves, make their own mistakes and learn from them. To help others in a mature way is to educate, empower and give them the necessary tools to be self-reliant.

We are loved beyond measure by our source – God. We have been gifted with freedom of choice to make our own decisions and to live our lives as we see fit. We should respect and honor the way others use their freedom of choice and allow them to live as they see fit as well.

## *The Bell-Curve*

Cycles are prominent in our lives. The purpose of life is yet another such cycle. Initially, while young, we are 100% in the receiving mode. Without our parents' contributions, we would not survive. As adults, our lives are balanced between giving and receiving – contributing and growing. We contribute services and we receive compensations in return. If we proceed in accordance with the cyclic nature of existence, our later years should be devoted to contributing 100% of the time to the welfare of others.

Humanity is on a bell-curve as well. We started in the Stone Age, progressed to the Bronze Age and then to the Iron Age. We began as primitive hunters and gatherers, discovered agriculture, became industrialized and are now in the Technology and Information Age. We advanced from primitive tool users to employing our minds and sophisticated equipment. Our knowledge is progressively increasing, our abilities mushrooming and our collaborations are burgeoning. What the far future holds for us is anyone's guess. It will reveal the ultimate purpose of humanity and the role each individual plays.

# WHY ARE WE BORN,
# LIVE AND DIE?

*Man's main task in life is to give birth to himself, to become what he potentially is. − Erich Fromm*

Science teaches that we are here as the result of natural selection, survival of the fittest and the evolutionary forces. This is true, but it applies only to the physical body. We are more than advanced beasts. There is a huge gap between us and our closest relatives − the primates. This is because humans have a spark of divinity within them.

We are a breakaway species far in advance of any other species. There is nothing remotely close to us. There are no other species with equal or lesser technological advancement, artistic achievement and linguistic proficiency. How could the evolutionary forces have favored us at the exclusion of all else? If our evolution was due to random forces, there should be some other species close behind us. There isn't. How come? Could it be that our evolution is directed by a unique feature we have − consciousness?

It is a puzzle why the human species is unique. Why is humanity a single species when all other lifeforms are a multiplicity of species? Why are we the only species with speech, technology, culture and civilization? There must be a unique aspect to us. This aspect is difficult to pinpoint. It cannot be attributed to brain alone, or DNA. All living beings have DNA as their blueprint. Many species have far more genes than we do, yet we stand unique in our capabilities.

Why do we have religions? Why do we have sophisticated rituals? Why do we concern ourselves with death and the afterlife? Why do we seek value and meaning in what we do? Why do we have hopes and dreams for a better future? Where does our appreciation for the arts, sciences and beauty come from?

Can it be that these are attributes stemming from our soul?

Can it be that we, as souls, are the drivers of the carriage and the residents of the temple that is the body?

Religion, on the other hand, teaches that we were created and placed in a garden to manage it.

> *The LORD God took the man and put him in the garden of Eden to work it and keep it. Gen 2:15*

Religion gives us a second reason for being here which is to multiply, to fill the earth and to have dominion over everything.

> *And God blessed them. And God said to them, "Be fruitful and multiply and fill the earth and subdue it, and have dominion over the fish of the sea and over the birds of the heavens and over every living thing that moves on the earth." Gen 1:28*

Living according to this dictate – multiply, fill the earth, and subjugate it – will create havoc. Earth is a balanced, harmonious coexistence of all of its inhabitants. Multiplying and filling earth with our kind is irresponsible, arrogant and dangerous. Quantity at the exclusion of balance and quality is reckless. This answer as to why we are here, is unacceptable.

Furthermore; If we accept that God is all, there cannot be any creation which implies a separate existence. Hence, we cannot be created and placed here. If we are placed here, then it is against our will. Since we have free will, it must be our choice to be here.

Both science and religion fall short in adequately explaining the mystery of the human species. There is another option: we are here as spirits in a physical body because we want to be here, but why?

If we encounter an object we have never seen before and we want to know what it is and why it is here, we study its features and functionality. In our case, we must look at our synchronicities, passions, unusual experiences, skills, talents and abilities. These are pieces of the puzzle that is our life.

How do these pieces fit together?

What picture emerges?

Synchronicities are revelatory. They are critical junctures in our lives and are opportunities that can redirect our course. My life is replete with synchronicities. One or two synchronicities could be due to chance, but a multitude of synchronicities that define our lives is beyond the realm of chance. My life is what it is because of the actions I took as a result of these synchronicities. By examining the unusual events in our lives, and by paying attention to what works and what does not, will force us to admit that chance is overrated. Chance does play a part in our lives, but it is not as often as we tend to believe. Examining the major incidents in our lives, we can easily see a clear direction, a purpose for our lives. This purpose does not have to be earth-shattering. It can be as simple as making a difference in someone's life. Because everyone is interconnected, that small contribution, over the long run, will become significant.

The synchronicities in our lives are due to forces we put in place even if we are not aware of them. Just as we have a subconscious that guides our daily activities, we have a Higher Self that is guiding us to the best possible life we can have. Our Higher Self is the force behind our synchronicities – the major forks in our lives. The decisions we made at these junctures got us to where we are. Were these decisions whimsical, according to subconscious knowledge or a hidden plan?

## *Why Are We Born?*

We are born to have an earthly experience – why else?

Earth is a magnificent, wondrous place to experience physical existence – to see, hear, touch, smell and taste. We can be transformed by the touch of a first born, intoxicated by beauty, moved to tears by a melodious song, lose our bearings by a kiss and be raised to heaven by an intimate embrace. The senses are the gateway to exhilarating or excruciating experiences. It is indeed a privilege to be alive on Earth. Yet, it is not about eating, drinking and merriment. These are the icing on the cake. The cake is our particular reason to be here – the specific experiences we need to grow, to mature, to gain mastery and to contribute.

Each individual has his or her lessons to learn and contributions to make. Some have to learn patience, others decisiveness. Some have to learn forgiveness, compassion and acceptance. Others have to learn assertiveness, fearlessness and independence. Some have to learn gratitude and appreciation while others have to learn to serve with a glad heart. Some have to overcome impulsiveness. Others have to learn to receive and give freely and generously. Some have to learn boundaries and how not to be a victim. Most have to learn relationships – how to amicably relate, interact and live with others.

We contribute in various ways. Some contribute financially, others through service and example. Any creative act is a contribution if others can enjoy and benefit from it. This can be in arts, sciences or in mentoring. We are all teachers whether we know it or not. We are observed and imitated. My grandson, who is just 18 months old, knows how to pick up remotes, point them at devices, and then press buttons.

We are also students in the school of life. We learn from others, initially via imitation, then through observation, study and education. Many continue to do this throughout their lives. While the order in nature is to imitate while young and impressionable, we must cease to do so once we reach adulthood. As adults, we are expected to examine what we have been indoctrinated with, keep the valuable ones and discard the rest as baggage that we do not need to burden ourselves with.

We are born into a physical body for a specific reason. It is our responsibility to discover what that is and live it. Our skills, passions and synchronicities will show us the way. Even if we do not see an ultimate purpose for our lives, what we do see is the very next step that we can take. As we take one step, the next step is revealed.

## Why Do We Live?

We live to grow, to mature and to make a difference. The body grows following a natural bell curve from a fertilized egg until adulthood then it begins to decline. Our minds, emotions and spirit do not grow following the same bell curve. They never mature on their own. They require attention, nurturing and action. We must strive to mature emotionally, mentally and spiritually.

This would be easy if we were not burdened. We live with heavy "baggage" that we carry around. Just as a seed must shed its outer coating in order to grow, we must shed our "baggage" which is emotional, mental, and spiritual. We are burdened with physical handicaps, emotional "blockages", mental deficiencies, and spiritual "dark clouds." These handicaps limit us. Emotional, mental and spiritual burdens can be lightened, even eliminated. To cleanse ourselves of these, we should avoid negative thoughts and release undesirable emotions. We should examine our thoughts, carefully entertaining the empowering ones and weeding out the debilitating ones by starving them of our attention. Spiritually, we must realize that we are born in love, not sin. Belief in sin is an unnecessary burden that can be easily replaced with the ennobling belief that we are born pure. Being born out of love, we have no sin to worry about. If sin is transgression against God or divine laws, then we have nothing to fear. Babies could not have had the chance to transgress yet. If sin is inherited because we are descendants of Adam and Eve; a loving, merciful God will never punish us for "sins" committed by our original forebearers. The only way we can be born in sin is if by sin we mean ignorance. Ignorance is our only "sin." Ignorance denotes immaturity. We are born with our eyes "closed." We cannot see or understand clearly. We require earthly, oftentimes, painful experiences to wake us up, force us to open our spiritual eyes, see, understand and know the truth.

Some are born with one, others with two and a few with five "talents" to start our earthly sojourn. Regardless, what matters is not what we start life with, rather what we do with what we have. We are expected to at least double what we started with by the end of each life time. By growing, learning and contributing, we increase our "talents." By at least doubling our "talents", the Master, our Higher Self, will be well pleased. That is what the parable of talents is all about.

*"For it will be like a man going on a journey, who called his servants and entrusted to them his property. To one he gave five talents, to another two, to another one, to each according to his ability. Then he went away. He who had received the five talents went at once and traded with them, and he made five talents more. So also he who had the two talents made two talents more. But he who had received the one talent went and dug in the ground and hid his master's money. Now after a long time the master of those servants came and settled accounts with them. And he who had received the five talents came forward, bringing five talents more, saying, 'Master, you delivered to me five talents; here I have made five talents more.' His master said to him, 'Well done, good and faithful servant. You have been faithful over a little; I will set you over much. Enter into the joy of your master.' And he also who had the two talents came forward, saying, 'Master, you delivered to me two talents; here I have made two talents more.' His master said to him, 'Well done, good and faithful servant. You have been faithful over a little; I will set you over much. Enter into the joy of your master.' He also who had received the one talent came forward, saying, 'Master, I knew you to be a hard man, reaping where you did not sow, and gathering where you scattered no seed, so I was afraid, and I went and hid your talent in the ground. Here you have what is yours.' But his master answered him, 'You wicked and slothful servant! You knew that I reap where I have not*

*sown and gather where I scattered no seed? Then you ought to have invested my money with the bankers, and at my coming I should have received what was my own with interest. So take the talent from him and give it to him who has the ten talents. For to everyone who has will more be given, and he will have an abundance. But from the one who has not, even what he has will be taken away. And cast the worthless servant into the outer darkness. In that place there will be weeping and gnashing of teeth.' Matt 25:15-30*

We start our journey on Earth as a seed. We are "buried" in the soil of our earthly experiences to learn, to grow and to contribute. We grow best when we engage in frequent self-examination:

    a. What are we good at and what are we doing with our talents, skills and abilities?

    b. What are our weaknesses? What do we need to work on? What areas do we need to improve or be better at?

    c. What handicaps do we have?

    d. Are we selfish, stubborn, angry or impatient?

    e. How effective are we at managing our resources, especially time?

    f. How are our relationships? Are they based on love, trust and appreciation?

    g. Do we communicate clearly and effectively?

    h. Are we supportive, compassionate and understanding?

    i. Do we understand where others are coming from? Can we see their point of view?

    j. How do our spouse, offspring, siblings and friends view us?

    k. What contributions are we making to our family, friends, community and the world?

    l. Do we appreciate enough? Are we thankful enough?

    m. Compared to five years ago, where are we on our journey to enlightenment?

    n. Are we living with a passion?

o. What is our purpose for living?

It is obvious that we are diverse, even at birth. We are equal only under the law. We can even say that life is not fair and it would be true. This, however, is not due to a capricious God. This is because of our previous history from past lives and what we need to do this time around.

Each lifetime is a brief interlude, a candle in the wind. It can be snuffed unexpectedly at any time. For some, life is too short. Regardless of how long we live, it is what we do with our stay and what we leave behind that matters most. Knowing, loving and expressing ourselves are treasures that do not spoil. Seeking them is a worthwhile endeavor.

## When Do We Die?

We physically die when we either complete our self-selected assignments or, because we have free will, we make unwise decisions that lead to our untimely demise. Since we know for a fact that we can shorten our lives by ill-advised activities, we can lengthen our lives as well. We can extend our lives if we have a strong enough reason to live and do all we can to maintain a healthy body, emotions, mind and spirit. The choices we make whether consciously or subconsciously, impact not only the quality of our lives, but also its duration. Having freedom of choice is a double-edged sword and a major responsibility.

We must play a role in when we die. If it were up to our genetics alone, we could live for thousands of years just as some species of trees do. The body is constantly renewing itself and there is no reason for this to stop other than by our own unconscious design.

Just like any actor who assumes a role knows exactly when and how that role will end, so it is with us. Prior to birth, we accept the role we will play on the stage of life. Once born however, forgetfulness sets in. Most live and die not knowing what their roles are. Yet, we act out our roles extemporaneously and once our mission is fulfilled, it is time for us to leave. We do and the body dies.

# WE ARE IN A THEATER

*All the world's a stage, and all the men and women merely players. They have their exits and their entrances; And one man in his time plays many parts.*

*— Shakespeare*

The world is a theater. In this theater there are actors, spectators, helpers and directors. We always play a role in the theater of life. Most, however, are spectators. They are being entertained. Helpers remain behind the scenes, in the background. Actors play an important role in the theater of life. The most important roles, however, are that of the creators and the directors. While the vast majority are consumers, spectators, observers, imitators and survivalists, creators and directors are leaders and trend-setters. Being a creator means writing our own script. Being a director is to intelligently guide our life, playing different roles at different times. Depending on the situation, we can act behind the scenes, we can take center stage or we can simply observe.

In the theater of life, we can:

1. Follow what is trendy and allow events to dictate our course;
2. Observe others, imitate, put on a show and create a drama;
3. Conform, please others and strive to be accepted;
4. Participate, act with intention and make a difference not only in our lives, but in the lives of others;
5. Direct, create and shape our destiny through

imagination, creativity, will and action.

In the theater of life there are plenty of spectator seats. There is one stage reserved for the actors – artists, scientists, industrialists, leaders and innovators. Unlike actors who have limited freedom in what and how they render their parts, we have more freedom but only if we utilize it.

Our stay in the theater of life is temporary. Soon the curtains will fall and we will have to leave. Being in the theater of life is an opportunity. We can occupy a seat as spectators and be entertained, or we can climb onto the stage of life and play an active role. We are born with freedom of choice. At any moment, we can choose to redirect the course of our lives for a more desirable outcome. We can shape our future by using our imagination, will and action to direct the course of events in our favor. We have a choice. Will we decide wisely and act intelligently?

It is amazing to watch some young or even child actors. They are outstanding performers. Two such examples are: **Anne with an E** and **A Little Princess**. We know they are putting on an act, but it does not seem so. The acting is realistic. Since actors can assume many roles in a lifetime, they cannot adequately perform if they are inundated by the memories of all their previous acting roles. Hence, forgetfulness of past performances is paramount.

Each lifetime is a birth into a new theater with new roles to play. We too must forget our previous roles in other lifetimes or else we will not be able to perform adequately. While actors have limitations, are directed, and must follow a script, we are less limited but also can be guided. We have obvious guides as customs, tradition, education, authority and expectations. These influence our day-to-day activities with or without our conscious knowledge. We also have not-so-obvious guides who will not intercede unless they are invited to do so. These guides are our Guardians and the Higher Self who whispers to us as The Voice Within. Their guidance must be sought for the major events in our lives. When implored, they whisper to us at the appropriate junctures in our lives. Upon hearing the voice, we have a choice to act accordingly, or we can ignore the promptings and do as we wish. **Listening to The Voice Within**

**is the surest way to stay on course and live a productive and impactful life.**

Earth is a unique theater. It is the proverbial Garden of Eden. It affords us unique opportunities that we must wade through. It is replete with temptations. Every imaginable fruit is available to be plucked and savored – fruit for pleasure, joy, learning, growth, knowledge and wisdom. Also, the fruit of despair, pain, agony, disillusionment, betrayal and misery. Often, we do not know the nature of the fruit and the consequences that will follow until we are tempted and yield to the temptation.

There is no theater like Earth to experiment, to experience, to learn and to grow. Also, there is no theater like Earth to contribute and to make a difference – the dual purposes of life.

◆ ◆ ◆

## The illusion of reality

We enter the theater of life, choose a seat, sit down and get comfortable.

In front of us is a gigantic screen. Soon the lights are dimmed and, on the screen, a movie is projected.

We watch the action unfold.

The moving pictures come to life. The music with stereo sound, the scenery and environment make us believe we are witnessing "live" events right before our eyes.

We are so engrossed by the projected "reality" that we forget we are in a theater.

We identify with the actors and are moved.

We live the events projected in front of us. We laugh and we cry.

Then the movie ends.

The lights are turned on.

We get up and are ready to leave.

Suddenly, we realize that it has all been an illusion.

Just as in a theater, in our daily lives we see images projected onto the screen of our consciousness. Even though they are images or moving pictures, we react to them as if they are real.

We see the live images move. We hear the stereo sound. The colors dazzle us.

We are drawn into the drama unfolding before us. We react favorably to what we consider to be good and unfavorably to what we consider to be bad.

Our bodies register our reactions.

Sooner or later, the curtain of life falls.

Physically, we die.

We wake up to a different reality.

We look back at our life on Earth and realize that it has all been a dream, a play in a theater.

We, along with everyone else, have been acting the entire time without realizing it.

We were putting on a show. Each had a part to play.

The villains and the heroes are all actors doing their part to create the necessary environment.

On this side of the curtain, there are no friends and no foes.

All are family! Each is doing their part to aid our growth and enable us to contribute.

While in the physical body, we are mostly asleep. Once we leave the body behind, we wake up to a different reality.

Happy awakening!

# WE ARE ON A JOURNEY

*Every path may lead you to God, even the weird*
*ones. Most of us are on a journey. We're looking*
*for something, though we're not always sure what*
*that is. The way is foggy much of the time.*
*I suggest you slow down and follow some of*
*the side roads that appear suddenly in the mist.*
*— Gordon Atkinson*

The Sun, the Earth, the solar system and the galaxies are on a journey through space. So are we. Our journey is eternal punctuated by numerous excursions. Each excursion is a short or long lifetime depending on what we need to accomplish.

Our journey starts at birth when we find ourselves on the highways and byways of life. Our journey ends when we come to a dead end. Since we do not know when our journey will end, it is best to live as if this trip is the only one we will make. This way we make the most of our opportunities.

Successful journeys require planning and preparation prior to commencing. For the journey of life, we do the planning and preparation prior to birth. We are born with specific goals in mind. We wait for the perfect circumstances before we incarnate. Yet, as soon as we are born, we forget our planning. We even forget why we are on the road. This is because:

1. We are on unfamiliar terrain. It is all new for us, thus exciting. We have no idea what is in store for us;

2. Improvisations can lead to exciting and unexpected results;

3. We could not remember our plans even if we wanted to because our brains and memory centers are not developed at birth.

Journeys are affected by:

1. Physical, emotional and mental states – the condition of the driver;
2. Weather and the condition of the road;
3. Obstacles and challenges along the way;
4. Vehicle condition and road choice;
5. Maps, or the Global Positioning System (GPS) used;
6. Entrance and exit points;
7. Purpose of the journey and ultimate destination.

The more physically, emotionally and mentally fit we are, the better we can react to the conditions of the road. It is also easier to stay alert, on course and on schedule.

We choose when to start our journey based on the "weather" – the conditions we need to best achieve our purpose. We wait, or even postpone our journey of life until the situation is favorable. We want our journey to be relevant.

Having guideposts along the highway of life makes it easy for us to know how to proceed. Challenges are guideposts. They tell us what changes we must make, where a detour is called for, what to seek and what to avoid. Obstacles along the way are the challenges we must face and overcome. They are invited guests to test our ability to stay on course and maneuver these situations. If we act decisively, intelligently and are victorious, we demonstrate mastery. We leave these challenges behind and proceed onward until we face our next challenge.

The vehicle for our journey is the physical body. When our journey is completed, we leave the vehicle behind. The path we follow in life depends on how purpose-oriented we are. We can stay on course, or we can be distracted and lose our way.

Many use maps or a GPS on a physical journey. On the journey of life, our purpose is our guide. Some shun using maps. They live without purpose floating with the currents. Others follow the example of their parents and do the same. Some follow tradition and do what is expected of them. A few chart their own course, paving new roads that others can follow. Those with spiritual inclinations use The Voice Within and the promptings of the Higher Self to know what to do at critical junctures in their lives. These people are on an accelerated path to accomplish their life purpose.

Just as our entrance is at the most opportune time, so is our exit. We exit life when we deem it necessary. This is when our mission is completed; when our bodies have been used up; or when we are riddled with diseases, suffering and in pain. We can also exit due to an accident. Just as we can shorten our journey through despair, neglect and abuse, we can extend our stay by acquiring a new motive to live.

Even though each journey has its own destination (purpose), the ultimate destination of all of our journeys is maturity and the full expression of our spiritual faculties.

We are travelers on the highway of life. It is best to pack necessities only and not be burdened by excessive baggage that will slow us down. We have what we need for this journey – skills, abilities and opportunities. Pride, ego, jealousy, fear and ignorance are unnecessary baggage. They must go.

As we live and experience, we accumulate debris – burdens that we carry around, scales on our eyes and wax in our ears. With each journey, as we get to know ourselves better, we shed some of the scales from our eyes, and remove some of the wax from our ears. The scales and wax we carry around are burdens. These are ignorance, bias, prejudice, fear and handicapping beliefs. The challenges we face and the pain and agony we go through, help us shed some of these burdens. Since this can be a slow process, our journey can be long and arduous. When we finally release our burdens, we will be light, free and fully alive.

Being on a journey, especially to a foreign land, is important in many ways. It is educational. It exposes us to different cultures and it broadens our perspective. The more we travel, the more cultured we become.

## The Conversion of Saul

*But Saul, still breathing threats and murder against the disciples of the Lord, went to the high priest and asked him for letters to the synagogues at Damascus, so that if he found any belonging to the Way, men or women, he might bring them bound to Jerusalem. Now as he went on his way, he approached Damascus, and suddenly a light from heaven shone around him. And falling to the ground he heard a voice saying to him, "Saul, Saul, why are you persecuting me?" And he said, "Who are you, Lord?" And he said, "I am Jesus, whom you are persecuting. But rise and enter the city, and you will be told what you are to do." The men who were traveling with him stood speechless, hearing the voice but seeing no one. Saul rose from the ground, and although his eyes were opened, he saw nothing. So they led him by the hand and brought him into Damascus. And for three days he was without sight, and neither ate nor drank.*

*Now there was a disciple at Damascus named Ananias. The Lord said to him in a vision, "Ananias." And he said, "Here I am, Lord." And the Lord said to him, "Rise and go to the street called Straight, and at the house of Judas look for a man of Tarsus named Saul, for behold, he is praying, and he has seen in a vision a man named Ananias come in and lay his hands on him so that he might regain his sight." But Ananias answered, "Lord, I have heard from many about this man, how much evil he has done to your saints at Jerusalem. And here he has authority from the chief priests to bind all who call on your name." But the Lord said to him, "Go, for he is a chosen instrument of mine to carry my name before the Gentiles and kings and the children of Israel. For I will show him how much he must suffer for the sake of my name." So Ananias departed and entered the house. And laying his hands on him he said, "Brother Saul, the Lord Jesus who appeared to you on the road by which you came has sent me so that you may regain your sight and be filled with the Holy Spirit." And immediately something like scales fell from his eyes, and he regained his sight. Then he rose and was baptized; and taking food, he was strengthened.*

*Acts 9: 1-19*

## We Are on a Journey

We too are on a journey, not to Damascus, but a journey inward, to meet, become and express our Higher Self.

We are on a journey moving away from wars, violence and atrocities to peace, compassion and caring.

We are on a journey leaving behind our ego, selfishness and exceptionalism to inclusivity, acceptance and an appreciation of diversity.

We are on a journey away from siding with one group against another to solving problems and bringing people together.

We are on a journey moving away from a war-based economy to genuine, sustainable productivity.

We are on a journey moving away from enemies and destructive competition to genuine cooperation and joint ventures.

We are on a journey to transform ourselves from brutes to children of God.

We are on a journey away from doctrines to spirituality.

We are on a journey inward where we discover all we need to live happy, healthy and productive lives.

We are on a journey transitioning from being under the law to living in grace. When we do, we will not only know ourselves intimately, we will love ourselves unconditionally and we will express ourselves fearlessly. We will become enlightened (beings of light) and we will be home.

# WE ARE A WORK IN PROGRESS

*Have patience with all things, but chiefly have patience with yourself. Do not lose courage in considering your own imperfections but instantly set about remedying them - every day begin the task anew.*
*—Saint Francis de Sales*

We are not a finished product.
We are like a rock being chiseled away to reveal the beautiful "image" buried within.
We are like a rough diamond being shaped to reflect the exquisiteness concealed within.
We are an encyclopedia being written, one volume at a time. Each lifetime, we add one volume, a book or a booklet, a chapter or even a paragraph.
We are gods in the making.
We are not as free as we think we are.
We are not as powerful as we believe we are. Even miniscule viruses or bacteria can bring us to our knees.
We are prone to mistakes, accidents, diseases and tragedies.
We are on a trip. While some are on a rollercoaster, others cruise gently down the stream.
While some are altruistic, others are selfish. While some have an open mind, others are parochial and egotistical. While some are gentle and protective, others are bullies. Above all, many are hypocritical. We do not see the pole in our eyes, while we point out the eyelash in another's. We can all be better.

## *We Can Do Better*

*The gem cannot be polished without friction, nor man perfected without trials.  Chinese Proverb*

Human nature has not changed much since the days of Christ.
Collective growth is excruciatingly slow.
Our hearts are still hardened.
We have eyes, but cannot see clearly.
We have ears, but cannot hear distinctly.
Our eyes have scales and our ears are covered with wax.
Ignorance, bias and arrogance rule supreme.
If Christ were living amongst us, He would be crucified anew.
Not much has changed in the collective consciousness of humanity.

Even at this age, some nations attack other nations and attempt to subjugate them. The powerful cook up excuses to bulldoze the homes of the less fortunate and take over their land, building settlements for themselves. There are those who continue to believe and act as if they are privileged, better than anyone else, and are "chosen." The day when we see and treat everyone as truly equal is on the horizon. What hastens its coming is often pain and suffering. We can be better. We can act intelligently and we can be compassionate.

Fortunately, there are incredibly generous, caring, compassionate and loving individuals. These people are the salt of Earth. They are our hope for a better future. Even collectively, on occasion, we show tenderness and generosity. We need more of our loving and compassionate nature to shine through for a brighter, peaceful and civilized future.

# WE ARE NOT PERFECT

*Try as hard as we may for perfection, the net result of our labors is an amazing variety of imperfectness. We are surprised at our own versatility in being able to fail in so many different ways.*

*— Samuel McChord Crothers*

We are not perfect. We are born to work on our imperfections. Humanity is improving at a snail's pace. This is because we are like a gigantic ship that is set on its course. Changing direction is slow and tedious. Additionally, we are trying to move forward with our brakes on. Fortunately, there are individuals who are paving the way for quick advancement by their breakthroughs, contributions and example.

There is nothing perfect in us except for our souls. Our sight is far below average compared to many birds. Our hearing is nothing compared to dogs. Our smell is rudimentary compared to bears. Our senses of touch and taste are also limited. Our sense faculties function within limited ranges. However, imperfection can be an advantage.

Take our memory for example. We see Brownian motion when sunlight filters through at an angle. It is remarkable to see what is floating in the air. We are fortunate that we are not constantly reminded of this. Imagine being constantly aware of what is in the air that we are breathing. What if we are always cognizant of the multitude of cultures living within and on us – on our skin, inside our noses, ears, eyes, guts and almost everywhere else, billions of microorganisms cohabiting our bodies. It would be almost impossible for us to have normal lives. It is best that we forget this. Selective memory is a blessing indeed. Similarly, we see, hear, smell, taste and feel what is essential. It is fortunate that we lose awareness of the clothes we wear after a short time.

It is the nature of life to not stand still, to progress, to improve and to do more with less. We are meant to learn, to grow and to continuously progress. Those who do not admit their imperfections have a long way to go. Justification is a human "disease." So is blaming others for our faults. It is easy to make excuses. It is far better to admit our mistakes, learn from them and resolve never to repeat them. If we accept the purpose of life as the opportunity to learn, to grow, and to contribute, then we can better see our shortcomings and resolve to do better.

We must accept that no one is perfect (except for most babies) and that everyone can be better, starting with us. We must accept responsibility for our life, our actions and their consequences even if we were treated unfairly. It is easy to blame our parents, society, even God for our misfortunes. The better way is to forgive, to let go and to decide to excel in spite of our challenges.

On January 20, 2023, CBS aired the story of a young boy born without legs. He wanted to play basketball. Instead of complaining about what he cannot do, he was determined to do whatever he could to achieve his goal. He successfully made his high school basketball team. Imagine that!

> *As he passed by, he saw a man blind from birth. And his disciples asked him, "Rabbi, who sinned, this man or his parents, that he was born blind?" Jesus answered, "It was not that this man sinned, or his parents, but that*

WE ARE NOT PERFECT | 51

*the works of God might be displayed in him. John 9:1-3*

We are the works of nature manifesting the laws of God. We glorify God when we put what we have been given to best use, especially to benefit others. Life is an opportunity. We can sit idly and complain, or we can roll up our sleeves and do our best with what we currently have. The better we use that which we have, the more opportunities we will attract into our lives.

The first step to move forward is to admit that we are imperfect. We are in good company; so is everyone else. The adult thing to do is to acknowledge our shortcomings, resolve to do better, and take a step forward. Because we are imperfect, we should expect ups and downs, good days and not-so-good days. We will rejoice and we will suffer. We will be sick and we will be healthy. We are fortunate indeed when the positive outweighs the negative.

Millions suffer childhood neglect, abuse and traumas because babies are born to parents who cannot adequately care for them; they did not plan on having them or did not want them. It is no wonder that violence, crime and addictions are major problems in society. We seem to value freedom over responsibility when these two should go hand-in-hand. To drive, we need a driver's license proving that we are adequately prepared. Yet, there are no preparations or requirements to be parents. Anyone can have children whether or not they can handle the responsibility.

Preventing unwanted pregnancies should be a priority. Teaching responsible parenting should be part of our curriculum. Ensuring the well-being of babies and parents should be a main focus for society. Raising emotionally healthy children is in our best interest for a brighter future. We must put aside our personal beliefs – whether religious or political – and work together to create a healthier, safer and more abundant future for all.

Many, with noble intentions, demonstrate for the life of the unborn. **Pro-life should stand for quality of life.** If we want to protect the unborn, we must also ensure a proper environment for their wellbeing. What happens after a baby is born is extremely important for the future of that child. Without loving parents, proper nutrition, education and nurturing, where do these children end up? The best we can do for babies is to ensure that they get the love and the necessities they need to become well-adjusted and contributing members of society. This happens when children are born through choice, after planning by responsible adults who are ready for them.

While protecting the life of the unborn, why not include protection for adults as well? Saving babies and later allowing them to get killed by gun violence, drug addiction or war does not make much sense. We should prevent killing, not because it is a commandment, but because we truly value life, individuality and the privilege of an earthly experience. "Thou shall not kill" we are commanded. Why stop there? Why not eliminate torture, maiming and cruelty as well? We should live guided by intelligence, not commands.

Earth can be an Eden, but this will not happen on its own. It will require us to work together toward that end. We are the agents of change on earth. We can turn earth into a hell through war, crime, and brutality. We have done this far too many times. Some believe that wars are good for the economy. This comes at a high cost – lives lost. The only ones who benefit from wars are war-related businesses and the weapons manufacturers. We can have a far better economy for more people by cooperation. Joint ventures between nations is the way to go. It is time to grow up and assume responsibility for our actions and their consequences. We can change course and be more cooperative and peace loving.

## Disease, Pain, and Suffering

Disease, pain and suffering persist because we are emotional beings. We learn value when we pay a price, usually in pain and suffering. Disease, pain and suffering are not necessary, and with intelligent living, they can be minimized. Sporadic diseases strengthen our immune system. Pain and suffering can act as an incentive to let go and die in peace. If we are gripped with the fear of the unknown, we cling to our worn-out bodies and refuse to let go. If occasionally we must endure excruciating pain and suffering, we can use this toward spiritual growth that can even lead to enlightenment.

Bullies, whether individuals or nations, will not cease bullying unless they taste some of the poison they are dishing out to others. The pain and suffering of bullies can be a cure in this case.

## We Are not as Free as We Believe We Are

Christ told us that when we know the truth, it will set us free. How free are we? We have minds, eyes and ears, yet we can neither think, see or hear without a veil. We are engulfed by a cloud. We are enslaved by our unexamined beliefs, fears, ignorance, and biases. Not setting time aside to examine our beliefs, we accept what we have been spoon-fed and we blindly follow. Blind faith, fanatical belief and narrow mindedness are dangerous. Truth is something we can discover if we let go of our preconceived beliefs and allow the light to shine through.

To arrive at the truth, we can study nature and ourselves. However, we must have an open mind, a willing heart and the intention to know and realize the truth. We must be fearless. This is not easy for we are born into a culture that has established beliefs, traditions, customs, expectations and biases. These are important to have initially. Once we are adults, then we must choose what we accept, believe and adopt as a philosophy of life. Adulthood comes with freedoms and more importantly, independence and responsibilities.

Our subconscious has a great influence on how we act. It has stored memories, cultural and societal "biases". These influence how we behave. If we follow tradition, do only what is expected of us, then we are not free. Freedom requires that we detach, evaluate and act with intelligence. We can increase our freedom if we accept what we cannot change, and instead focus on what we can do. We can decide to think before we talk. We can elect not to react. We can choose what and when to eat. We can assume responsibility for our continued education, health and happiness. We can contribute to the wellbeing of others. It is far more important to focus on what we can do than complain about what is beyond our control. Knowing that we are not as free as we think we are, should give us pause to evaluate our thoughts, words and actions prior to expressing them. The more we use our available freedoms, the freer we become. In the process, we live happier and content lives.

Attachments limit our freedom. The more attached we are to other people's opinions, the less free we are. The more we seek approval and acceptance, the less free we are. The more we cling to unproductive situations, relationships and viewpoints, the less free we are. Learning to detach, to let go, and to maintain clear boundaries adds to our freedom. We control how free we are.

## We Are not as Powerful as We Think

We are not all powerful. Those who have experienced hurricanes, tornados, earthquakes and volcanos know how powerful nature can be. We are bombarded by viruses, bacteria and other microorganisms. We succumb to disease; we suffer; we age and we die. At times we are capable of the miraculous and at other times, we are unable to carry out the simplest of tasks. This is evident when we are incapacitated and are bedridden. There is a silver lining though. Even though individually we are not all powerful, together we are. Just as a cable is unbreakable when all the threads band together, so are we. The more we work together, the stronger we are.

## The March to Perfection

Even though we are not perfect, we should strive to perfect our body, emotions, mind and spirit. We can care for the body by providing it with what it needs to stay healthy, energetic and vital. We should seek material prosperity that satisfies our needs and allows us to enjoy living. We should cease accumulating once we have enough and dedicate ourselves to learning, improving and contributing. We nurture our emotions through loving relationships, by expressing positive emotions such as love and joy and by refraining from negative emotions such as envy, jealousy and hate. We cultivate our mind by feeding it enriching and empowering thoughts and images. Continuous education should be a lifelong endeavor. It is easy to find uplifting books in libraries or for purchase. Setting time aside for contemplation, meditation and prayer enlivens and rejuvenates the spirit. Being in nature marveling at God's creations is a sure way to enrich our souls.

We approach physical perfection in our youth. Emotionally, it might take us much longer to mature. Mentally, we can continue to grow until the last day of our life. Spiritually, we require many lifetimes to realize our true potential. Until then, we are a mere shadow of our true selves.

To grow spiritually, we must contend with ignorance. We do

not know who we are. We do not love ourselves enough. We rarely express ourselves as we would like to. Like the Prodigal Son, we prefer to be poor and hungry living with the swine rather than returning to our Father, His mansion, acceptance, love and abundance. Like everything else in life, we are free to do as we please. There is no judgment, there are only consequences. We can continue, like the Prodigal Son and remain lost, or we can start our journey to return home. It starts with taking the first steps – genuine self-knowledge, unconditional self-love and fearless self-expression.

## Everyone is Handicapped

Assumptions influence how we behave. If we assume that we and others are perfect, then we behave in a certain way. It is best to assume that no one is perfect.

What if we did not expect perfection from anyone, including ourselves?

What if we assumed that everyone is handicapped or challenged in one or more ways?

How would we act if we knew that someone was intoxicated, or under the influence of drugs? Would we expect them to act normal?

How would we act if we knew that someone had Alzheimer's? Would we expect that individual to remember everything?

How would we act if we knew that someone was blind, mute or deaf? Would we expect them to see, talk or hear?

What if we treated everyone with compassion, understanding and patience because they are challenged or handicapped?

Wouldn't that make our world a more pleasant place to be in? Wouldn't that be marvelous? What is stopping us?

Let's do it!

I am handicapped.
You are handicapped.
We all are handicapped.
In more ways than one.

# WE ARE CONNECTED

What I know now is that we're all interconnected and that's a really beautiful thing. We have links to everyone else in our lives and in the world. Different people have different journeys for different reasons. You can't judge, but you can celebrate that there are connections everywhere. – *Jane Seymour*

We are inseparably connected to our environment. We are also connected to each other. Some of our connections are direct and obvious. Most are not. It is easy to see the connections to our parents, children, spouse, siblings, relatives and friends. Yet, a few moments of reflection will show our other connections. If we live in a house or an apartment, we are connected to all those involved in manifesting our residence. If we wear clothes, we are connected to all those involved in making the clothes we wear; ditto for the food we eat, the water we drink, the cars we drive and the household machinery and other items we use. Our indirect connections extend to the producers, manufacturers, distributors and retailers.

We have no existence apart from our environment. We must breathe, drink, consume food and occupy space. Our bodies, emotions and minds are shaped by our environment. Even our genes respond to their environment. Which aspects of the genes are activated is determined by the environment in which the cells find themselves. Different environments activate different aspects of the genome. Even through our entire genetic material is in each cell, what aspects of the genome are active in a muscle cell are different from what is activated in a nerve cell. Therefore, we are what we are because of the environment we find ourselves in.

Our connections are physical, emotional, mental and spiritual. Our emotions are generated in response to the people and situations we encounter. Our minds are shaped by the educators we had, the books we read, the shows we watched and the plays and concerts we attended. Mentally, emotionally and spiritually we are connected to any place we have ever been to. Our memories are the threads that connect us to our larger self.

Our individuality is not distinct. We do not have isolated existences. We are our relations and our connections. Our existence is a web that extends over space and time. Like the queen bee, we are always at the center of this web. We tend to think of the center as our entire being when it is not. We are the entire web. This web links us to everyone and everywhere that we ever came in touch with consciously or unconsciously.

When we think of a person, we remember our connection to that person and all the events and circumstances that binds us. When we talk about our love for our family, sports, cooking or the arts, we are speaking of our connections, memories and relationships. When we reflect on our life, we are reviewing our memories which are our connections. By reflecting and remembering, we strengthen the fibers of the web that link us to people and events.

We identify with our bodies and assume that that is who we are. If we limit ourselves to our bodies, we sell ourselves drastically short. We are our relations as well. Our relations give rise to the boundaries of our larger bodies. We are a web directly connected to all we know and indirectly to all they know and are related to. After we die and the body is decomposed, our connections remain as the memories we leave in the hearts and minds of all those we came to know.

To demonstrate the extent of our connections, the following is a quote from my book: **A Passion for Living, a path to meaning and joy.**

### The TOMATO

*"I picked a tomato from my garden and looked at it. I did not look at it casually, but with a deep desire to really know what is this thing we call a tomato?!*

*I remember planting the seed. Then, after an ambiguous period of not knowing what was taking place in the soil, I saw a tiny seedling break the surface of the soil. It was as if it was declaring silently but resolutely "I am here and I am alive!" The plant grew in width and height until it became fully mature. It acquired many stems, branches and leaves and even though I could not see the roots, I knew they were there. Then many tiny yellow flowers formed beside the leaves on the stems.*

*After a few days, I saw tiny bulbous structures at the base of the flowers. At first small, hard and green, they grew to become large, soft and red.*

*I now hold one of them in my hand and look at it attentively, curiously and lovingly. What are you?*

*Red, soft and round.*

*The colors green and red displayed by you are not inherent in you. Color is due to light, absorption, refraction and the structures of my eyes and brain. At night, your color is not there, for it never was in you even when I saw it there. What I see as color is what you do not absorb when the rays of light reach you. You reflect the color I see. What you reject, I consider an essential aspect of you. What I see tells me as much about me as it does about you.*

*I cannot know how hard or soft you are until I touch you. By touching you, my own structure, my nervous system and how it functions, are revealed to me. I interpret my own sensations, thoughts and ideas as qualities of yours.*

*Looking at you when you were round, but small and green, I could not understand how you would be able to slowly transform yourself into a much larger round structure with a different color—red. I could see you getting larger on a daily basis. Even though, logically, I understand how you do that, I still do not fully realize the magic unfolding before my eyes.*

*I am told that you are a bunch of cells grouped together in a specific way. But these cells are not the same cells that formed you a while ago. When you were a tiny bulbous structure you had very few cells compared to now. How did you know how to create all these extra cells and add them to yourself? I am told that you are constantly changing and that you have been adding to yourself from the soil, the air and the sun. If life progresses only from life, how could the soil, the water, the air and the sun add to your body and life? How can you take inert elements and give life to them? Or, are all these elements and the sunshine alive as well?*

*Your journey from a tiny, green, knot-like structure until you became the red, soft and large tomato I now hold and observe, lasted about four weeks. During this journey, you constantly changed your features while extending in the three dimensions of space. During this time, you were also extending in the fourth dimension of time. Your journey appears to have started from when you were tiny, green and knot-like, but for your journey to begin the plant had to be first. For the plant to be, the soil, seed, water and sunshine had to be first. Where is the real beginning?! All beginnings and endings are mere apparent starts and ends. Since you are always in a state of change, your journey is ongoing. Your beginning with me was the seed I planted. That seed had to come from somewhere. It had its own journey. Your seeds and cells will have their own journeys as well. In a way, you had no true beginning and are not going to have an ultimate end. The cells that formed you were part of some other structures. Now they are going to be part of another. Before I picked you up, you were part of the plant. To remind me of your previous connection, you carry a "scar" the same way that I carry a belly button to remind me and others of my previous connection. The same way that I came from my mother, you came from your mother—the plant. The plant is connected to the soil just as you were connected to the plant. The soil, in turn, is connected to earth. Earth is connected to the solar system. The solar system is connected to the galaxies and the universe.*

*Where does it all end or start? Your atoms and cells, just like mine, are always combining, breaking down and recombining. Since nothing can be created nor destroyed, all that now is, has always been, only in different combinations, assuming different forms and existing in diverse spaces and times.*

*I look at you again. What makes you now must have been a part of everything else, one time or another; from the beginning, now and forever.*

*Behold, when I look at you, I see eternity.*

*Slowly I lift the tomato up and bring it closer to me. Now it is seen as separate and apart, as a tomato. I open my mouth and reverently consume the tomato. It is now* part of me. The eternity that was the tomato is now part of the eternity that is me. The journey continues. What constituted the tomato is now breaking down. The particles of the tomato will recombine and reappear in a different form. They will no more be known as a tomato, or seen apart by themselves. Henceforth, the particles will be called by a new name. They will take on my identity and the journey will go on until I, too, am dissolved, absorbed and recombined into other forms. Then, I too will appear in a different garment and be known by a new name.

I take a long and deep breath.

What is true of the tomato is equally true of the air I just breathed in and the sun whose rays are shining upon me. Soil, air and sunshine forming the tomato; tomato, air and sunshine forming me.

I am always becoming with everything else. Is air part of me? Is water or food part of me? They are not until I take them in and then they are.

How can I be so dependent on these elements and yet proclaim a separate existence? This is the paradox of the ages. I am, yet without all else, I cannot be.

Can I have a body without what I consume? Can I have emotions without others to interact with and an environment to respond to? How can I depend so much on others to stimulate and cause my emotions and yet think that I have a separate existence of my own? Is not my intelligence activated and developed as a response to my environment? Did not my senses form as a result of being in this world, immersed in earthly experiences?

I am in the image of my environment and my environment is in my image. Environment and I, like *chicken and egg, have always existed and coexist. We both assume various garbs, colors, shapes and form numerous associations. We take on unique identities for a while and then exchange them for new ones. As we exchange, we change, wake up and grow."*

What is true of the tomato is equally true of us. We have no independent existence. As a body, we are a corporation and as an individual we are a network.

We are a thread in the web of life. We are a link in the chain of existence. We are a fiber in the tapestry that is humanity. We are a spider continuously weaving the web of our connections. We are boundless and timeless, conscious only of our bondage to the body and to this timeframe. We choose to confine ourselves to space and time so we can have a unique set of experiences on an incredibly beautiful planet. We are an aspect of the divine having assumed a physical body to know what it is like to be human. Just as any experience is limited, so is our existence in human flesh. It is temporary. Soon we will depart and be free.

We can never be isolated and separated as an independent individual. Our existence is the result of our relationship to the environment. We are what we are because our environment is what it is. Because we live on Earth, we have a body weight due to gravity. Because of sunlight, we see color. Our lungs are adapted to breathe the air on this planet. Our organs, systems and the physical body are specific for this planet and our earthly environment.

## Relationships

Relationships are vital, yet difficult to master. This is because each person is in their own world, focused on what is important to them. People do not like to lose, be wrong or made to feel less than anyone else. They like to feel safe so they isolate themselves in a protective cocoon.

The best place to witness **perfect** relationships is in a **healthy** human body. We are made of cells. Each cell is like a miniature individual. It has organelles the same way that we have organs. It carries out the same functions that we carry out such as reproduction, respiration, digestion, elimination, defense, and interaction with the environment.

Cells "know" that they do not have an independent existence. They "know" that they are part of the body. They carry out their designated functions, their specialty, meticulously for the benefit of the entire body and in return they receive all that the body has to offer.

Our cells, tissues, organs and systems are connected and function as one. When any part of the body is in pain, we know it because every part is connected. Humans, plants and animals are also systems that are connected and function as one. We do not fully realize this yet. The day will come when we will wake up to this reality and act accordingly. When any part of our connections suffers, we will know it and act to relieve that pain. We are individuals, yet we are a vast web of interconnections. The web of our connections is our extended body – the tree of life with its vast network of connections. This tree has minerals, plants, animals and humans. They are diverse, seemingly independent, yet connected and interdependent.

We are not simply interconnected. Our lives depend of the benefits of this interconnectedness. We require touch, nurturing and intimacy to thrive. Our connections provide us the essential vitamins we need to make it as humans. Without these, we shrivel and we die.

# THE NATURE OF EARTHLY EXPERIENCES

*The essence of intelligence is skill in extracting meaning from everyday experience.* – Unknown

I t is marvelous to be in a physical body. There is no better way to appreciate a touch, a hug or a kiss. How else can we experience ideas and ideals such as justice, compassion, even anger and jealousy unless we are in a physical body? We cannot experience these mentally or in the astral world. How can we know what forgiveness is if we never have the opportunity to forgive someone who has wronged us? How do we know what empathy is if we have never experienced it? Can we master relationships if we have never physically lived with someone?

How can we know what type of parents or grandparents we would be if we have never raised children or had grandchildren? We can never know if we are patient, sympathetic, encouraging, intolerant, neglectful or abusive, unless we undergo the crucible of earthly existence and the revealing mirror of firsthand encounter.

There is no better way to know intimacy, love, beauty and joy than to experience them in a physical body. How can we raise our consciousness unless we undergo physical experiences? How we react to, and what we make of our experiences is the needle pointing to the degree of our maturity. Experiences are opportunities to go through, reflect upon, learn from and eventually gain mastery over. Our level of consciousness is like a mirror bouncing back to us the exact image of where we are on our journey to maturity.

We learn most from a variety of experiences under diverse circumstances. To gain mastery, we must practice. This might require many iterations, over several lifetimes. When we finally gain mastery, we reflect our mature and fully unfolded nature. It has been said that "when the student is ready, the master will appear." The truth is that when the student is ready, the student becomes the master. What manifests then is our Higher Self.

Being in a physical body confines us to the conditions, laws and limitations of physicality. Mastering these enables us to, not only perform better, but stress less and even excel.

The following items we need to be mindful of, apply and master.

## 1. We are Responsible for our Lives

We are not born with an owner's manual on how to best care for ourselves. We are born to imitate, learn from each other and via trial and error improve. Unfortunately, if who we imitate and learn from is flawed, then we will have more challenging lives. Regardless, once we become adults, we are responsible for our bodies, emotions, minds and behavior. We are responsible for our thoughts, words and actions. Being human, we will make mistakes. We are expected to learn from them, improve and not repeat them. It is far better to learn from the mistakes of others and live preventive lives.

We are responsible for all aspects of our lives – health, wealth and happiness. It is easy to make excuses and blame others. Yet our lives are our own to live as we see fit. It is our responsibility to decide where, how and with whom we live, who we choose to associate with, how we manage our time and other resources. Christ has stated in a parable that those who expertly manage what they have, even more will be given to them. And those who manage them foolishly, even the little they have will be taken away from them. In other words, use it wisely or lose it. We are free to do that, but it does not make our lives better. It is far more beneficial to leverage our handicaps and expertly invest our talents for multiple returns.

Being responsible for our lives is not easy, yet it is a fact of life few understand and even fewer accept and carry out proficiently. It is easy to make excuses, justify and blame others. We are free to do that, but it does not make our lives better. It is far more beneficial to use our history as a stepping stone to rise higher and have a broader perspective on life.

## 2. We Need Each Other

We need each other. We do not make our own shoes or clothes. When we are sick, we need the services of a doctor. We are a society – social beings, interdependent, each contributing and receiving multiple benefits in return.

We especially need companionship, contact and love. When receiving love, it is best to be gracious. When giving love, it is wonderful to give wholeheartedly. We should especially be thankful for any opportunity to experience intimacy.

## 3. Existence is Cyclic

Night follows day, then another day follows night, on and on indefinitely. Seasons follow each other in a cyclical fashion. So do years and centuries. We are born as infants and are nurtured by our parents. We grow up and have infants of our own to nurture. Our children grow up and continue repeating the cycle. We sleep and we wake up repeating this cycle daily. When we are awake, we experience. When we sleep, we dream. Day after day the cycle repeats. Cyclic existence is not repetition of the same. It allows for change and hopefully, for improvement. To avoid being stuck in a circle, we should act decisively to place ourselves into a spiral – rising with each cycle to new heights of awareness, skill and abilities.

## 4. Existence is Varied, Diverse and Complex

Each human is in a different grade in the school of life. Each person is acting out a unique role on the stage of life. Each one of us is a world unto ourselves, existing in a bubble based on our concept of self. These bubbles make communication between individuals easy if the bubbles are compatible and difficult if they are dissimilar. We often see, hear and experience based on the nature of our bubble which acts as a veil between us and others. We need to see and accept people for who they are without an intervening veil.

Differences are normal, natural and welcomed. They are the spice of life. They make life challenging, but worthwhile. They provide an opportunity to see, hear and interact with others as genuine, unique individuals. By using our differences for the common good, everyone benefits. Our stay on earth becomes more interesting, rewarding and enjoyable. The human body is a diversity of cell types, tissues and organs. These diverse elements work together harmoniously for the maximum benefit of all. We can do the same in society and in the world.

## 5. Mysteries Abound

Where did we come from? What happens when we die? Do we go anywhere? What is space? What is time? What is matter? What is energy? What is consciousness? Mysteries abound.

We are surrounded by mysteries. Not having answers is

OK. This is our opportunity to find answers. It is an occasion to creatively contribute to solutions. We can have the answers we seek if we persist, continue to earnestly ask and incessantly knock at the appropriate doors. Just as our knowledge is based on all who preceded us, we can add to the knowledge for those who will follow. We can be trail-blazers.

## 6. Change is the Law of Life

Nothing is ever the same. Everything is in motion. We can never step into the same moment twice. Change provides newness, opportunity and alleviates boredom. We can welcome change or we can dread it. Regardless, change will happen. It is the law of matter, energy and consciousness.

## 7. There is a Microcosm and a Macrocosm

Humans occupy a mid-level between that which is huge and that which is miniscule. The world of the macrocosm is the world of expanding outward while the world of the microcosm is the world of spiraling inward. Both the micro and the macro worlds are governed by physical, mental and spiritual laws. Just as there is outer space, there is also inner space. We are at the perfect place to study and understand both worlds.

## 8. Without Consciousness, Nothing Matters

Consciousness is the witness to all that happens. Without consciousness, it matters not whether there is a universe or not. Without a witness to existence, there is no existence as far as we are concerned. Without our awareness, there is no reality. We are fortunate to be conscious. Without it, we cannot know anything.

## 9. Intention is the Pilot

Like birds in flight guided by their intentions, our pilot is our intentions. We steer our lives in the direction of our intentions. Intentions can be conscious or subconscious.

Being aware of our intentions by examining them, we can guide our lives in a chosen trajectory.

## 10.   Experience and Practice Pave the Way to Mastery

There is no alternative to experience. It is the best way to learn and to grow. Being in the world and facing actual events is how we find out what kind of a person we are. We must be tested to see how much we have learned. Earth is a testing and proving ground. The road to mastery is paved by our successes and failures and the lessons we learn.

Our time on Earth is our opportunity to be the best version of ourselves. As we live, we will face many choices. These are our opportunities to make the "right" decisions. There is no punishment for choosing "wrong". There are, however, consequences. If we learn from our mistakes and do not repeat them, then it is worth it. Otherwise, we might face similar situations until we master the challenges that we need to overcome. Experience and practice pave the way to mastery. We can make our stay on Earth a joyous journey or an arduous one.

## 11. Now is all We Have

We can remember the past and project into the future. In reality, now is all we have. Now is where we can act, re-write our past and shape our future. Now is the time and the place because there is no other. It is our center of power. It is our constant companion wherever and whenever we are.

## 12. We are Never Alone

We are never alone. We exist and function on multiple dimensions. We are never static. We have our thoughts to keep us company. We live in a community surrounded by people and nature. Our bodies are communities. Our mind is a treasure trove of memories and tools we can call on. We can remember, imagine and visualize. We have family and friends. Most importantly, we have a spark of God within us. It prompts and whispers to us as The Voice Within. We have nature to appreciate and enjoy. We also have a Higher Self that we can call on at any time. And if we believe it, we even have guardian angels helping us at all times. However, because of our free will, no entity will intervene in our lives unless and until they are invited to do so. We must ask.

We are not alone, yet we can choose to be alone. We can enter the "closet" and shut the door whenever we like.

# PART II

## Know Yourself Intimately

1. Levels of Knowing
2. Trinity
3. We Are a Trinity
4. The Physical
5. The Astral
6. The Spiritual
7. I Am
8. Knowing Our Source
9. We Are in the Image of our Source
10. We Have Three Names
11. The Three Names of God
12. How Can We Know for Certain?

# LEVELS OF KNOWING

*We shall not cease from exploration, and the end of all our exploring will be to arrive where we started and know the place for the first time.* — *T. S. Eliot*

"You know you should give up smoking." I know, I know.

"You know you should take better care of yourself." I know, I know.

"You know you should call or visit your mom more often." I know, I know.

It is customary to say: "I know," but do we really know? Belief is not the same as knowledge. One could hear or read about something and believe it to be true when it is falsehood.

There are at least five forms of knowing:

1. Artificial;
2. Superficial;
3. Intermediate;
4. Intimate; and
5. Revelatory.

Artificial knowing is machine knowing. It is not knowing at all. We can ask machines with artificial intelligence questions and get answers, but do they really know what any of it means? This "knowing" is dumb, programmed and out of a data base. It does not involve comprehension. An example of artificial knowing is using the internet to find answers.

Superficial knowing is to perceive intent and meaning. It is shallow, background knowledge and often is an instinctual response. Superficial knowing is reflexive with no real emotion attached to the knowledge. It is not something we apply to our lives and live accordingly. An example of superficial knowing is remembering what day of the week it is.

Intermediate knowing has emotional value. It is internalizing, thinking about, reflecting on, analyzing and reasoning before accepting. It is embedded knowledge that helps us to be cognizant, to believe and to act accordingly. An example of intermediate knowing is having the skill to solve problems.

Intimate knowing is the deepest form of knowing. It is experiential and pivotal. It is knowing at our core. When we know at this level, we are transformed. We are reborn. We are no longer our old self, but a new being. It is as if a missing piece of a puzzle is found and the picture is complete. With this knowing there is no doubt, facts are self-evident, crystal clear and need no explanation. When we know at this level, we feel free, light and liberated.

To illustrate this form of knowing, here are a few examples from the Bible:

> Now Adam **knew** Eve his wife, and she conceived and bore Cain. Gen 4:1

> When Joseph woke from sleep, he did as the angel of the Lord commanded him: he took his wife, but **knew** her not until she had given birth to a son. And he called his name Jesus. Matt 1:24-25

> Then said Mary unto the angel, "How shall this be, seeing I **know** not a man?" Luke 1:34

When Adam **knew** Eve, she conceived. When Cain **knew** his wife, she conceived. Joseph did not **know** Mary until after Jesus was born. Mary did not understand how she could conceive since she had not known a man through intercourse.

Knowing is wholistic, a right-brain function. When we know, we simply accept it. We do not wonder, question or doubt. When Joseph woke up from his dream, he knew what he needed to do. He acted accordingly without hesitation or doubt.

> *And when they were departed, behold, the angel of the Lord appeareth to Joseph in a dream, saying, Arise, and take the young child and his mother, and flee into Egypt, and be thou there until I bring thee word: for Herod will seek the young child to destroy him. When he arose, he took the young child and his mother by night, and departed into Egypt: Matt 2:13-14*

This "knowing" is not simple understanding. It is acquiring wisdom and becoming enlightened. The ancients equated this KNOWING to the sexual act. The state of an individual changes dramatically as a result of a person's first sexual experience. To express the difference in the two states dramatically, the ancients chose the state of virginity to represent one state while experience would represent the other state. The state of lack of experience, innocence, having one's eyes closed and not knowing is represented by virginity. Gaining in worldly knowledge through experience represents having one's eyes opened, loss of innocence, wakefulness and knowing good and evil.

Finally, there is revelatory knowing. This is when we have an inspiration, an intuition and a gut feeling. This is a gift from our Higher Self that we know to be true. An example of revelatory knowing is the organization of this book and several of the ideas contained within.

## What Happens When We Know?

When we **know**, it is like finding the part of ourself that was missing. It is like the Prodigal Son returning to the "Father." It is like the question finding its answer. It is like the door being opened after insistent knocking. It is like remembering something that we had forgotten. When we **know**, there is no doubt. We become wise and can discriminate between good and evil. When we **know**, we feel light, liberated and a new version of us is born.

When Adam and Eve ate of the forbidden fruit, their eyes opened and they knew that they were naked. They were naked all along, but could not see it. They needed that pivotal experience so their eyes would open and they could see for the first time.

When we know, four related things take place.

First: The knowledge acquired changes our internal mental and psychic organization. This change is reflected in the neural networks of the brain. The neurons form new associations to reflect the knowledge gained.

Second: We become proportionately transfigured by the knowledge gained and its impact. We give birth to new areas of ourselves every time we know. We acquire added power, freedom and responsibility. Eventually, when we gain enough knowledge, we are totally reborn into a new being, a being of light and power.

Third: Each time we gain knowledge, we reflect our newly gained insights in our daily lives. We help others gain the same knowledge through our example. Some scientists believe that when we learn something new and repeat our new behavior, we create a "morphic resonance" that covers the globe and makes it easier for others to discover the same knowledge.

Fourth: We acquire an added responsibility equal to our new knowledge. When we receive, we must give back in service to others. We must contribute. This is a spiritual obligation.

## How Do We Know?

There are many ways we acquire knowledge:

- Through science we get facts;
- Through religion we acquire faith and belief;
- From personal experiences we glean truths;
- Philosophy gives us understanding;
- From inspiration we get new insights;
- From dreams we can have revelations;
- Using our imagination, we attract solutions;
- Being spiritual leads to transformation.

The path to knowledge should be multiple streams. We should be adept in many branches of knowledge. Curiosity, interest and continuous education not only expand our horizon, they keep us youthful as well.

Personal experience is first-hand knowing. It is direct and powerful. It is the difference between reading about a country and visiting it. It is the difference between seeing a picture of a mango and tasting it. We can read all about the mango, but until we savor it, we do not truly know what a mango is.

It takes experience to become wise. Experience enables us to see what was evident all along. Only crucial, profound and transformative experiences compel us to open our eyes so we may see clearly, unobstructed by past history, heritage or prejudice. The type of experience we need for our eyes to open varies from person to person. Some require several repetitions before they change while for others, one intense experience is all it takes.

There is no substitute for personal experience. In spiritual matters, this is the preferred route to the truth.

## *Cardinal Knowledge*

Like Adam and Eve, we find ourselves in a garden – Earth. Our eyes are closed, but we do not know it. Once we have transformative experiences, we will know and we will gain wisdom and understanding. Our eyes will open. We will become God-like. But what exactly do we need to know? We need to know ourself, who we truly are.

Hence, the cardinal knowledge is the knowledge of self.

How then can we know ourself? What path should we take? Which system should we follow?

We can take several approaches all at once. This way, the concept will sink in, our understanding will be grounded, and we will realize the merits of each approach.

Knowing ourself is instrumental in shedding our ignorance and being reborn as new beings of light. To the extent that we know ourself to that extent can we accept and love ourself. And to the extent that we accept and love ourself, to that degree we can accept and love others. Once we know, accept and love ourself, nothing will stop us from expressing ourself.

We do not suddenly wake up and know ourself. It can happen, but mostly we wake up gradually. Each experience, each encounter, each aha is a credit we deposit in the bank account of our knowing. Just as liquid water requires a certain amount of energy before it transforms into steam, and for solid ice to become liquid water, so it is with us. We must undergo a change in phase. When we accumulate enough experiences and a critical point is reached, the scale tips. We undergo a transformation. We shed our old skin, we gain wisdom, our eyes open, we see clearly and we know that:

**We are a living soul animating a physical body.**

## *Example of Knowing*

If we conduct a survey asking people, "How did you meet, and how did you know you wanted to marry your spouse?", many will relate fascinating anecdotes of synchronicities. They will also tell us that, at some point, they **knew** who they were going to marry. Where does this knowledge come from?

If we survey the same people years later to find out whether or not they made the right choice, what will we find out?

If it was the right choice, what are the reasons?

If it was not the right choice, what are the reasons?

Some marry for a few years while others marry for a lifetime. Regardless, there are always benefits accrued. Three in particular are:

1. Offspring, shared experiences, and memories;
2. Valuable life lessons learned;
3. Achievements that would not have been possible by either spouse alone.

In early 1972, I met my cousin in Canada. He took me with him to Sherbrooke, to visit a family with four daughters. After a brief visit, my cousin knew which one of the four he wanted to marry. He did marry her and they remain happily married to this day.

How did my cousin know which one to choose?

What happened to him to make him decide?

Who exactly is the knower?

What is evident is that when we know, something unusual happens. Something clicks. We feel different, we change and we are transformed.

Obviously, not all marriages last a lifetime. Regardless, there are always unusual gifts bestowed: Learning more about ourself, about the other and becoming more mature.

# TRINITY

*Reason, observation, and experience; the holy trinity of science.*

*– Robert Green Ingersoll*

To celebrate my retirement from the Federal Government, my wife and I took a trip to Egypt. Among the many wonders we visited, the Great Pyramids stood out. These are one of the wonders of the ancient world because of their massive size, the vast number of gigantic stones and the large number of workers it must have taken to build them. These however, are the obvious aspects of the pyramids and are part of the wonder, but not the most significant. The amazing features of the pyramids are the skill, planning, and the ingenuity of knowing how to do it – the blueprint, the design, the sequence of events and mastery of the interdependencies. These are the unseen, the intangible aspects of the Great Pyramids. The obvious aspect of the pyramids is the first leg of a trinity. How the pyramids were built is the second leg. Finally, "why" the pyramids were built is the third and most important aspect.

Looking at any structure, be it a house, a bridge or a computer it is easy to note the obvious – the material component. Yet, what we see is not all that there is. We soon realize that a house, a bridge or a computer are more than their material parts. They embody specific laws without which they would not stand. The analysis, design, and the physical laws incorporated in these structures are as important as the materials used. For without the laws that determine how much concrete to use, what the proportions should be, the sequence of events, and how and where to lay the foundation, a house or a bridge will not stand. Even though the laws and the knowledge are hidden from view, their handiwork is self-evident. An even more important third aspect is why the house, the bridge or the computer were built in the first place. Purpose and utility constitute the third leg of this trinity. These are the driving force behind the manifestations.

We know of the material components because we can see them. They occupy space and, over time, change. They must be maintained. The laws, intentions and the skills of the "creators" are never seen. Neither are their hopes, dreams and purpose. These do not occupy space and do not succumb to the ravages of time. They are intangible. Thus, we have a trinity of:

1. What something is made of;
2. How it is made; and
3. Why it is made.

## The Universe as a Trinity

Cosmology states that existence had its origin in a singularity. This is a small extremely dense "ball" which exploded as the "Big Bang". The Big Bang, just like a fertilized ovum, burst into activity and expanded at a furious pace resulting in the formation of the galaxies and the universes. Because the universes are organized and orderly, the "Big Bang" could not have been a random explosion. It must have been orderly and the beginning of an unfoldment. An organizing intelligence must have been in the singularity from the beginning. It is evident in every aspect of existence. Organization, law and order are indicative of mind and intelligence.

Hence, the original trinity was:

1. Singularity as substance, vibratory energy and matter;
2. Imbued laws, order and organization;
3. Space in which everything exists and can expand into.

## Trinity in the Beginning

*In the beginning, God created the heavens and the earth. The earth was without form and void, and darkness was over the face of the deep. And the Spirit of God was hovering over the face of the waters. Gen 1:1-2*

Looking at the quote above, we have:

1. The deep – space, in darkness;
2. Primordial water filling the deep;
3. Spirit hovering over water.

"In the beginning" there was only the deep full of water and in darkness. Spirit was hovering over the deep. The deep, full of water, was in darkness – asleep and dormant. Water was primordial.

The deep was in darkness which pervaded all. Darkness is the absence of light, never the source of it. Light is ever present. It cycles between wakefulness and sleep. When "awake", it is light. When "asleep", it is darkness. We reflect this duality of sleep and wakefulness in our daily lives. Just as we cycle between sleep and wakefulness, so does the cosmos. The cycle is like a see-saw. When the sleep cycle is over, wakefulness begins. When light appears, darkness is dispelled, instantly.

The reference in the Bible to water is significant. This water is not what we are used to. It is primordial. According to J. C. Cooper author of **An Illustrated Encyclopedia of Traditional Symbols:**

> *"The waters are the source of all potentialities in existence; the source and grave of all things in the universe; the undifferentiated; the unmanifest; the first form of matter, ... All waters are symbolic of the Great Mother and associated with birth, the feminine principle, the universal womb, the prima materia, the waters of fertility and refreshment and the fountain of life. Water is the liquid counterpart of light"*

**"Water is the liquid counterpart of light".**

Eve, in Genesis, symbolized Primordial water. Eve is the mother of all the living. On Earth, the mother of all the living is ocean water where life began. Hence, water is the mother of life and it is also the source of all potentiality. That is why the deep is full of primordial water. It is common knowledge that without water, there is no life. Since water is the liquid counterpart of light, without light, there is nothing.

This is why the first act of creation in the Old Testament was the creation of light. There are two types of light: tangible and intangible. Tangible light is material emanating from stars such as our sun while intangible light is spiritual. The intangible light precedes the tangible light. Hence the first act of creation was not tangible light, rather intangible light.

> And God said, "Let there be light," and there was light.
> Gen 1:3

This was on day 1. This light could not have been physical light since the stars were not created until day 4. This light was intangible, spiritual light.

## Intangible Light

Intangible light is spiritual light which is of two forms:

1.  Wisdom and understanding. That is why we

say "I see" meaning I understand. It is also equivalent with the Logos and the intellect;

*The LORD by wisdom founded the earth;*
*by understanding he established the heavens;*
*by his knowledge the deeps broke open,*
*and the clouds drop down the dew.  Prov. 3:19-20*

2.  Radiance, effulgence, and illumination. That is why Jesus and the saints are pictured with a halo of radiance about them. In fact, their aura is a specific radiance of light.

With spiritual light, everything is imbued with law, order, life, intelligence and consciousness. In the New Testament, the embodiment of spiritual light is the Holy Spirit, the Word, the Logos, or Wisdom (Sophia) and the Christ Consciousness.

*In the beginning was the Word, and the Word was with*
*God, and the Word was God. He was in the beginning*
*with God. All things were made through him, and*
*without him was not any thing made that was made.*
*In him was life, and the life was the light of men. The*
*light shines in the darkness, and the darkness has not*
*overcome it.*                                    *John1:1-5*

A Word is a trinity of sound, vibration and meaning or intent. Logos is a special word or an utterance – it is the word of God. Words flow from the mind.  Logos flows from the mind of God as a trinity of sound, vibration and the message it conveys.


## Tangible Light

Tangible light is physical light which is also in two forms:

1. wave;
2. and particle.

Tangible light is the source of energy and matter and what the cosmos is made of. Living entities consist of both types of light. Materially, tangible light and spiritually, intangible light. Those with radiant intangible, spiritual light are awake, "alive" and enlightened. Those without much spiritual light are in the dark, asleep and "spiritually dead".

## The Ultimate Trinity

At times, almost all of us experience a knowing. "I know this is the house I want." "I know this is the person I am going to marry". "I know I am in love". "I know I should quit this job". "I know this is the trip I have been waiting for".

Knowing happens. We might not fully understand how or why, but we accept it.

Knowing is a trinity of:

1. Knower;
2. The Knowing; and
3. The Known.

We know that we are the knower, but what we do we mean by we as knower? Is it our brain that knows? Is it our emotions? Or, is it the physical body? If we take the time and look into this, we come to realize that the knower is beyond the brain, the emotions and the body. When we know, this knowing engulfs us. It is like a **field** permeating us,

**Everything we experience takes place in a field**. This is a scientific fact, but it is also easy to see it for ourselves. While awake, we are accustomed to think that our experiences are taking place out there in the world. They are not. They are taking place in our minds and **the mind is a field**. We know this to be a fact when we sleep and dream. All dreams take place in the mind. Yet, while dreaming we believe that we are experiencing space, time and movement out there. In the daytime, the conscious mind "projects" on this field its creations. While dreaming, the subconscious mind "projects" our dream dramas on this field.

A basic understanding of what the field and mind are is to consider them aspects of consciousness. Consciousness is the most fundamental aspect of reality. Without it, there is no reality. Without a witness to existence, nothing matters. Consciousness is described as a fluidic field. This field is everywhere. It is the creative, intelligent substrate of existence. Mind is the creative aspect of consciousness. It assigns dimensionality to the field and fashions our experiential realties. What results are various condensations of Light. Thus, consciousness is a trinity:

1. Consciousness as fluidic field, the substrate;
2. Consciousness as fashioner, Mind;
3. Consciousness as the fashioned, Light.

Regardless of how creation took place, it involves a trinity. Most likely, creation started as a seed. Seeds (wheat kernel for example) are a trinity of an outer coat (bran), an intermediate nutrient layer (endosperm) and an inner layer (germ) containing the nucleic acids and other essentials. Everything can be created through trinities by varying sequence, proportion and intensity. Triplets of nucleotides compose amino acids which form all the proteins. The three primary colors of **red, green, and blue** can be combined in different proportions to make other colors. Similarly, from the various combinations of **electrons**, **protons** and **neutrons** all physical manifestations result. Perhaps that is why in Christianity we have the trinity of Father, Son and Holy Spirit.

# WE ARE A TRINITY

*Who am I? Not the body, because it is decaying; not the mind, because the brain will decay with the body; not the personality, nor the emotions, for these also will vanish with death.*

*– Ramana Maharishi*

I t is easy to make a statement such as: "We are a Trinity." It is much more difficult to make such a statement from conviction – knowing it is a fact based on personal experience and supported by evidence. The ultimate question is "Are we advanced beasts or is there more to us?"

Even as a child I wanted to know if and how we are different from animals. Are we just like them, or is there something special about being a human?

> *I said in my heart with regard to the children of man that God is testing them that they may see that they themselves are but beasts. For what happens to the children of man and what happens to the beasts is the same; as one dies, so dies the other. They all have the same breath, and man has no advantage over the beasts, for all is vanity. All go to one place. All are from the dust, and to dust all return. Eccl. 3:18-20*

It is obvious that we have a body just as any animal. We also have hidden aspects that are even more important than the physical body. The body is a mere receptacle, a housing for our memories, skills, abilities, beliefs, knowledge and relationships. Examining the body would never reveal who we really are: the fact that we are spouses, parents, siblings, who we love, who we are loved by, what we believe and what are we capable of. These are hidden aspects that upon inquiry might be discovered. We also have a secret aspect that does not reveal itself to inquiry – what our private thoughts, beliefs, experiences are and what our future accomplishments will be.

For many years I struggled with the concept of soul. Is soul real or is it fiction? Are we a mere physical body or is there more to us? Fortunately, I have a childhood memory of an incident I can never forget. I found myself hovering in midair looking down at my physical body lying motionless on the ground. The neighbor found me and began screaming that I was dead. In response, I screamed back that I was not dead. Suddenly I realized that she could not hear or see me. Even worse, I could not move any part of my body on the ground. That is when I realized that without the part of me that was floating, the physical body had no volition of its own. It could not move, talk or be alive. This incident proved to me the existence of the astral body.

Years later I had another, even more unforgettable experience that proved to me the existence of yet a third aspect to my being. For a week I had the haunting knowing that I was going to die. I could not shake this "knowing" off. It haunted me day and night. An inner "knowing" urged me to put my house in order and write down my final instructions. I resisted and refused to accept that I will soon die. I was afraid and did not want to leave my family behind. Then it happened, but instead of dying, I had a near-death-experience.[1]

Even though the experience itself was life altering, what puzzled me most was the clarity and persistence of the voice alerting me of my impending demise.

What was this "knowing" and where was the voice coming from?
What was the source of its knowledge?
Why was I being alerted?

The knowledge that I was about to die was like nothing I had ever experienced before. It was overwhelming, total and unshakable. There was nothing I could do to stop it until I had my near-death-experience.

Even though this distinct voice was persistent and lasted for a week, it was not the first or last time that I encountered it. Looking back at my life I realize that all of my major decisions, without question, were the result of acting according to this voice. This voice was a power that not only "spoke" to me, it also arranged all my synchronicities. It is responsible for my life being what it is. Here are a few examples:

1. What was the likelihood of my being sent to a monastery in Lebanon after my mother's death?
2. Why did I have an atrocious chanting voice that played a major role in my decision to leave the monastery?
3. What is the chance that a group of psychology students from the American University of Beirut (AUB) would visit my High School? Had they not visited when they did, I would never have attended college (AUB).
4. Having come from a monastery, what made me join the US Army?
5. Why did I have an irresistible urge to join the Rosicrucian Order AMORC?
6. What was the voice that guided me to my future wife?
7. Where did the unwavering desire to write, teach and publish books come from?

The answer to all of the above is The Voice Within. Since this voice was specific to me, coming from I know not where and always with the absolutely best advice I could receive, I am led to the inescapable conclusion that there must be a third aspect to me that is "all-knowing, wise and personal." I am only aware of this part of me when I need it most. "It" decides to reveal itself to me. Its presence is a secret. It is the source of my inspiration when I write or teach and is the source of the answers that I receive after persistent inquiry. Without this part, I would not be able to write, teach or be who I am. Hence, I am a trinity of three aspects: an obvious physical body, a hidden astral body and a secret spiritual aspect. These three are "layers" I wrap myself with. They are three interwoven spheres surrounding my inner core, my I Am.

Once, as a result of a motorcycle accident, I lost consciousness and when I came to, my memory was wiped clean. I did not know my name, where I lived or who anyone was. Even though my memory was gone, I still knew that I, as an individual, existed.

There is an aspect of us we never lose – who we are. We never forget that we are an individual. When we are young and we look in the mirror, we recognize ourselves. When we are old and we look in the mirror, we know who we are. Looking at pictures of ourselves from any age, we always recognize ourselves even though the body never stops changing. We do not have to think, imagine or need anyone to tell us that we exist. We know that the essence of who we are has been with us throughout our life – always the same, never changing, evolving or ceasing to be. This essence is our true identity, our soul, our I Am.

The French mathematician and philosopher René Descartes declared: "I think, therefore I am" (cogito, ergo sum). Even if we do not think, we still know that we are. We know ourselves even in our dreams. This I Am is our nucleus, our core, the background against which all of our other aspects are superimposed. Our I Am is surrounded by three components as if we are wearing three layers of clothing: an outer jacket, a shirt and an undershirt.

1. A physical component – the outer jacket. A material body we have had since conception.
2. An astral component – a shirt. An energetic light body that we are developing.
3. A spiritual component – an undershirt. A highly evolved light body that is the closest to our core identity.

The physical body is what we need to exist on planet Earth. It is condensed light vibrating at a very low frequency. The physical body is dense, material and limited in its functionality. Upon death it disintegrates and is gone forever. The lifespan of the physical body varies with a higher limit of around 120 years.

The astral body is similar to the physical body except that it is much finer with higher frequency and far more capabilities. The astral body is energetic light with intermediate density. It is the source of our life and vitality. It survives death as long as it remains associated with the spiritual body. Together, the astral and the spiritual reincarnate into a new physical body.

The spiritual body is closest to our core, the I Am. It has the highest frequency and the most abilities. The spiritual body is permanent. It never dies. It is the source of our consciousness, houses our individuality, character and personality. It is also the source of our higher emotions such as love and empathy and our higher mental faculties such as visualization and imagination. Without a spiritual body, we have no permanent existence.

I Am is our core and essence. It is surrounded by the spiritual body which in turn is surrounded by the astral body which is surrounded by the physical body. These three coexist and intermingle. The spiritual penetrates the astral which in turn infiltrates the physical.

These three components correspond to the three worlds that we inhabit:

1. The physical world;
2. The astral world; and
3. The spiritual world.

We are a trinity of physical, astral and spiritual. The first is obvious, the second is hidden but can be seen as the aura. The third is secret, known only to a very few. Our physical body being material can be experienced, analyzed and studied. It occupies space and is continuously changing. Our astral component is evident during astral travel and out-of-body experiences. Our most important component, the spiritual, is non-existent or is vestigial in most. It reveals itself during inspiration, intuition, guidance, hunches and gut feelings. These flow from our Higher Self, through the astral to the physical brain. Unless we are attuned and can adequately receive and make use of the inspiration, The Voice Within will remain silent. We hear The Voice Within when we cultivate our minds via education, curiosity, desire and persistent questioning. The more attuned we are to the Higher Self, the better the connection and the clearer the inspiration.

# THE PHYSICAL

*It's also helpful to realize that this very body that we have, that's sitting right here right now... with its aches and its pleasures... is exactly what we need to be fully human, fully awake, fully alive.*
*– Pema Chodron*

The human body has been in the making since the beginning of life. It has evolved into its current state. It is perfectly adapted for life on earth. It is matter made up of the elements of Earth. It is dust and to dust it returns after the animating spirit departs.

*By the sweat of your face you shall eat bread, till you return to the ground, for out of it you were taken; for you are dust, and to dust you shall return. Gen 3:19*

Our body is the house we live in. It can be a meager hut or a castle. It is meant to be a temple.

*Jesus answered them, "Destroy this temple, and in three days I will raise it up." The Jews then said, "It has taken forty-six years to build this temple, and will you raise it up in three days?" But he was speaking about the temple of his body. John 2:19-21*

The body is an amazing abode. Just as a house has a foundation, an electrical system, plumbing, heating and air conditioning, secure doors and windows, walls and a roof to delineate and protect it, so does the body. The body has a digestive system to extract nutrients from food, a circulatory system to distribute essentials throughout the body. It has security and defense, respiratory, urinary, eliminatory, endocrine, immune, muscular, skeletal, nervous, and reproductive systems, all harmoniously working together. Just as a house is plugged into a source of power, electricity, so is the body. It is connected to the astral body via an "umbilical" cord.

The living unit in the body is the cell which is a center of operations. We have trillions of cells with about two hundred different types carrying out specialized functions. Organization and specialization are the key ways the body carries out its activities. Cells organize into tissues, organs and systems all working together to ensure the utmost effectiveness and efficiency to maximize survival, adaptability and progress.

We have two major centers of operation: the heart and the brain. These two centers are indicative of the two aspects of our being: reason and intuition, thinking and feeling, the arts and the sciences, feminine and masculine qualities. With the brain we can think, reason, compare and contrast. More importantly, we can concentrate, contemplate, visualize, imagine and meditate. With the heart we can feel and have emotions. More importantly, we can empathize, be compassionate and love. Mental creation requires the combined use of the faculties of mind and heart.

The more extensively we study the body and its components, the more in awe we are of the intricacy of design, the sophistication of the inter-communications and the marvel of cooperation that makes the body what it is. There are extensive intra and extra cellular communications within and among cells at all times. The language of the communications is chemical and electrical.

Even though we know a great deal about the workings of the body, life and consciousness remain mysteries because, for many, the focus is only the physical body. They do not acknowledge that we have astral and spiritual components.

Are we merely sophisticated machines? Are our cells employees working in an organization or factory to enable life? Why are we programmed to age and die even though we continuously produce new cells to replace the worn-out ones?

A computer is a machine. It houses powerful software along with an operating system that runs the hardware. The operating system is the same for most computers. It is an essential aspect of the machine or else it won't turn on. The human operating system is a product of evolution. It is designed for survival. It continues to evolve and improve with use. The specialty software is unique and an add-on for tailored operations. Each computer has different added software depending on what is desired to be performed. In humans, we have physical specialized software such as enzymes, hormones and catalysts and mental specialized software in the form of habits, beliefs and knowledge. These act as programs or sub-routines that automate and simplify our lives. They propel us beyond survival to thrive and make the most of our experiences.

Yet, we do not function like sophisticated machines. Unlike machines that are programmed to perform any task indefinitely, we get bored. We seek value and meaning. We want to contribute to what we believe in. We crave contact, association, appreciation and above all, acceptance, intimacy and love. We cannot survive without affection. Our life must have meaning or else we do not see any sense in carrying on. Besides, what machine gets hunches, gut feelings, intuitions and inspirations?

The body we live in might be a machine, but we are not

machines. We are the machine users. We are the driver, maintainer and the master of the machine. For as long as we occupy our temple, the machine, the body lives. As soon as we depart, the machine as body, dies. We are endowed with life, self-awareness, freedom of choice and consciousness. These not only set us apart from machines, they make us human. These are properties of our astral and spiritual components.

## Our DNA

The nucleus houses the blueprint of the body in the form of DNA (deoxyribonucleic acid). DNA is the lead architect. It has the information to make proteins in various forms such as antibodies, enzymes and hormones. Discovering the sophistication of DNA as a language capable of writing any "encyclopedia" is magical.

Our entire genetic blueprint is contained in each cell. Genes are the stored information needed to replicate and assemble proteins that are needed for living functions. Even though genes are the blueprints, the aspects of the blueprint that are activated is determined by the environment in which the cells find themselves. Different environments activate different aspects of the genome. Therefore, the body is what it is, because of the environment we find ourselves in.

Just as we extract nutrients from food to build our cells, we distill our experiences into memories. Thoughts, feelings and intent propel us to action. Actions distill into habits; habits distill into attitudes; attitudes distill into expectations; expectations distill into beliefs and knowledge and ultimately into lessons learned and instinct. These are incorporated into our character and personality and are imprinted into our DNA. These are carried forward in our gametes, the sex cells. Physically, we are in the image of our blueprint, the DNA.

The body grows and maintains itself by the intelligence in

its blueprint, the DNA. This DNA is an extremely long, thin filament in the form of a double helix compacted in the nucleus of each cell. It is like a long ladder twisted upon itself. DNA cannot be a simple chemical compound. It has intelligence far beyond how to make proteins. It "knows" when to increase hormone production so special features and characteristics can manifest at specific times in the lifecycle of the body. It "knows" when to set off certain functions such as the onset of adolescence, menstruation and menopause. It "knows" how and when to decrease hormone production with age. It "knows" what type of hair to grow, where and when. It "knows" when to turn some hair white while others maintain their normal color. It "knows" how to preserve the rhythms and cycles of the body, when to sleep, when to wake up, when to age and when to die.

Most amazingly, DNA "knows" how to preserve measurements and ensure symmetry. Have you ever wondered why your fingers, arms, legs, eyes and ears grow only to a specific size? And how do they remain absolutely symmetrical? These are not easy tasks. That is why it is believed that DNA is not only physical residing within the nucleus of each cell, but it is also multidimensional spread out as a field surrounding the body. This field enables the DNA in one cell to communicate with the DNA in any other cell. This field is variously known as the L-field or the Life field. It is related to the aura and the astral body. DNA is conscious. Its consciousness impacts living matter.

## The Physical Body

Living in the body, we mostly function in survival mode, struggling and competing for crumbs. We forget that we are the drivers. We can impact the state of our body via our thoughts, emotions and visualizations. This influence is evident, but slow to take effect. We can augment this and greatly enhance it by the intensity of our emotions and by the laser-sharp focus of our mental images. While many function by instinct and react to situations, others use reason, logic and memory to facilitate their activities. We can employ our advanced spiritual and mental faculties such as concentration, visualization and imagination to innovate, to create and to live impactful lives.

We are a miracle, a true wonder and a marvel to behold. Each cell is a factory with hundreds of thousands of reactions taking place every second. Our bodies are a conglomeration of matter and energy, emotions and feelings, mind, will, skills and abilities. These are the worker bees while we are the queen bee. If we move, our subjects follow. If our motion is calculated, we get to where we want to be, otherwise we flounder.

Important things to remember about our bodies:

1. The body is made up of octillions of atoms and trillions of cells. It is resilient, adapts to its environment and it can heal itself.

2. We are a community of trillions of cells. These cells are individuals combining forces to form our corporate bodies. Our bodies house vast numbers of temporary and permanent settlers in the form of microorganisms that live within us symbiotically or parasitically. Our bodies are diverse communities coexisting peacefully, productively and harmoniously. Perhaps we can learn from our bodies and do the same.

3. There are about 200 different cell types organized into tissues, organs and systems. Our cells are "listening" to us, especially to our subconscious and are doing our bidding. Our cells are trainable. Practice and repetition establish new neural

connections, strengthen their pathways and create habits that can serve or hinder us.

4. Specialization is the key to the effectiveness and efficiency of the body. Sharing, cooperation and excellence are the overriding qualities. Division of labor is an important aspect of this highly efficient and effective body.

5. The body is a corporation with headquarters and specialty sub-divisions. Red blood cells transport oxygen. Muscle cells enable movement. Neurons facilitate nerve impulses. Sex cells ensure the continuation of life through reproduction.

6. The skin, the largest organ, acts as the barrier between the body and the environment. It is highly intelligent and facilitates what goes in or comes out. It senses the weather and keeps us cool or warm. Our skin is the interface between two different worlds, yet these worlds are intimately connected and are in constant interface. Thus, if it is hot outside, our skin relays the message to our internal organization which adjusts itself by perspiring. The skin enables us to touch, feel and be intimate.

7. We have thousands of miles of blood vessels that circulate nutrients, oxygen and chemicals throughout the body.

8. We have billions of neurons that enable us to, not only exist on earth, but flourish as well.

9. The body symbiotically cooperates with microorganisms to break down food using

chemicals which they produce. It "knows" how to extract energy from food. It "knows" how to use oxygen for combustion. It "knows" how to sanitize and how to get rid of waste. It has several defense systems that work cooperatively and symbiotically with an overwhelming number of microorganisms that live everywhere in and on the body to keep us safe and healthy.

10. Microorganisms within us have tremendous value. We cannot live or function without them. We have more microbes in the body than our own cells. Microorganism genes are more abundant in our bodies than our own genome.

11. According to Arahad O'Connor (The Washington Post 9/20/2022) "studies show that our gut microbes transform the food into thousands of enzymes, hormones, vitamins and other metabolites that influence everything from your mental health and immune system to your likelihood of gaining weight and developing chronic diseases." "Gut microbia even affect your mental state by producing mood-altering neurotransmitters like dopamine which regulates pleasure, learning and motivation, and serotonin, which plays a role in happiness, appetite and sexual desire. The composition of your gut microbiome can even affect how well you sleep."

12. Just as cells are in constant contact with the environment through their cell membranes, we are in constant contact with the environment. Communications are ongoing.

13. The senses, along with the skin are our windows to the external environment.

14. There is a lot more to our bodies than we are aware of. The intricacy of its design defies comprehension. We could spend months studying the chemical composition of the cellular components. There is an embedded intelligence everywhere.

15. Even though the body is highly intelligent and is on auto-pilot, it needs care. To function at optimum, it requires nutrition, elimination, exercise, cleanliness, rest, play, intimacy and merriment. Being social, we need intimacy, sex and love.

16. Sex is not only for physical pleasure and procreation. It is a means for intimacy and togetherness.

17. The body is on a journey. At different stages on its cyclic existence, it manifests various abilities and tendencies. It is in full bloom at maturity. Yet, it is prone to ups and downs, diseases and infirmities.

18. Above all, the body is our abode. We live in the body. Its health and well-being are our responsibility.

## Exercise

To have an inkling of how wondrous our bodies are, look up the answers to the following questions:

1. How many miles of blood vessels do we have?

2. How many nerve endings are at the bottom of our feet?

3. How long is the thread of DNA in each cell? Multiply that by the number of cells in the average body to find out the length of DNA contained in the human body.

## The Purpose of the Physical Body

We are creative just as our source, God is. However, we are infant creators. Just as infants are not allowed to play with fire and must wait until they grow up to use fire, we must mature before we can instantaneously mentally create. We must practice, learn and improve. This necessitates our being in a physical body. While in the body, our creations are temporary. We must learn from our temporary creations before we graduate to creating permanent structures. We start slow creating with "sand" before we venture forth to create with "concrete".

All creations are mental in origin prior to manifesting in the physical. Every thought, emotion and intention is causative. Earth is the laboratory where we practice mental creation, mostly without much awareness. Manifestations take place after all obstacles are removed and the path is clear for the components to come together. This takes time and only happens if the contradicting forces do not cancel each other out. We learn the reality of our creativity in the astral world where thoughts and intentions manifest instantly. The manifestations, however, do not last because they are based on individual effort driven by selfish desires. Conflicting creations cancel each other out. As long as we are selfishly focused on ourselves, our creations will not endure. Manifestations in the spiritual world are permanent because they are the result of the cooperative effort of many spiritual beings collaborating to create beautiful and harmonious environments. To make sure that what we manifest in the spiritual world is well thought out, we must learn how to mentally create with intent and in consideration of others. This is why we must incarnate into a physical body where we practice. We are like children when in the physical world. We are like adolescents when in the astral world. We must be mature adults in the spiritual world. As children in a physical body, we are ignorant of how we are mentally creating our experiences. As adolescents in the astral body, we learn how mental creation takes place and how responsible we are for our experiences. Once our spiritual bodies are fully developed, we collaborate with others and begin to create in earnest. We create for the benefit of others.

Just as while learning to drive a car, we practice locally before we venture onto the highway, so it is with mental creation. Our local, safe practice arena is the physical world. Here is where we practice using our minds and emotions often without realizing how creative we are. This is because the results of our creativity do not manifest immediately. In the astral world, we discover the power of our thoughts, emotions and intentions to create. It is here that we realize we are the creators of our reality. Here, we discover the haphazard nature of individual creations and the importance of co-creation. Finally, in the spiritual world, we apply lessons learned to mental creations. In the spiritual world, creations are detailed, harmonious and permanent necessitating the contributions of many evolved individuals. This is why we must master relationships while in the physical body. In the spiritual world we will need to cooperate to co-create beautiful, harmonious and permanent structures and environments.

# THE ASTRAL

*Humans are amphibians - half spirit and half animal.
As spirits they belong to the eternal world, but as
animals they inhabit time.* – C. S. Lewis

We know the astral exists because millions have experienced it. If you ever were out-of-your-body or had dreams where you were flying or floating, then you have experienced the astral. The astral reveals a fundamental truth that escapes the vast majority of people - we create our reality.

The astral body is an energy body analogous to the physical body in that it has similar senses. It is aware, can see, hear, smell, taste and feel. Because it is conscious energy, it instantly reacts to intention and desire. The astral body can move from place to place at the speed of thought. It can hover and it can go through solid objects.

Since the astral body instantly reacts to intention and desire, then we are definitely creating our reality regardless of which world we exist in. The physical also reacts to intention and desire. However, the impact is minor and the manifestation is slow. In addition to time lag in the physical world, we must contend with many obstacles such as other peoples' desires and intentions. The astral world teaches us that we reap in accordance to what we sow in the form of thoughts, intentions and expectations. Yet most of what we sow are unconscious, unintended and accidental.

Those who find themselves out-of-the-body realize that the moment they desire to be in a specific place, they are instantly transported there. If they think of a person, they instantly find themselves in the presence of that person. **What does this tell us? We create our own reality. This is an incredible revelation that we must take to heart. If we create our own reality in the astral world via thoughts and intentions, it must be so in the physical world as well. In other words, we are responsible for our lives**.

This fact is revealed in our sleep and dreams. Our dream creations are the consequences of our thoughts, feelings, desires and intentions. Just as we create our dream experiences, we create our fortunes and misfortunes in the physical world. We are powerful indeed. We are in charge of our destiny. Yet we are mostly oblivious to the fact of our power. Fortunately, the astral, spiritual and the dream worlds reveal the truth – we create what we experience.

We are co-creators with divinity. However, what we create individually is often haphazard, weak and temporary. It does not endure. What we create in the astral world is our individual reality alone, not shared by anyone else. It takes place in our local field of consciousness. Others cannot see it or experience it. Creating permanent realities is a joint venture. It requires the cooperation of many. Unless we master relationships and work together for a common good, we are not ready for the spiritual world where co-creating is a must.

◆ ◆ ◆

The astral body is intimately connected to the physical body via a "silver cord" which can be seen while out of the body. Once back in the body, the silver cord is nowhere to be found. The astral body shines through the physical, extending beyond it. It appears as the human aura. When in physical proximity with others, our astral bodies (auras) intertwine and assess each other. Those with compatible auras attract, those with incompatible auras repel. This explains attractions and repulsions between people. Spouses who have been together for many years and are in love have their auras constantly intertwined which makes it easy for them to read each other's thoughts and intentions. The astral bodies of twins are in communion. They are aware of their connections. Telepathic communications take place via the astral bodies. In fact, being aware of anything establishes an astral link to that thing.

When we love deeply, the connection of the astral bodies is strong. When we hate passionately, the hate is in the astral body. We are always linked to our parents, children, siblings and those with whom we have emotional attachments by astral "cords". When a child or sibling is born, the connections are established in the astral bodies. When we lose a family member or someone close, we feel it in the astral body. This link extends even to our favorite pets, places, foods and activities. While some of the links are via a thread and are casual, others are via a cord and are profound. In some cases, parents' proclivities such as lack of self-confidence seems to affect a child's self-confidence as well. When one acquires self-confidence, the other seems to do the same instantly. We are entangled through our astral bodies just as entangled particles are. Our entanglements are unaffected by space or time.

Moods, thoughts and emotions have an immediate impact on the astral body. Hence, how we choose to think and feel has an impact on the astral body which in turn influences the physical body and its wellbeing. The astral body also determines our health, energy and vitality (magnetism.) What renders us magnetic is the nature of our thoughts and emotions. What we radiate are thoughts, feelings, intentions, expectations, hopes and dreams. These attract to us what we experience. If we radiate positive expectations, then that is what we draw to ourselves. If we believe in doom and gloom, then that is what we attract.

If we pollute ourselves with negative emotions such as jealousy, envy, hatred, fear and anger, then our astral bodies become polluted. We can cleanse our astral bodies by giving thanks for all of our blessings including our challenges. By thinking optimistic thoughts and by feeling positive emotions such as empathy, love and joy, our astral bodies become purified. What we dwell on, whether positive or negative, we empower. This influences the rate of our vibration, the makeup of the astral body and the nature of our experiences.

## Astral World

The astral world is where we came from to be born on Earth and it is where we go after we die. It is also home to ghosts, apparitions and nature spirits. We experience the astral world while out-of-the-body, during near-death-experiences, in dreams and while under the influence of drugs and hallucinogens. The astral body can take us anywhere by merely thinking of a place, desiring something, or intending to experience something. This is why it is critical to develop focus, thought control and clear intentions while living. We will need these in the astral world or else we will find ourselves all over the place, confused and at a loss of what is happening to us.

Some, through practice, develop the ability to willfully free their astral bodies and travel to the astral world. They return to their physical bodies having gained insights and the certainty that life does not end with the death of the physical body. They know that life continues.

Upon death, the silver cord is severed and the astral body is freed from the physical. Initially, the departing entity experiences exactly what that person expected to experience. This is in according to their belief. Pious Christians experience the presence of Holy People such as Saints and Christ. Others find themselves in the presence of personalities according to their faith. Evil people, expecting punishment, experience fear and trepidations. Fortunately, these experiences are temporary created by the imaginings and expectations of the deceased. After a period of adjustment, personal illusions disappear. We are confronted with the reality of the astral world. We realize that Earth has been a place to learn and to contribute. Looking at our lives, we decide how we performed. We determine our reward and our punishment. For many, this is the first time they fully realize that they create their reality.

## Spirit world

What Exactly Are Spirits?

The foundation of all existence is light. There are different degrees of light based on vibratory rates. The physical, astral and spiritual bodies are light energies vibrating at varying rates. The physical body and the material world are light energies vibrating at extremely slow rates. The astral body and the astral world are light energies vibrating at a higher rate. The spiritual body and the spiritual world are light energies vibrating at a very high rate. I Am does not vibrate.

We are light. As we live and experience, we stamp this light and format it in our image and likeness based on the experiences we have, the memories we form, and the lessons we learn. Our thoughts and feelings imprint our body of light. If these are positive and good, we vibrate at a higher rate. If they are negative and evil, we vibrate at a lower rate. Our rate of vibration is reflected as a color. Good spirits have brighter and lighter colors. Evil spirits have darker and heavier colors. Hence spirits are light beings with a specific vibratory rate and color.

We become spirits, ghosts and apparitions after we leave our bodies behind. Most spirits are neutral in the sense that they are a mixture of good and evil. Some spirits are mostly good while others are predominantly evil. It is more appropriate to label the evil spirits as ignorant and immature. The astral world is not a uniform world. There are various "houses" in the astral world. It is layered based on the various vibratory rates of its occupants. The good spirits vibrating at higher rates occupy the higher realms.

> In my Father's house are many rooms. If it were not so, would I have told you that I go to prepare a place for you?
> John 14:2

Evidence of spirits is in our Holy Books, religious beliefs and daily lives. Thought-forms can even be a factor in our moods and dispositions. This is evident in cases of "possessions" which were not only in the ancient times, but are with us today disguised as temperament.

Unless we guard our minds, other people's or entities thought-forms can influence our mood and behavior. We are spirits inhabiting physical bodies. We have freedom of choice as to how we behave. If we choose goodness, we are good spirits. If we choose evil, we are evil spirits. If we have a strong personality, we are solely responsible for who and what we are. If we have a weak personality, the door is open for external entities to influence us or to even take possession of our minds and direct our actions. Our struggle to choose between good and evil is ongoing.

> Put on the whole armor of God, that you may be able to stand against the schemes of the devil. For we do not wrestle against flesh and blood, but against the rulers, against the authorities, against the cosmic powers over

*this present darkness, against the spiritual forces of evil in the heavenly places. Eph 6:11-12*

## Evidence of Spirit in Folklore and Religion

**Primitive religions** believe in animism and nature spirits.

**Folklore** contains fairies, imps, elves and gnomes.

**Zorasterism** espouses Ahura Mazda and Ahriman, good and evil spirits.

**Hinduism** identifies many gods which are spirit entities.

**Buddhism** recognizes the existence of non-physical realms, entities, intelligences and various states of existence.

**Judaism** is replete with angels and spirits in various guises as in the burning bush, angels appearing as men (Sodom and Gomorrah) and spirits appearing in people's dreams (Abraham and many others).

Similarly, **Christianity** has many angels and spirits appearing to perform various functions such as announcing the Virgin birth.

**Islam** also has angels and spirits including Jinni. It was Gabriel who appeared to Muhammad and gave him the Koran.

In **Mormonism**, it was the angel Moroni who gave Joseph Smith the book of Mormon.

## Good Spirits

There are many good people in the world. These are caring, considerate, peace-loving, helpful and generous individuals. What is different about these people is their mental framework, noble spirit and their comforting aura. These people are carriers for "good spirits."

We know good spirits by their nature, the fruit of their actions.

> But the fruit of the Spirit is love, joy, peace, patience, kindness, goodness, faithfulness, Gal 5:22

Good spirits never possess individuals. They simply and silently whisper to us and inspire us. They present us with positive options. They instruct us to choose good.

We are temporarily "possessed" with good spirits when our spirit soars with joy and when we are in love and radiating. We are full of good spirit when we are touched by beauty, choose to do good, help, serve and give gladly. We invite good spirits when we pray, meditate, or express gratitude. We are agents of the light any time we choose to do good.

## Evil Spirits

There are evil people in the world. Those who kidnap, torture and kill other human beings are carriers of evil spirits. What is different about these individuals is their mental framework, their hardened hearts, mean spirit and their repulsive auras. Evil is a disease of the mind and the spirit. Evil-spirited people have dark, heavy astral bodies. They lack compassion, empathy and do not care about anyone other than themselves.

Just like the good spirits, we know evil spirits by their nature. Christ admonished us that "by their fruit you can know them." If the fruit is evil, then the source is evil.

> You will recognize them by their fruits. Are grapes gathered from thornbushes, or figs from thistles? Matt 7:16

It is incomprehensible how someone can kidnap others, abuse and torture living beings and then kill and dispose of the bodies. These individuals are not only possessed by evil; they are evil personified.

Nations can also be possessed by evil spirits when they act with evil intent. Any nation that places politics, money and profit ahead of morals and principles has lost its conscience and is promoting evil. Any nation that supports "friends" who are committing atrocities against innocent people is evil spirited. Any nation that invades another country just because they can is evil spirited. Any nation that espouses divisions among other nations in order to gain an advantage or cause conflict in order to sell weapons is possessed with evil spirits. Any nation that, because of their power, takes advantage of other nations is acting in the spirit of evil. When the mighty act for their own advantage at the expense of the weak, they are possessed with evil.

There is evil in the world and it is evident. Wars, crime and violence are symptoms of the predominance of evil. How can we continue to kill? We justify. We call it war, self-defense, or payback. Regardless, killing is barbaric and justification is an excuse. We can justify anything. Yet, if we proclaim that we are a God-fearing people and that we abide by God's commandments, then how can we justify killing, including mass killings, when the commandment is clear: "Thou shalt not kill"?

Evil is conniving, deceitful and intelligent. Evil uses its intelligence to deceive. Just as when we place a frog in hot water, it jumps out, but it will cook to death if the water temperature is raised gradually, this is also how evil functions. Committing evil acts gradually and in small measure instead of all at once, makes the world look the other way and the perpetrators of evil get away with their acts.

We must decide between peace and war, love and hatred. Occasionally, we need to look in the mirror. It takes courage to introspect, examine, open our eyes and hearts to see clearly, understand, and know the truth. Are we living good lives, or are we contributing to evil? We are major players in the balance of good vs. evil. The struggle between God and Satan is in fact a struggle within us. We are endowed with freedom of choice. We tilt the balance one way or the other based on what we think, how we feel and the choices we make.

If we dwell on the negative, we are siding with evil. If we twist an event to appear negative when it is not, we are inviting evil. If we intentionally lie, we are contributing to evil. Cheating on a spouse for self-gratification is evil. Lusting after what is not ours is definitely being possessed by an evil spirit. In fact, partaking of any vice is considered a "sin" because it invites evil into our lives.

> No one can serve two masters, for either he will hate the one and love the other, or he will be devoted to the one and despise the other. You cannot serve God and money. Matt 6:24

Who are we serving? Politics? Money? Wealth? Selfish interests? Evil or Good? What do we want Earth to be? A heaven or a hell? It is up to us and we have a clear choice.

The difference between good and evil is in the results. Good leads to compassion, kindness, generosity, health, happiness, and wellbeing. Evil produces misery, pain and suffering. The choice is clear. Which will it be, Good or Evil?

In the days of Christ, committing a sin was considered being possessed by an evil spirit. Some had one evil spirit while others had many, a legion of them.

> Jesus then asked him, "What is your name?" And he said, "Legion," for many demons had entered him. Luke 8:30

Oftentimes, Christ healed by driving evil spirits out of people possessed by them.

> *In that hour he healed many people of diseases and*
> *plagues and evil spirits, and on many who were blind he*
> *bestowed sight. Luke 7:21*

**These evil spirits are attributes we house within us.**

Throughout history, two excesses have been part of the human nature: sex and alcohol. Excesses are evil. A modern-day evil is avarice – excessive love of money, wealth and power. There is nothing wrong with sex, alcohol and money in moderation. It is the unrestrained pursuit of these and the addiction to more and more and never being gratified that is evil. Where is the good of unbridled consumption of alcohol and other intoxicants?

We can be wealthy and enjoy our money, but we cannot love them to the exclusion of all else. Wealth is a means to do good. It is not an end in itself. With wealth, we can enjoy life and contribute our best. When we have enough, then that should suffice. What we have in excess, we can use for the benefit of others.

Another aspect of evil is bullying and the misuse of power. Subjugating others to our will is evil. Biased support or favoring one group against another is evil. This can be carried out by individuals and by nations. Some nations intentionally support division and strife in order to sell weapons. This is evil.

## Evil Intent – The Lord

There are innumerable atrocities committed in our world. Wars, massacres and genocides do not dot our landscape, they are prominent. Are these due to human nature alone? Are we that barbaric, hard-hearted and stupid? Or, has there been meddling in our affairs and continues to be so by evil-intending spirits?

> *Now the LORD said to Abram, "Go from your country and your kindred and your father's house to the land that I will show you. And I will make of you a great nation, and I will bless you and make your name great, so that you will be a blessing. I will bless those who bless you, and him who dishonors you I will curse, and in you all the families of the earth shall be blessed. Gen 12:1-3*

Who is this Lord who asks a family to leave their country and kin to move to another area already occupied by other people?

Who is this Lord who upon witnessing people working together as one to build a tower, descends and confuses their languages so they will not understand each other?

Who is this Lord who intentionally hardens hearts so he can inflict calamities on nations like he did in Egypt?

What is the idea behind relocating people to an area already occupied, ordering genocide of the innocent and even the slaughter of wildlife?

An incredible amount of suffering ensued to the descendants of the people who followed the dictates of this Lord and to the natives of the areas they moved into. Countless numbers of people would have been saved had this incident not happened.

This Lord is not interested in the welfare of humans. He has an obsession to be obeyed, feared and worshipped.

According to Michael Gellert, author of: **The Divine Mind**, *exploring the psychological history of God's inner journey:*

- There are 613 commandments in the Old Testament;

- "Theologian Raymund Schwager counts approximately one thousand episodes of Yahweh's violence in the Hebrew bible – more, he says, than the incidents of human violence." These were direct responses to man's deeds. An additional one hundred events involve Yahweh commanding people to kill on his behalf. (By my own count at least seventy-five of these were acts of genocide, if we consider decimating single towns as separate episodes)".

According to Joe Kovacs, author of: **Shocked By The Bible**, the most astonishing facts you've never been told, the biggest killer in the Bible is God Himself:

- Scripture states that God ordered capital punishment for men, women, and even young children— sometimes in very large numbers. It might disturb modern people (especially opponents of capital punishment), but thousands, perhaps millions, of humans beings experienced death either by God's direct hand or His edict;

- The flood destruction: *"And all flesh died that moved on the earth, birds, livestock, beasts, all swarming creatures that swarm on the earth, and all mankind. Everything on the dry land in whose nostrils was the breath of life died. He blotted out every living thing that was on the face of the ground, man and animals and creeping things and birds of the heavens. They were blotted out from the earth. Only Noah was left, and those who were with him in the ark." Gen 7: 21-23;*

- *Then the LORD rained on Sodom and Gomorrah sulfur and fire from the LORD out of heaven. And he overthrew those cities, and all the valley, and all the inhabitants of the cities, and what grew on the ground. Gen 19: 24-25;*

- *The plagues of Egypt and the murder of their first -born. "So Moses said, "Thus says the LORD: 'About midnight I will go out in the midst of Egypt, and every firstborn in the land of Egypt shall die, from the firstborn of Pharaoh who sits on his throne, even to the firstborn of the slave girl who is behind the handmill, and all the firstborn of the cattle. There shall be a great cry throughout all the land of Egypt, such as there has never been, nor ever will be again. But not a dog shall growl against any of the people of Israel, either man or beast, that you may know that the LORD makes a distinction between Egypt and Israel.' Exodus 11:4-7.*

We cannot deny that evil intent exists. We cannot continue to live in ignorance and fear. We have, and continue to pay a heavy price in lives lost. We must wise up and live, not governed by commands, edicts and dictates of evil-intending deities, but by intelligence, conscience and compassion. By their deeds we judge and know these spirits as good or evil.

This is our opportunity to use our God-given minds to wake up, throw away our fears and apprehensions. We must choose between good and evil. The distinctions are clear and obvious. Unless we choose the good, lives will continue to be lost, families ruined and the planet possessed by evil spirits. We have been manipulated too long. We are not pawns. We are children of the Almighty God. It is time to act and live accordingly.

We can treat our challenges as opportunities. We can abandon bullying in favor of compassion. We can move from exclusion to inclusion and from focusing on differences to recognizing similarities. We can look at our difficulties as tests in the school of life. We either confront them head on and solve them (pass the test) or we succumb and suffer (fail). We will confront the same difficulties over and over until we master the situation and make the most of the opportunity to advance the cause of good.

## *Spirits as Carriers of Qualities*

**A:     Divine Spirits as Carriers of Abilities, Intelligence and Knowledge.**

> *The LORD spoke to Moses: See, I have called by name Bezalel son of Uri son of Hur, of the tribe of Judah: and I have filled him with divine spirit, with ability, intelligence, and knowledge in every kind of craft. Exod 31:1-3*

Just as there were good spirits in the Old Testament, there were also evil spirits:

**B.     Evil Spirits as Tormenters.**

> *Now the spirit of the LORD departed from Saul, and an evil spirit from the LORD tormented him. And Saul's servants said to him, "See now, an evil spirit from God is tormenting you. 1 Samuel 16:14-15*

> *The next day an evil spirit from God rushed upon Saul, and he raved within his house. 1 Samuel 18:10*

We can be influenced not only by good or evil spirits but by the thoughts and emotions of others. Our astral bodies are receptive to the extent that we are open for suggestions. We can guard against unwanted intrusion by surrounding ourselves with light and by having a strong personality.

## Spirits in Animals

Spirits seem to enter not only people, but animals as well. In the New Testament, expelled evil spirits find home in swine. In the Old Testament, we have a spirit enter a donkey – a talking donkey just as in Shrek.

Balaam, the Donkey, and the Angel

*God's anger was kindled because he was going, and the angel of the LORD took his stand in the road as his adversary. Now he was riding on the donkey, and his two servants were with him. The donkey saw the angel of the LORD standing in the road, with a drawn sword in his hand; so the donkey turned off the road, and went into the field; and Balaam struck the donkey, to turn it back onto the road. Then the angel of the LORD stood in a narrow path between the vineyards, with a wall on either side. When the donkey saw the angel of the LORD, it scraped against the wall, and scraped Balaam's foot against the wall; so he struck it again. Then the angel of the LORD went ahead, and stood in a narrow place, where there was no way to turn either to the right or to the left. When the donkey saw the angel of the LORD, it lay down under Balaam; and Balaam's anger was kindled, and he struck the donkey with his staff. Then the LORD opened the mouth of the donkey, and it said to Balaam, "What have I done to you, that you have struck me these three times?" Balaam said to the donkey, "Because you have made a fool of me! I wish I had a sword in my hand! I would kill you right now!" But the donkey said to Balaam, "Am I not your donkey, which you have ridden all your life to this day? Have I been in the habit of treating you this way?" And he said, "No."*

*Then the LORD opened the eyes of Balaam, and he saw the angel of the LORD standing in the road, with his drawn sword in his hand; and he bowed down, falling on his face. The angel of the LORD said to him, "Why have you struck your donkey these three times? I have come out as an adversary, because your way is perverse before me. The donkey saw me, and turned away from me these three times. If it had not turned away from me, surely just now I would have killed you and let it live." Then Balaam said to the angel of the LORD, "I have*

*sinned, for I did not know that you were standing in the
road to oppose me. Now therefore, if it is displeasing to
you, I will return home." The angel of the LORD said to
Balaam, "Go with the men; but speak only what I tell you
to speak." So Balaam went on with the officials of Balak.
Numbers 22:22-35*

## Gateway to the Spirit World

It is possible to access the astral world through meditation,
sleep deprivation, exhaustion, dance, prayer, dreams,
medications, drugs, and hallucinogens. Some have entered the
spirit world accidentally, while others, like the Shamans, do it
deliberately.

## Seances and Mediums

Many have attempted to contact the spirit of the dead
via seances. It is important to keep in mind that, even if
successful, spirits do not know anything more after they die
than they did while they lived.

*(Saul Consults a Medium)*

*Now Samuel had died, and all Israel had mourned
for him and buried him in Ramah, his own city.
Saul had expelled the mediums and the wizards from
the land. The Philistines assembled, and came and
encamped at Shunem. Saul gathered all Israel, and
they encamped at Gilboa. When Saul saw the army of
the Philistines, he was afraid, and his heart trembled
greatly. When Saul inquired of the LORD, the LORD
did not answer him, not by dreams, or by Urim, or by
prophets. Then Saul said to his servants, "Seek out for
me a woman who is a medium, so that I may go to her*

*and inquire of her." His servants said to him, "There is a medium at Endor."*

*So Saul disguised himself and put on other clothes and went there, he and two men with him. They came to the woman by night. And he said, "Consult a spirit for me, and bring up for me the one whom I name to you." The woman said to him, "Surely you know what Saul has done, how he has cut off the mediums and the wizards from the land. Why then are you laying a snare for my life to bring about my death?" But Saul swore to her by the LORD, "As the LORD lives, no punishment shall come upon you for this thing." Then the woman said, "Whom shall I bring up for you?" He answered, "Bring up Samuel for me." When the woman saw Samuel, she cried out with a loud voice; and the woman said to Saul, "Why have you deceived me? You are Saul!" The king said to her, "Have no fear; what do you see?" The woman said to Saul, "I see a divine being coming up out of the ground." He said to her, "What is his appearance?" She said, "An old man is coming up; he is wrapped in a robe." So Saul knew that it was Samuel, and he bowed with his face to the ground, and did obeisance.*

*Then Samuel said to Saul, "Why have you disturbed me by bringing me up?" Saul answered, "I am in great distress, for the Philistines are warring against me, and God has turned away from me and answers me no more, either by prophets or by dreams; so I have summoned you to tell me what I should do." Samuel said, "Why then do you ask me, since the LORD has turned from you and become your enemy? The LORD has done to you just as he spoke by me; for the LORD has torn the kingdom out of your hand, and given it to your neighbor, David. Because you did not obey the voice of the LORD, and did not carry out his fierce wrath against Amalek, therefore the LORD has done this thing to you today. Moreover the LORD will give Israel along with you into the hands of the Philistines; and tomorrow you and your sons shall be with me; the LORD will also give the army of Israel into the hands of the Philistines." 1 Samuel 28:3-19*

# THE SPIRITUAL

*My life is the story of a man who always wants to carry too much. My spiritual quest is the painful process of learning to let go of things not essential.*
*— Gordon Atkinson*

The spiritual body is the astral body transfigured. We must create it and it takes effort. Since the spiritual body is of a much higher rate of vibration than the astral body, to build it up, we must shun negativity, evil and selfishness and instead cultivate the highest faculties of mind and emotions. These include proper attitude, effective prayer, single-minded meditation, detachment, concentration, pure intention, empathy, sympathy, compassion, tolerance, patience, acceptance, forgiveness, joyful living, unselfish loving and anonymous philanthropy.

Not everyone has a detectable spiritual body. Evil people have a mere vestige, if any. Saints and masters are living spiritual bodies. The quality of the spiritual body is a reflection of the consciousness of the individual. This ranges from heightened awareness all the way to Christ Consciousness. Unlike the astral aura, the spiritual aura is magnetic, powerful, extending far beyond the physical body. It can be sensed by people from a distance and they can be affected by it.

With a spiritual body, individuals are in constant communion with their Higher Self which resides in Christ Consciousness. They have access to the proficiencies they developed over eons of reincarnations. After Christ's baptism and the descent of the Holy Spirit on Him in the form of a dove, He was transformed from a human to the Son of God. He began expressing His advanced spiritual abilities – healing, forgiving sins, and raising the "dead". The Holy Spirit is the embodiment of the highest spiritual capabilities.

The spiritual body is conscious, intelligent light energy with the brightest colors ranging from purple to white. It can see, hear, smell, taste and feel. However, these senses are far more advanced than the physical, especially inspiration and intuition. Because the spiritual body is energy, it instantly reacts to thought, desire and intention. The spiritual body can move from place to place at the speed of thought. It can go through matter easily. Functioning from the spiritual body, our eyes and hearts are open. We are powerful and creative.

## The Spiritual World

The spiritual world is governed by laws that are different than the physical laws. Here giving does not diminish the giver, rather, the giver receives spiritual gifts in return. What we focus on, we empower. What we dwell on, increases and multiplies. The more we love and serve, the better we feel. In physical law, one plus one equals two. In the spiritual realm, one plus one can equal a number greater than two. The intense vibratory rate of spiritual beings can change the organization of matter giving rise to instantaneous manifestations that appear as miracles.

## Spiritual Attributes

Spiritual beings are imbued with the Christ Consciousness. They can move "mountains," calm tempests, walk on water, change water into wine, appear and disappear at will, manifest items out of thin air, multiply the few into the many, heal, forgive and even raise the "dead."

> *They shall take up serpents; and if they drink any deadly thing, it shall not hurt them; they shall lay hands on the sick, and they shall recover.*     Mark 16:18

> *Behold, I give unto you power to tread on serpents and scorpions, and over all the power of the enemy: and nothing shall by any means hurt you.*     Luke 10:19

In the Old Testament, Elijah brought back to life the Widow's Son who had died (1Kings 17). In the New Testament, Christ restored life to a girl (Mat 9: 18-26). He brought back to life the daughter of the leader of the synagogue (Mark 5:5-43). He raised the Widow's Son at Nain (Luke 7:11-17). The most miraculous of all was bringing Lazarus to life after being dead for a few days (John 11:38-44).

Spiritual beings never act to impress or gain notoriety. Their mission is to serve, enlighten, support, dispel evil, be compassionate, forgive, empower and above all, exude love and joy. Spiritual beings spiritualize everything they come in contact with. They transform the base into the noble, the ugly into the beautiful, lust into love and grief into joy.


## Spiritual World Order

Christianity has assigned rank and order to spiritual beings. The Cherubim are winged angels and the Seraphim are angels with six wings. Since angels are spiritual beings that can appear and disappear and be anywhere, anytime, at will, they have no need for wings. Humans gave them wings to indicate the ability to fly. Then there are the Principalities, Powers, Dominions, Arch Angels such as Michael, Gabriel, Raphael, Uriel and finally Angels who act as messengers from God. Our understanding of the spiritual world is sketchy at best. Allegedly, each order has its own powers and capabilities. Perhaps, what distinguishes spiritual beings from one another is not rank and ability, but rather function and responsibility. Each might have a specific role and a function to carry out.

## The Holy Spirit

The Holy Spirit is the consciousness and mind of God. It is the source of All-Knowledge, power and capabilities. It is symbolized as a dove and when it descends on an individual or a group of them, they are transformed into spiritual beings – children of God.

> *And when Jesus was baptized, immediately he went up from the water, and behold, the heavens were opened to him, and he saw the Spirit of God descending like a dove and coming to rest on him; and behold, a voice from heaven said, "This is my beloved Son, with whom I am well pleased."* Matt 3:16-17

Mary was impregnated with the Holy Spirit. In other words, her offspring was destined to grow up with God-like qualities.

> *And the angel said to her, "Do not be afraid, Mary, for you have found favor with God. And behold, you will conceive in your womb and bear a son, and you shall call his name Jesus. He will be great and will be called the Son of the Most High..."* Luke 1:30-32

The Holy Spirit can take the form of divided tongues of fire as it did when it descended of the disciples at Pentecost:

> *When the day of Pentecost arrived, they were all together in one place. And suddenly there came from heaven a sound like a mighty rushing wind, and it filled the entire house where they were sitting. And divided tongues as of fire appeared to them and rested on each one of them. And they were all filled with the Holy Spirit and began to speak in other tongues as the Spirit gave them utterance.* Acts 2:1-4

We can be gifted with the Holy Spirit and become spiritual all at once. More likely, we must spiritualize ourselves gradually by our own effort.

## Angels and Demons

Angels and demons are spiritual beings and as such reside in the spiritual world. Lucifer, who we consider to be the Devil, is the bearer of Light. He is an archangel just as Michael and Gabriel are. He resides in the spiritual world along with the other angels and archangels. Evil cannot reside in the spiritual world.

Angels are always good. Demons, on the other hand, are good disguised as evil. They aid our development and hasten our maturity. They do this by tempting, testing and fanning desires within us as an opportunity for us to use our freedom of choice and make intelligent decisions.

We are accustomed to believe that angels are in heaven while demons are on Earth. We also believe that angels help us while demons test and tempt us. That is why the Devil is also known as the tempter. We encounter the tempting role of demons in the Garden of Eden where Satan appeared as a Serpent and tempted Eve.

> *Now the serpent was more crafty than any other beast of the field that the LORD God had made. He said to the woman, "Did God actually say, 'You shall not eat of any tree in the garden'?" And the woman said to the serpent, "We may eat of the fruit of the trees in the garden, but God said, 'You shall not eat of the fruit of the tree that is in the midst of the garden, neither shall you touch it, lest you die.'" But the serpent said to the woman, "You will not surely die. For God knows that when you eat of it your eyes will be opened, and you will be like God,*

*knowing good and evil." So when the woman saw that the tree was good for food, and that it was a delight to the eyes, and that the tree was to be desired to make one wise, she took of its fruit and ate, and she also gave some to her husband who was with her, and he ate. Then the eyes of both were opened, and they knew that they were naked. And they sewed fig leaves together and made themselves loincloths.     Gen 3:1-7*

The serpent did not deceive. It told the truth. The serpent, by presenting a temptation, acted to test the human resolve. This is the exact role Satan played in the life of Job – to test Job's resolve. To tempt is to test. Tests are opportunities to find out how an individual would choose. If we choose "right" we are rewarded and are triumphant, otherwise we learn from our mistakes and prepare to face our next challenge. We might make several "wrong" choices before we become wise and make better decisions.

When Judas Iscariot was tempted, he failed. He succumbed to temptation. He allowed others to influence his judgment. He displayed his weak character for all to see. When Jesus was tempted, He was triumphant. Satan, in this case, was "good" disguised as evil, for the triumph of Christ revealed Who Christ was and how above temptation He was. Temptation in itself is never bad or evil. It is merely a test of our resolve, a measure of our "spiritual" attainment. We are tested in academia to find out whether or not we have mastered specific subjects and are ready to advance.

Evil can never exist in the spiritual world. The vibrations are simply too high. Hence, God did not create the Devil, Satan, or Lucifer as evil spirits. Evil spirits exist on the physical and astral plains because humans entertain evil thoughts and act in evil ways. We become the evil spirits by contaminating our pure spiritual light with evil thoughts and deeds.

God is pure Goodness and Love. Good angels assume tempting

roles to test our resolve and give us an opportunity to choose wisely or foolishly. When they do, they are not evil or the Devil. They are angels in disguise.

The book of Job is among the most ancient of the biblical books. Here we discover the true purpose and function of Satan.

> Now there was a day when the sons of God came to present themselves before the LORD, and Satan also came among them. The LORD said to Satan, "From where have you come?" Satan answered the LORD and said, "From going to and fro on the earth, and from walking up and down on it." Job 1:6-7

The fact that Satan was in God's council with the Sons of God is an indication that he was an invited guest. He plays an important role in God's plan and the overall purpose of why we incarnate on Earth and face challenges. It is the reason we are endowed with freedom of choice. The test is which would we choose – good or evil?

At times, it is difficult to know an angel from a demon. Christ, for example is definitely the embodiment of the good. He never judged, condemned, killed or hurt anyone. He accepted everyone as a child of God. He is Light indeed. He is Life. He is Love, forgiveness and compassion. The power He had, He only used for good.

On the other hand, we have a deity who floods Earth with the specific purpose of eradicating humanity, rains devastation on entire cities and hardens hearts to inflict suffering and calamities. He even orders the murder of innocent first-born children. He commands his chosen people to carry out numerous genocides against innocent people to take over their land and give it to his "favored." He is a deity who demands blood sacrifice, blind obedience and commands "his people" to never worship anyone else. A deity who notices people working together, united as one, becomes insecure and decides to come down and confuse their language to thwart their efforts. These acts are, not only evil spirited, mean and nasty; they embody Evil incarnate. Yet, this god of the Old Testament is the one many worship and adore.

Angels and Demons, good and evil, exist as our opportunity to use our freedom and decide. It is our responsibility to choose between God and Devil, Angels and Demons, Old Testament and the law or the New Testament and grace. These coexist and provide us the opportunity to compare and contrast. How we choose and how we live determines whether we are agents of light or contributors to evil and darkness.

In the theater of life, like in any drama, some actors assume villainous roles, but only for the duration of the play. These actors are not evil. They play the role of evil so the drama can unfold. We, the audience, decide who is good and who is evil. Once the drama is over and we leave the theater, we know that it was all an act.

Good and evil are consequences of our thoughts and actions. They reside within us. We must evaluate our thoughts and emotions promoting the good and rejecting the evil. Just as actors assume villainous roles, angels do the same. At times, they appear as good angels, and at other times, as evil spirits. It is up to us to evaluate and choose wisely.

## The First Tempter

We assume that the serpent in the Garden of Eden was the first tempter. He was not. The real tempter in the Garden of Eden was the god of the Old Testament.

> The LORD God took the man and put him in the garden of Eden to work it and keep it. And the LORD God commanded the man, saying, "You may surely eat of every tree of the garden, but of the tree of the knowledge of good and evil you shall not eat, for in the day that you

*eat of it you shall surely die." Gen 2:15-17*

Why would the Lord God put a good-looking tree in the midst of a garden with alluring, delicious fruit if not to tempt? And why did the Lord God create the serpent and allow him to enter the garden in the first place? Was it placed there by the Lord to test the first humans on His account?

> *Now the serpent was more crafty than any other beast of the field that the LORD God had made.* Gen 3:1

> *He said to the woman, "Did God actually say, 'You shall not eat of any tree in the garden'?" And the woman said to the serpent, "We may eat of the fruit of the trees in the garden, but God said, 'You shall not eat of the fruit of the tree that is in the midst of the garden, neither shall you touch it, lest you die.'" But the serpent said to the woman, "You will not surely die. For God knows that when you eat of it your eyes will be opened, and you will be like God, knowing good and evil."* Gen 3:2-5

It is interesting that the end result of succumbing to the temptation was not what the Lord had told the couple, that they would die, for they did not die. What happened instead was exactly what the serpent had predicted, even the Lord admits to this.

> *Then the LORD God said, "Behold, the man has become like one of us in knowing good and evil. Now, lest he reach out his hand and take also of the tree of life and eat, and live forever—" therefore the LORD God sent him out from the garden of Eden to work the ground from which he was taken.* Gen 3:22-23

Adam was tempted by Eve but he did not have to succumb. He could have resisted. It was his choice. Besides, why not eat of the fruit of the tree that will open the eyes, make one wise and know the difference between good and evil?

*So when the woman saw that the tree was good for food, and that it was a delight to the eyes, and that the tree was to be desired to make one wise, she took of its fruit and ate, and she also gave some to her husband who was with her, and he ate.*      *Gen 3:6*

The Lord is the tempter. We admit to this when in the Lord's Prayer we ask God "not to lead us into temptation." Temptations are tests of our resolve. They are a measure of our spiritual growth. We need to be tempted so we learn to distinguish good from evil. Some advocate a blind faith in everything that is written in "holy" books. Why then do we have brains to reason with? Myths, fables and stories are not historic facts. When I was a child, especially after watching the movie **Samson and Delilah**, I wholeheartedly believed that it was a historical event. Samson's strength was in his hair! Cut it off and his strength is gone. Allow it to grow back and he regains his strength. Samson's strength was never in his hair. This is an allegory. The secret is revealed in the deeper meaning of the word "Nazarite".

*There was a certain man of Zorah, of the tribe of the Danites, whose name was Manoah. And his wife was barren and had no children. And the angel of the LORD appeared to the woman and said to her, "Behold, you are barren and have not borne children, but you shall conceive and bear a son. Therefore be careful and drink no wine or strong drink, and eat nothing unclean, for behold, you shall conceive and bear a son. No razor shall come upon his head, for the child shall be a Nazirite to God from the womb, and he shall begin to save Israel from the hand of the Philistines."*      *Judges 13:2-5*

Nazarites are children dedicated, while still in the womb, to the service of God. In the Middle East, when a boy is born as a result of supplication to God when normal pregnancy is not possible and the request is granted, the child becomes a Nazarite, dedicated to God. At the age of thirteen, the boy is taken to church or the temple and his hair is ceremoniously cut for the first time. Jesus was a Nazarite, dedicated to serve God. There is no special power in hair. The power resides in the person imbued with the Holy Spirit.

## A Closer Look at Our Lives

Do spiritual beings influence our lives?

Near Eastern cultures are replete with the stories of angels, both good and evil. Aristotle called them intellogences while Socrates named them daimons. These spirit entities appear physically or in dreams. Here are a few examples from the Bible:

> For our struggle is not against enemies of blood and flesh, but against the rulers, against the authorities, against the cosmic powers of this present darkness, against the spiritual forces of evil in the heavenly places. Ephesinian 6:12

> But during the night an angel of the Lord opened the prison doors, brought them out, and said, "Go, stand in the temple and tell the people the whole message about this life." Acts 5:19-20

> In Caesarea there was a man named Cornelius, a centurion of the Italian Cohort, as it was called. He was a devout man who feared God with all his household; he gave alms generously to the people and prayed constantly to God. One afternoon at about three o'clock he had a vision in which he clearly saw an angel of God coming in and saying to him, "Cornelius." He stared at him in terror and said, "What is it, Lord?" He answered, "Your prayers and your alms have ascended as a

*memorial before God. Acts 10:1-4*

Angels have played critical roles in establishing our religions. In a dream, they appeared to Abram and asked him to him leave his homeland. They appeared to Mary announcing her eminent pregnancy. They appeared to Mohammad and gave him the Quran. They appeared to Joseph Smith. Even without appearing, they inspire and channel through individuals.

There is also meddling in human affairs that we might not be aware of. Here is an example of Lucifer incarnating as the king of Tyre, a city in Southern Lebanon:

## Lucifer as King of Tyre

*Moreover the word of the LORD came to me: Mortal, raise a lamentation over the king of Tyre, and say to him, Thus says the Lord GOD: You were the signet of perfection, full of wisdom and perfect in beauty. You were in Eden, the garden of God; every precious stone was your covering, carnelian, chrysolite, and moonstone, beryl, onyx, and jasper, sapphire, turquoise, and emerald; and worked in gold were your settings and your engravings. On the day that you were created they were prepared. With an anointed cherub as guardian, I placed you; you were on the holy mountain of God; you walked among the stones of fire. You were blameless in your ways from the day that you were created, until iniquity was found in you. In the abundance of your trade, you were filled with violence, and you sinned; so I cast you as a profane thing from the mountain of God, and the guardian cherub drove you out from among the stones of fire. Your heart was proud because of your beauty; you corrupted your wisdom for the sake of your splendor. I cast you to the ground; I exposed you before kings, to feast their eyes on you. By the multitude of your iniquities, in the unrighteousness of your trade, you profaned your sanctuaries. So I brought out fire from within you; it consumed you, and I turned you to ashes on the earth in the sight of all who saw you. All who know you among the peoples are appalled at you; you have come to a dreadful end and shall be no more forever.*      Ezekiel 28:11-19

Are we then controlled and manipulated? Not necessarily. Spirits must be asked, invited or allowed in order to come. If we keep our "doors" wide open, anyone could walk in. If, on the other hand, we guard ourselves against any intrusions, then no one can intrude. As always, we have freedom of choice. By cultivating strong personalities, we build a shield around ourself. Our aura strengthens and acts as an armor and our magnetism attracts only the good.

Earth is our testing ground. It is where we prove ourselves. If we live blindly following without questioning and act on influences without evaluation, then we are manipulated and are pawns. We have a choice. We can wake up and act intelligently instead.

## Heaven and Hell

Heaven and hell as places for reward and punishment do not stand the scrutiny of reason. Not all good people are equally good and not all evil doers are equally evil. There are gradations of good and evil. Lumping all good people into one place and all evil people into another without distinction between minor and major acts of goodness and evil cries in the face of justice. The concept of eternal reward or eternal punishment for temporal acts does not make much sense. Reward and punishment must be commensurate with the acts perpetrated. Heaven and Hell are human concepts that do not have any resemblance to how a loving deity is or acts. If God is Love, then there is absolutely no judgment, punishment or reward by God. Only humans mete rewards and punishments. Hence, we do it to ourselves. We create our own rewards and punishments based on how we act and what we sow. We reap the consequences, good or bad. Hell is a human creation. It serves to frighten people into submission. Through fear, we accept what we are told and follow. We must never forget that once we die, we are no longer physical. We become spirits and spirits do not burn. Only physical beings experience the pangs of burning fire. **Heaven and hell are what we experience while alive and physical in a body and on Earth.**

We are already in hell when we have to endure the consequences of a horrific accident and we are near total disability. We are already in Hell when we are terminally ill, suffering incredible pain and without any hope for a cure or recovery. Any parent who loses a son or a daughter to senseless violence, drunk driving, or drug abuse is already living in hell. Hell is real while we are alive on earth. We do not need another one after we die.

Earth can be a heaven as well. We are blessed with incredible beauty, both in nature and in living beings. Experiencing pure joy, contentment and happiness is being in heaven. Spiritualizing our senses to see beauty, hear uplifting music, experience intimacy, feel ecstatic and smell intoxicating fragrances is being in heaven. Seeing beauty in a smile, perfection in a child, wonder in a flower, magic in laughter, and enchantment in touch and caress is being in heaven. There is beauty everywhere. All we need are eyes that see, ears that hear and hearts that feel.

Good and evil are doors to fast moving elevators. We choose one and it takes us "up" to heaven. We choose the other, and it takes us "down" to hell. While good is light and creative, evil is dark and destructive. They are the opposite poles of the same thing. One is positive and the other negative. Both are needed and coexist as Creator (Brahma) and Destroyer (Shiva) and in between is the Preserver (Vishnu). This is why the Lord can claim credit for light and darkness, good and evil.

> *that people may know, from the rising of the sun and from the west, that there is none besides me; I am the LORD, and there is no other. I form light and create darkness, I make well-being and create calamity, I am the LORD, who does all these things. Isa 45: 6-7*

Heaven and hell, good and evil are our own creations. We have, not only the power to choose between them, but also the power to transmute evil into good and hell into heaven. We are the agents of good and evil, light and darkness. What we do and how we choose to live matters.

# I AM

*There is one spectacle that is grander than the sea, that is the sky; there is one spectacle grander than the sky, that is the interior of the soul.*

*— Victor Hugo*

I Am can never be known for it is the one who knows. It cannot be seen because it is the one who sees. It cannot be studied, because it cannot be analyzed, compared or contrasted. Our I Am is an inseparable aspect of God. It is the spark of divinity within us.

We do not have an I Am. I Am is who we are. There is only one I Am that is the same for everyone. This I Am is God. It is the undifferentiated, absolute, changeless essence of being. It is timeless pervading all. It never changes because it does not vibrate. It is like a multi-faceted jewel with each of us being a facet. I Am can never be individualized in actuality. It can never incarnate wholly as a human. The unlimited can never be confined to limited bodies. It is the essence of light shining forth as emanations. The further the emanation from its source the lower its vibratory rate terminating in nature as matter.

Nothing cannot give rise to something. Matter/energy can never be the source of matter/energy. Since matter and energy exist, their source must be intangible. The ancients termed this intangible source **spirit**. This is why God is intangible, unknown and spirit.

If God is spirit, how can we relate to or even pray to a spirit? What do we visualize? Is this relationship intimate and personal? It helps to have a picture of God in our minds to relate to when we pray. God as I AM is intangible. Intangibles are beyond our comprehension. Yet if we personalize an intangible and associate it with a tangible, then we can relate to, identify with and understand the intangible. The intangible and abstract become tangible and personal. Christ did just that when He referred to God as His Father. He made it personal and intimate. Since God as I AM is a trinity, I like to make it personal and intimate as well by referring to It as Love, Beauty and Joy. This way, we can easily imagine these and relate to them. Viewing I AM (God) as Love, Beauty and Joy makes the intangible tangible, the incomprehensible comprehensible and the unapproachable, personal, intimate and within our experience.

Love, Beauty and Joy are eternal ideals. Anytime we experience these, we are in the presence of God as I AM. Thus, by merely experiencing Love, seeing Beauty and feeling Joy we are in the presence of I Am. And where there is Love, Beauty and Joy, there is God. **Love, Beauty and Joy transform any place into a holy place.**

> *Then he said, "Do not come near; take your sandals off your feet, for the place on which you are standing is holy ground." Exod. 3:5*

Love, Beauty and Joy are alive, active and all-encompassing. For love is appreciation, beauty is celebration and joy is enjoyment. If we can love even the unlovable, see beauty even in the ugly, and experience joy regardless of the situation, then we can find God anywhere, anytime, within and without.

Similarly, we cannot know our I Am. It is unknowable. We can however, picture our I Am as a trinity of Love, Beauty and Joy.

Experiencing these puts us in touch with our I Am.

God calls Himself: "I Am that I Am." In other words, I am whatever I want to be. I AM can be anything. To simplify our understanding of I AM, we can visualize I Am surrounding itself with three layers – spiritual, astral and physical orbs, worlds or "bodies" as progressively slower rates of vibration. If we use the sun as a symbol of the I Am just as Akhenaten did in ancient Egypt, then the orb, the light and the heat constitute the trinity of I Am as the sun. The orb would be the physical, the Light would be the astral and the warmth would be the spiritual. The rays emanating from the sun and extending outward as "hands" would represent souls. Each soul is a localized version of the I Am. Each ray is an "individual facet" of the sun, a "fragment" of orb, light and warmth.

I AM is who we are. We have three components – physical, astral and spiritual. Physically, our most precious asset is our DNA. Astrally, our most precious asset is our freedom of choice – how we choose to think and feel. Spiritually, our most precious asset is our consciousness. We are most intimately linked to our consciousness. Without it, nothing matters. Consciousness is the most obvious attribute of I AM.

# KNOWING OUR SOURCE

*The more I study religions the more I am convinced that man never worshipped anything but himself.*

– Sir Richard Francis Burton

What if we have a million dollars in the bank and never use it? Are we wealthy?

What if we are left a huge inheritance, but we never claim it? Does it matter what we inherited?

Our source is the unfathomable Cosmic Intelligence, the "King" of the universes. Our potential is vast as evidenced by our DNA. Just as we only express a fraction of our DNA, so it is with our capabilities. We are princes and princesses, but do not know it and are living like paupers.

We might readily admit that our soul is of God. That knowledge, however, is superficial. We live in accordance with what we innately know and believe. Hence, we reflect, not our source, but our limited understanding. A watermelon seed has no choice but to be a watermelon. We, on the other hand, do have a choice in whose image we grow up to be.

Those who know God, know Him as Love, Beauty, Joy, Intelligence and Compassion. Those who believe in God, know Him with human qualities: demanding, wrathful and judgmental.

Our life is a reflection of what we know and believe. Some wonder which is more important – faith or action. If we believe, but do not act accordingly, what is the value of that belief? In fact, action is a reflection of faith. Faith alone, however, without action will never save us. Action based on the correct faith, will.

Are we in the image of God or is God in our image?

What is our understanding of God?

Each individual views God in their own unique way based on their education, culture and understanding. Simply, we can place the concepts of God in three categories:

1. Primitive, tribal;
2. Enlightened; and
3. Spiritual.

Primitive, tribal gods are created in the image of the people who worship them. These gods have human qualities. They have commandments, are demanding, vengeful, vindictive, punishing and uncompromising. They are fickle just as primitive people are. It is acceptable for primitive people to believe in such gods, but modern, educated people? Why then do many people believe in such gods even today? Is this because we seldom read the books we believe in? We rarely examine what we accept and live by. We get used to our beliefs and we find comfort in the familiar. We create and believe in primitive gods because we want them to look after us, favor us, provide for us and protect us. However, these gods do not respect an individual's freedom to choose. They judge, punish and rain death and destruction on entire cities. Some, as Yahweh did, even order genocides in order to favor their tribes. These gods instill fear in their followers. They demand worship out of fear, not love.

The following is among the first 10 commandments in the Old

Testament:

> *You shall have no other gods before me. Exo 20:3*

This commandment is a demand that people worship him and no other.

Compare this to the following:

> *Arjuna, all those who worship other gods, with deep faith, are really worshipping me, even if they do not know it.* **Bhagavad Gita**, *Stephen Mitchell*

With a tribal god, we better obey or else:

> *But if you will not listen to me and will not do all these commandments, if you spurn my statutes, and if your soul abhors my rules, so that you will not do all my commandments, but break my covenant, then I will do this to you: I will visit you with panic, with wasting disease and fever that consume the eyes and make the heart ache. And you shall sow your seed in vain, for your enemies shall eat it. I will set my face against you, and you shall be struck down before your enemies. Those who hate you shall rule over you, and you shall flee when none pursues you. And if in spite of this you will not listen to me, then I will discipline you again sevenfold for your sins, and I will break the pride of your power, and I will make your heavens like iron and your earth like bronze. And your strength shall be spent in vain, for your land shall not yield its increase, and the trees of the land shall not yield their fruit.*

> *Then if you walk contrary to me and will not listen to me, I will continue striking you, sevenfold for your sins. And I will let loose the wild beasts against you, which shall bereave you of your children and destroy your livestock and make you few in number, so that your*

*roads shall be deserted.*

*And if by this discipline you are not turned to me but walk contrary to me, then I also will walk contrary to you, and I myself will strike you sevenfold for your sins. And I will bring a sword upon you, that shall execute vengeance for the covenant. And if you gather within your cities, I will send pestilence among you, and you shall be delivered into the hand of the enemy. When I break your supply of bread, ten women shall bake your bread in a single oven and shall dole out your bread again by weight, and you shall eat and not be satisfied.*

*But if in spite of this you will not listen to me, but walk contrary to me, then I will walk contrary to you in fury, and I myself will discipline you sevenfold for your sins. You shall eat the flesh of your sons, and you shall eat the flesh of your daughters. And I will destroy your high places and cut down your incense altars and cast your dead bodies upon the dead bodies of your idols, and my soul will abhor you. And I will lay your cities waste and will make your sanctuaries desolate, and I will not smell your pleasing aromas. And I myself will devastate the land, so that your enemies who settle in it shall be appalled at it. And I will scatter you among the nations, and I will unsheathe the sword after you, and your land shall be a desolation, and your cities shall be a waste.*
*Lev 26:14-33*

In the enlightened concept of God, God is gentle, loving and non-judgmental. He belongs to everyone as the Heavenly Father of all. Christ always referred to God as His Father. The personification of this father is not the Middle Eastern concept of father: authoritarian, autocratic and disciplinary. The Father Christ had in mind was the one in the Prodigal Son:

*And he arose and came to his father. But while he*

*was still a long way off, his father saw him and felt compassion, and ran and embraced him and kissed him. And the son said to him, 'Father, I have sinned against heaven and before you. I am no longer worthy to be called your son.' But the father said to his servants, 'Bring quickly the best robe, and put it on him, and put a ring on his hand, and shoes on his feet. And bring the fattened calf and kill it, and let us eat and celebrate. For this my son was dead, and is alive again; he was lost, and is found.' And they began to celebrate. Luke 15:20-24*

The son takes his inheritance, squanders it and returns home empty handed. Yet this Father never judges him, never rebukes him. Instead He runs toward him with open arms and embraces him. He puts a ring on his finger, a robe over him and orders the fatted calf slaughtered to celebrate His son's return.

In the Spiritual concept of God, God is no longer an idea, but is an embodiment. Personalizing God as Our Father makes God personal and approachable. Personalizing the trinity as Love, Beauty and Joy makes God transcendent and experiential. Whoever loves, embodies God. Anytime we are intoxicated by Beauty and are buoyed with Joy, God incarnates within us. God shines through that which is loving, beautiful and joyous. The spiritual knowing of God is not a belief taught in books or places of worship. It is personal and expressed in daily living. We know God personally because we have known Love, seen Beauty and experienced Joy.

## What is sin?

Sin is the tainting of our pure I Am, the speck of God within, by superimposing "false images" upon it and living accordingly.

"Thou shalt have no other gods" implies that the pure, loving, beautiful and joyous God should never be replaced by imposters. The only God we need to worship is the God of Love, Beauty and Joy. Imposters take the form of the lesser gods: wealth, power, greed and lust.

## What is blasphemy?

Can anyone really blaspheme against God or a Holy Book? Are we that naive to assume that God is insulted by what we say or do? Are we that powerful to impact God? It is hard to imagine how ignorant some can be. So, when individuals accused of blasphemy in some countries are lynched or stoned to death, we wonder what age are we living in. The stone age?

We can never blaspheme against God. God is so above our pettiness. We should stop defending God who does not need defending and concern ourselves with what is at hand – eliminating ignorance, overcoming fear, getting rid of superstition, caring for our families, raising healthy, confident and enlightened children and opening our hearts and minds to Love, Beauty and Joy.

# WE ARE IN THE IMAGE
# OF OUR SOURCE

*In the beginning Man created God; and in the image of
Man created he Him. – "Aqualung" - Jethro Tull*

T he universe began as a seed. So did we. Just as the rapid
expansion and organization of the Big Bang resulted
in the formation of the galaxies and the universes, so
did we. Our seed, the fertilized ovum, exploded into activity
and expanded through multiplication at a furious rate that
ultimately resulted in the human body. Neither the universe,
nor we, are a finished product. We are works in progress.

Christ realized the true nature of being when He stated:

> *"Now the parable is this: The seed is the word of God."*
> *Luke 8:11*

The meaning of this powerful verse becomes clear once we
reverse the order of the two words "seed" and "word."

> "Now the parable is this: ***The word of God is the seed***."

This makes perfect sense. God does not speak words that are
written in books. God's words are the seeds scattered all over
as you, as me, as the tree, as the cat, as the mountain, as the
earth, and as the universe. Everything started as a "seed" and
continues to unfold. Seeds are storehouses of potentiality.

Life is like a pomegranate with each seed on its own journey
of unfoldment. Unlike the pomegranate, life is a diversity of

seeds. We too are like a pomegranate. The seeds lying within us are skills, talents and abilities which are at various stages of unfoldment – many dormant while others are partially developed. Just as seeds require an environment to grow in, so do we. We have internal and external environments. Our growth and unfoldment depend on the environments we create or find ourselves in, the choices we make and the actions we take.

We have two types of seeds. Our material seed is our genetic code, the DNA. Our spiritual seed is the spark of God within. DNA, our material seed, makes us of earth. The spark within makes us of heaven. Hence, physically we are of earth and spiritually we are of heaven or God.

Genesis chapter 1, verses 26-27 state that God created us in His image:

> Then God said, "Let us make man in our image, after our likeness. And let them have dominion over the fish of the sea and over the birds of the heavens and over the livestock and over all the earth and over every creeping thing that creeps on the earth." So God created man in his own image, in the image of God he created him; male and female he created them.

The word for "man" in Hebrew is Adam which signifies man in the generic sense. In other words, it is a reference to humanity. According to Christianity, Judaism, and Islam, God created Adam or the first human out of clay, mud, wet sticky stuff, a droplet of semen or a clump of blood.  These refer to the physical body. We also have an intangible aspect – the animating breath of God.

> then the LORD God formed the man of dust from the ground and breathed into his nostrils the breath of life, and the man became a living creature.   Gen 2:7

Being in God's image takes on a deeper meaning when we look

at the words in Syriac (Aramaic).

> *And God said, "Let us make man (Heb. Adam) in our image, after our likeness:"*

This verse in Syriac is: ***Nebad nosho b salman akh da mouton.***

Salman (our image), Salmo (image) can mean:

       a. Image, figure, form, a picture;

       b. To impress an image as coin;

       c. To give a shape; and

       d. To form.

The word for "Our likeness" in Syriac is ***da mouton*** which means: to give a likeness or shape and to imprint a figure on the coin. In other words, to be in the image of God is to be imprinted with the figure and likeness of God.

What is the figure or the likeness we are imprinted with? In other words, if we are like a coin, what is the imprint that we are stamped with?

A seed is "stamped" with the potentiality of its source. An acorn is "stamped" with the potential to grow into an oak tree. A watermelon seed is "stamped" with the potential to grow into a watermelon. Physically, we are "stamped" with our DNA to grow into a human being. Spiritually, we are "stamped" with the potential to grow and express our divinity.

The seed starts as an ovule or a fertilized ovum. Soon, it divides and multiplies into a large community of harmoniously co-existing organized "cells". These give rise to the oak tree, the watermelon and to the human. Only then are the potentials of the acorn, watermelon seed and the fertilized ovum realized.

We are in the image of our source as seeds. We become like our source once grown and fully developed. While an acorn can become an oak tree and a watermelon seed can become a watermelon, we cannot be like our source until the body that is humanity is fully developed and matures. We start our journey as an "image" of divinity. Our progression is to be a fully developed, mature humanity in full cooperation, harmoniously existing and progressively manifesting the qualities of divinity as Love, Beauty, Joy, knowledge, wisdom and power.

The same way that a tree passes its likeness to its progeny as seeds containing DNA and genes, God has endowed us with His DNA in the form of our personal seed, our soul, our unique identity with the potential to manifest divinity.

# WE HAVE THREE NAMES

*You can know the name of a bird in all the languages of the world, but when you're finished, you'll know absolutely nothing whatever about the bird... So let's look at the bird and see what it's doing – that's what counts. I learned very early the difference between knowing the name of something and knowing something. –Richard Feynman*

W hat is in a Name?

A name is a special word and a word is a symbolic representation of a concept, an object or an entity. It is how we distinguish one idea, item, or person from another. From this we can see that to give something a name is to set it apart from all else, ***to give birth to it***, or to cause it to be, in the sense that it is distinct, separate and apart from all else.

We are inundated with words. Some dictionaries boast of having over half a million entries. We give everything a name.

*So out of the ground the LORD God formed every animal of the field and every bird of the air, and brought them to the man to see what he would call them; and whatever the man called every living creature, that was its name. The man gave names to all cattle, and to the birds of the air, and to every animal of the field; but for the man there was not found a helper as his partner.* Genesis 2:19-20

What a daunting task! Adam must have had an encyclopedic

reservoir of names to give to all the living creatures. We follow in the footsteps of Adam by giving names to everything we encounter. Studying the red blood cell for example, we discover the various names we use to describe each stage in the life cycle of this one cell type from its inception in the bone marrow until it matures and loses its nucleus. Have you noticed how many different names we use for the various apples, grapes, melons, or even the cars we use and the types of houses we live in?

Each variation seems to require a new name. We have different names for the roles we assume – mother, wife, daughter, sister, friend, aunt, employee, patient and so forth. When a woman is pregnant with a child, she is carrying a fetus. When the fetus is born, it is called a baby. The baby becomes an infant, then a toddler, a child, an adolescent, a teenager, a young adult and then an adult. The adult grows and ages and is known as middle aged, then an old person. The old person later is known as a senior citizen. The names we use make it easy to know what and who we are referencing. It does not change the person. The person is still the same. The changes a person goes through are continuous. They never cease. Yet, we pick stages to come up with new names. This is for convenience. The same is true with our age. We do not age a year at a time or a month at a time, or even a day at a time. Our growth, or aging, is continuous. Yet, we count our age in years.

We also give various names to our spiritual aspects. We, for example, have spirit, breath, soul, soul personality, mind, consciousness, awareness, emotions, thoughts, hopes, dreams, and aspirations. How different are these one from another?

According to Barbara G. Walker, author of **The Women's Encyclopedia of Myths and Secrets:**

> *"For the purposes of magic and religion, the name of anything was considered identical with the thing*

*itself, a spiritual "handle" by which the thing or the supernatural being could be manipulated."*

*"Each Egyptian's soul-name, the ren, was breathed by a mother on her child as it was first put to her breast; therefore, the Goddess of soul-names was Renenet, who governed lactation. Without its ren, the child would have no identity and would not be allowed to eat. Even the gods needed mothers to give them names, otherwise they would pine away and die. The same belief is found in India: the "thousand-eyed god" named Existence cried immediately after he was born, "Give me a name, for without a name I will not eat food."*

*"Names were confused with souls almost everywhere... Egyptians said "To speak the name of the dead is to make them live again." ... "No greater harm could be done to an Egyptian than to erase the carving or writing of his name. To destroy the very letters meant destruction of the soul."..."The Mother of Gods controlled her offspring by knowledge of their secret names."..."Both Jewish and Christian Gnostics focused on the power of divine names to bring about healing, exorcism, absolution, and salvation."*

There is an ancient Pharaonic text that states:

*"Each human being writes his name, the name that is his for a lifetime, in one of the knotted loops on the infinite thread of infinity."*
*Egyptian Mysteries, Lucie Lamy*

A name contains a bundle of information. Initially a name has little significance to us. As we accumulate experiences, the name becomes more significant in that it houses a considerable number of memories. By constantly incorporating experiences as memories, we are continually rewriting our names and recreating ourselves.

## Our Three Names

We have three names, each associated with one of our bodies. Our **obvious name** is associated with the physical body. This is our given name. It is a repository for our experiences for this lifetime. If we undergo a transformation, we reflect this great change by acquiring a new name as happened in the Bible when Jacob became Israel and Abram became Abraham and Sarai became Sarah.

Our **hidden name** is associated with the astral body and represents our essential characteristics in this lifetime. It embodies our purpose for being here on earth and our current mission. For some, this hidden name is Healer, Teacher, Peace Maker, Seeker, Student, Architect, Designer, even Disruptor or Wild Card. Living our hidden name imbues us with energy and vitality. This name does not change often and can last for several lifetimes.

Our **secret name** is associated with the spiritual body. This name is our soul name and what the ancient Egyptians called the REN. This name does not change. It is who we are for eternity. It is our identity. It is a brilliant light radiating a unique rate of vibration with a special color and hue.

## The Three Names of Jesus Christ

Jesus Christ is not an actual historic name. Jesus or Joshua is a first name which means savior. Christ is a title conferred on anyone anointed. Kings of old were anointed with oil, usually by a prophet, to establish their authority as regals.

Jesus is given three different names in the bible:

After a long list of genealogy, Matthew 1:16 states:

> and Jacob the father of Joseph the husband of Mary, of whom Jesus was born, who is called the Messiah.

_**Messiah**_ is the first name.

In Matthew 1:20, the angel announcing Mary's pregnancy to Joseph says:

> "Joseph, son of David, do not be afraid to take Mary as your wife, for the child conceived in her is from the Holy Spirit. She will bear a son, and you are to name him Jesus, for he will save his people from their sins."

_**Jesus**_ is the second name.

Continuing with Matthew 1:22 we find out that there is yet a third name for Jesus.

> All this took place to fulfill what had been spoken by the Lord through the prophet: "Look, the virgin shall conceive and bear a son, and they shall name him, Emmanuel which means, "God is with us."

_**Emmanuel**_ is the third name.

## Meaning of the Names

1.  Messiah is the **Obvious Name** of Christ. Messiah is from the Aramaic _mĕšîhâ_ or Hebrew _māšăh_, meaning the anointed one. The same word is used in Arabic where MASAHA means to anoint. Jesus is a Messiah, the anointed one, in the sense that he is a king. To be king is to be ruler over a kingdom. Jesus never had an earthly kingdom. He was never King of the Jews. Christ's kingdom was a spiritual one, a kingdom where He was king over His physical, emotional, mental and spiritual faculties, a kingdom where love rules.

2.  Jesus is the **Hidden Name** of Christ. Jesus is the

same as Joshua meaning savior. This appellation, Jesus, shows us the purpose for Christ's life, his life mission, to be an example of what is possible for us to be – to love, to serve and to pursue a spiritual life. Jesus being light saves us from our ignorance by showing us the way to salvation via spirituality.

Jesus meaning savior, can be construed as the purpose for which Jesus was born, that Christ came to "save his people from their sins." This is shortsighted. He came so we may have life and have it abundantly. He came to set an example of what is possible for us to be as children of God. **There is only one sin we need to be saved from – ignorance which blinds eyes, deafens ears and hardens hearts.** When we give up our ignorance and open up to spirituality, Christ saves us from our "sin." No one needs salvation from a sin that is a transgression against God. How can any human ever transgress against God? God, the creator of the universes can never command humans or demand anything from us, not even worship. Unless we worship God freely, voluntarily and gladly, it does not count. Christ came to save us from ourselves – our ignorance, blindness, and hard heartedness.

3.   Emmanuel is the **Secret Name** of Christ. This name which in Aramaic (Syriac) is **Aman O Eel** means God is with us or within us. This secret name holds the key to the entire scriptures and the whole life story of Jesus. In fact, this is the Good News of the New Testament. The Kingdom of God is within us. God is not in a faraway place – heaven. God is not only with us or within us. God is everyone disguised as this or that. There is nothing but God and all is God. If we completely

understand and live by this one fact, we will be not only saved, but transformed as well.

Jesus Christ is the prototype, the model, the Word, and the Way for the transformation of the Human into the divine. This happens when we know who we are. We are the Child in whom the Father is well pleased. The sooner we know ourselves intimately, love ourselves unconditionally and express ourselves fearlessly, the sooner Christ's mission will be fulfilled. Our Earth will be transformed into Heaven.

## The Power in a Name

There are many passages in the New Testament where Christ asks us to do things in His name. When we do something in someone's name, we do it on their behalf; we have their power and authority to carry out that function.

Here are some references to **in my name**.

> For where two or three are gathered in my name, I am there among them.  Matt 18.20

> I will do whatever you ask in my name, so that the Father may be glorified in the Son. If in my name you ask me for anything, I will do it.  John 14.13-14

> But the Advocate, the Holy Spirit, whom the Father will send in my name, will teach you everything, and remind you of all that I have said to you. John 14.26

> On that day you will ask nothing of me. Very truly, I tell you, if you ask anything of the Father in my name, he will give it to you. Until now you have not asked for anything in my name. Ask and you will receive, so that your joy may be complete.  John 16.23-24

**"In my name"** means according to my way, method, approach, and technique. In other words, with the kind of understanding Christ had, functioning from the same level of awareness as Christ. In other words, expressing His mission in life, to love and to serve.

It is common in Christian churches to invoke, not only the name of Christ, but also the Holy Trinity. In many churches, worshipers cross themselves repeatedly while saying: "In the name of the Father, the Son and the Holy Ghost." Obviously, people would not do that if they did not believe in the efficacy of invoking these holy names. The clergy invoke the holy names to cleanse, purify, baptize, forgive sins and to ward off evil spirits.

> *And these signs will accompany those who believe: in my name they will cast out demons; they will speak in new tongues; they will pick up serpents with their hands; and if they drink any deadly poison, it will not hurt them; they will lay their hands on the sick, and they will recover. Mark 16:17-18*

> *The seventy-two returned with joy, saying, "Lord, even the demons are subject to us in your name!" Luke 10:17*

For the ancients, names were imbued with power. Yet, the actual power does not reside in the name, rather in the belief of the one pronouncing the name. If we truly believe in the power of Christ, then invoking His name is powerful. Otherwise, it is an inert word. Moslems invoke the name of Allah because that is who they believe in. It is the belief and conviction that matters, not the actual word or name uttered. Ultimately, what matters is the faith we have. It is laudable to have faith in God; it is equally important to have faith in ourselves, in our skills, talents and our abilities.

Finally, *"For where two or three are gathered in my name, I am there among them. Matthew 18.20"* is a spiritual law. It is the law of abundance. When two or more people come together in the spirit of Christ, in love, then the product to their efforts is more than the sum of its parts separately. This is clearly evident in my life. Alone, I could have achieved little. With my wife, working together in love, we accomplished a great deal and continue to do so.

This spiritual law is a direct rebuke of mindless competition. Cooperating and working together for a common good is far better than competing amongst ourselves to outdo each other. This is especially true of nations. Instead of brute competition, cooperation yields far better results. Joint venture amongst nations is the way to peace and prosperity.

# THE THREE NAMES OF GOD

*The Tao that can be told is not the eternal Tao; the name that can be named is not the eternal name. The Nameless is the origin of Heaven and Earth; the Named is the mother of all things.     −Lao Tzu*

God does not have a name. What God has are attributes. How many attributes does God have? As many as we want. Since we can reference a thing or a person by their attributes, an attribute can substitute for a name.

It is customary, in several cultures, to refer to people by their attributes. For example:

Hello friend.

Hi cousin and depending on age, good morning, Uncle or Aunt.

When we were in Egypt, I referred to our tour guide as "brother." He, in turn, referred to me as Uncle.

Being a trinity, God has three names or attributes:

1.  An obvious name which corresponds to the physical;
2.  A hidden name which corresponds to the astral;
3.  A secret name which corresponds to the spiritual.

# The Obvious Name

**The obvious name** is the one by which a thing or an entity is known. We give people, animals, and things names so that we may distinguish between them.

Everybody has an obvious name. This is our given name. God, too, has an obvious name. Some of God's obvious names are God, Allah, Brahma, Elohim, El Shaddai, Adoni, Ahura Mazda and so forth.

The Kabbalists state that God has 72 names and knowing these names gives us power. Moslems, on the other hand, state that God has 99 names. Even though there are several lists available noting the alleged 99 names of Allah, they are not all consistent and there is some argument over what actually represents a Name of Allah. The following list of the 99 names of Allah is taken from **The Wikipedia**:

> *1. ar-Raḥmān (The Beneficent/ All-Compassionate/ Most Gracious) 2. ar-Raḥīm (The Most Merciful/ Ever-Merciful/ Merciful/ Most Clement) 3. al-Mālik (The King/ Lord/ Sovereign/ Dominion/ Master) 4. al-Quddus (The Holy/ All-Holy/ All-Pure/ Sacred/ All-Sacred) 5. As-Salām (The Giver of Peace/ Peace/ All-Calm/ Ever-Tranquil) 6. al-Muʿmin (The Granter of Security/ the Giver/ Faith/ Supreme Believer (of Belief)/ Giver of Belief/ All-Assurer) 7. al-Muhaymin (The Controller/ Absolute Authority Over All/ Guardian Over All/ Absolute Master/ Eternal Dominating) 8. al-ʿAzīz (The Exalted in Might and Power/ Exalted/ Powerful/ Almighty/ Mighty) 9. al-Jabbar (The Omnipotent/ Supreme Power/ Possessor of Having All Power/ Strong) 10. al-Mutakabbir (The Possessor of Greatness/ Supreme/ Justly Proud) 11. al-Khaliq (The Creator/ Creator of the Universe/ Maker/ True Originator/ Absolute Author) 12. al-Bariʿ (The Initiator/ Evolver/*

*Eternal Spirit Worshipped By All, Have Absolute Power Over All Matters, Nature and Events) 13. al-Muṣawwir (The Fashioner/ Shaper/ Designer/ Artist) 14. al-Ghaffar (The Repeatedly Forgiving/ Absolute Forgiver/ Pardoner/ Condoner [He Who is Ready to Pardon and Forgive]) 15. al-Qahhar (The Subduer/ Overcomer/ Conqueror/ Absolute Vanquisher [Possessor of Who Subdues Evil and Oppression] 16. al-Wahhab (The Absolute Bestower/ Giver/ Grantor/ Great Donor) 17. Ar-Razzaq (The Provider/ Sustainer/ Bestower of Sustenance/ All-Provider) 18. al-Fattaḥ (The Opener/ Opener of the Gates of Profits/ Reliever/ The Victory Giver) 19. al-Alim (The Knowing/ All-Knower/ Omniscient/ All-Knowledgeable/ Possessor of Knowing Much of Ever Thing/ All-Knowing) 20. al-Qabiḍ/ al-Qabidh (The Restrainer/ Withholder/ Straightener/ Absolute Seizer) 21. al-Basiṭṭ (The Extender/ Expander/ Generous Provider) 22. al-Khafidh (The Abaser/ Humiliator/ Downgrader [Possessor of Giving Comfort, Free from Pain Anxiety or Troubles]) 23. Ar-Rafi'/ Ar-Rafee (The Exalter/ Upgrader [of Ranks]) 24. al-Mu'izz (The Giver of Honor/ Bestower of Honor/ Empowerer) 25. al-Mudzhill (The Giver of Dishonor/ the Giver of Disgrace) 26. As-Sami'/ As-Samie (All-Hearing/ Hearer of Invocation) 27. al-Basir/ al-Baṣṣir (The All-Seeing/ All-Seer/ Ever-Clairvoyant/ Clear-Sighted/ Clear-Seeing) 28. al-Ḥakam (The Judge/ Arbitrator/ Arbiter/ All-Decree/ Possessor of Authority of Decisions and Judgment) 29. al-'Adl (The Just/ Authorized and Straightforward Judge of Dealing Justly) 30. al-Laṭwif [al-Laṭeef/ (The Gentle/ Benignant/ Subtly Kind/ All-Subtle) 31. al-Khabir [al-Khabeer] (The All-Aware/ Well-Acquainted/ Ever-Adept) 32. al-Ḥalim [al-Ḥaleem] (The Forbearing/ Indulgent/ Oft Forbearing/ All-Enduring. 33. al-'Azim, al-'Aẓẓim, (The MostGreat/ Ever-Magnificent/ Most Supreme/ Exalted/ Absolute*

Dignified) 34. al-Ghafur (The Ever-Forgiving/ Oft-Forgiving) 35. ash-Shakur (The Grateful/ Appreciative/ Multiplier of Rewards) 36. al-Ali (The Sublime/ Ever-Exalted/ Supreme/ Most High/ Most Lofty) 37. al-Kabir (The Great/ Ever-Great/ Grand/ Most Great/ Greatly Abundant of Extent, Capacity and Importance) 38. al-Hafiz (The Preserver/ Ever-Preserving/ All-Watching/ Protector/ Guardian/ Oft-Conservator) 39. al-Muqit [al-Muqeet] (The Nourisher/ Feeder) 40. al-Hasib (The Bringer of Judgment/ Ever-Reckoner [the One Who Takes Account of All Matters] 41. al-Jalil (The Majestic/ Exalted/ Oft-Important/ Splendid) 42. al-Karim [al-Kareem] (The Noble/ Bountiful/ Generous/ Precious/ Honored/ Benefactor) 43. Ar-Raqib [Ar-Raqeeb] (The Watchful/ Observer/ Ever-Watchful/ Watcher) 44. al-Mujib (The Responsive/ Answerer/ Supreme Answerer/ Accepter of Invocation) 45. al-Waasi'/ al-Waasie] (The Vast/ All-Embracing/ Omnipresent/ Boundless/ All-Encompassing) 46. al-Hakim/ al-Hakeem (The Wise/ Ever-Wise/ Endowed with Sound Judgment) 47. al-Wadud [al-Wadoud/ al-Wadood] (The Affectionate/ Ever-Affectionate/ Loving One/ Loving/ the Lover/ the One Who Tenders and Warm Hearts) 48. al-Majid [al-Majeed] (The All-Glorious/ Majestic/ Ever-Illustrious [Oft-Brilliant in Dignity, Achievements or Actions]) 49. al-Ba'ith / al-Ba'eith [al-Baa'ith/ al-Baa'eith] (The Resurrector/ Awakener/ Arouser/ Dispatcher) 50. ash-Shahid [Ash-Shaheed] (The Witness/ Testifier/ Ever-Witnessing) 51. al-Haqq (The Truth/ Reality/ the Only One Certainly Sound and Genuine in Truth) 52. al-Wakil [al-Wakeel] (The Trustee, The Dependable, The Advocate) 53. al-Qawi [al-Qawee] (The Strong) 54. al-Matin [al-Mateen] (The Firm, The Steadfast) 55. al-Wali [al-Walee] (The Friend, Helper) 56. al-Hamid [al-Hameed] (The All Praiseworthy) 57. al-Muhsi [al-Muhsee] (The Accounter, The Numberer of All) 58. al-

*Mubdi'* [al-Mubdie] (The Originator, The Producer, The Initiator) 59. *al-Mu'id* [al-Mu'eid/ al-Mu'eyd] (The Restorer, The reinstater Who Brings Back All) 60. *al-Muhyi* [al-Muhyee] (The Giver of Life) 61. *al-Mumit* [al-Mumeet] (The Bringer of Death) 62. *al-Hayy* (The Living) 63. *al-Qayyum* [al-Qayyoum/al-Qayyoom] (The Subsisting, The Independent) 64. *al-Wajid* [al-Waajid] (The Perceiver, The Finder, The Unfailing) 65. *al-Majid* [al-Maajid] (The Illustrious, The Magnificent, The Glorious) 66. *al-Wahid* [al-Waahid] (The Unique, The Single) 67. *al-Ahad* (The One, The Indivisible) 68. *As-Samad* [As-Ssamad/ As-Swamad] (The Eternal, The Absolute, The Self-Sufficient) 69. *al-Qadir* [al-Qaadir] (The All-Powerful, He Who is able to do Everything) 70. *al-Muqtadir* (The Determiner, The Dominant) 71. *al-Muqaddim* (The Expediter, He Who Brings Forward) 72. *al-Mu'akhkhir* [al-Mo'akhkhir] (The Delayer, He Who Puts Far Away) 73. *al-Awwal* (The First, The Beginning-less) 74. *al-Akhir/al-Aakhir* (The Last, The Endless) 75. *Az-Zahir/ Az-ZZahir/ Az-Zwahir* (The Manifest, The Evident, The Outer) 76. *al-Batin/ al-Battin* (The Hidden, The Unmanifest, The Inner) 77. *al-Wali* [al-Waali] (The Patron, The Protecting Friend, The Friendly Lord) 78. *al-Muta'ali* [al-Muta'aali] (The Supremely Exalted, The Most High) 79. *al-Barr* (The Good, The Beneficent) 80. *At-Tawwab* [At-Tawwaab (The Ever-Returning, Ever-Relenting) 81. *al-Muntaqim* (The Avenger) 82. *al-'Afu* [al-'Afou] (The Pardoner, The Effacer, The Forgiver) 83. *Ar-Ra'uf* [Ar-Ra'ouf/ Ar-Raw'ouf] (The Kind, The Pitying) 84. *Malik ul-Mulk* [Maalik ul-Mulk] (The Owner of all Sovereignty) 85. *Zul-Jalali wal-Ikram/ Dzhul-Jalali wal-Ikram* (The Owner, Lord of Majesty and Honour) 86. *al-Muqsit* [al-Muqsitt] (The Equitable, The Requiter) 87. *al-Jami'/ al-Jamie* (The Gatherer, The Unifier) 88. *al-Ghani* (The Rich, The Independent) 89. *al-Mughni* (The Enricher,

*The Emancipator) 90. al-Mani'/ al-Manie (The Preventer, The Withholder, The Shielder, The Defender) 91. Ad-Darr [Adh-Dhaarr] (The Distressor, The Harmer, The Afflictor) 92. An-Nafi'/ An-Nafie (The Propitious, The Benefactor, The Source of Good) 93. An-Nur [An-Nour] (The Light) 94. al-Hadi [al-Haadi] (The Guide, The Way) 95. al-Badi'[al-Badiy'/ al-Badiye] (The Originator, The Incomparable, The Unattainable, The Beautiful) 96. al-Baqi [al-Baaqi] (The Immutable, The Infinite, The Everlasting) 97. al-Warith (The Heir, The Inheritor of All) 98. Ar-Rashid [Ar-Rasheed] (The Guide to the Right Path) 99. As-Sabur/ Aṣ-Ṣṣabur/ Aṣ-Ṣwabur (The Timeless, The Patient)*

Since most of these names are attributes of God, it is easy to see why knowing these names gives us power. Knowledge is power. Knowing the attributes of a being is partial knowing of that being. These attributes are embodiments of qualities that humans believe are of the nature of God. Some of these attributes are opposing qualities: {*The Abaser/ Humiliator/ Downgrader (22) and The Exalter/ Upgrader of Ranks (23)}, {The Giver of Honor (24) and The Giver of Dishonor (25)}, {the Giver of Life (60) and The Bringer of Death (61)}, {The Expediter (71) and The Delayer (72)}, {The First (73) and The Last (74)}, {The Manifest (75) and The Unmanifest (76)}, {The Distressor, The Harmer, The Afflictor (91) and The Propitious, The Benefactor, The Source of Good (92)}*).

## Sounding the Names

According to **The Gospel of Islam** by Duncan Greenlees, it is believed that the repetition of specific names of Allah produces varying effects and benefits for the devout chanter. For example:

· Sounding of the phrase *Ya-Rahman* (God the Beneficent) 100 times is said to result in the acquisition of a good memory and freedom from care and worry.

· Calling out *Ya-Salaam* (The Source of Peace) 160 times to anyone who is ill will bring him or her to health.

· Repetition of *Ya-Mutakabbir* (God the Majestic) by a man before having intercourse with his wife will see him blessed by Allah with a righteous child.

· Devout use of *Ya-Ghaffar* (God the Forgiver) will result in forgiveness of all sins.

· Calling out the name *Ya-Fattah* (God the Opener) will result in the heart of the petitioner being opened for victory to be bestowed by Allah. (Significantly, *Al-Fattah* was the name chosen by Yasir Arafat for the military arm of his Palestine Liberation Organization [PLO].)

· For personal protection, calling out the name *Ya-Hafiz* (God the Preserver) 16 times is recommended.

These names are obvious and anyone can pronounce them. These are the names most use when they pray, think of and when hallowing the name of God. Uttering the obvious name of God without much feeling and emotion is praying from the lips alone. It is devoid of power.

## The Hidden Name

The hidden name represents the most dominant characteristic of an entity. It is the grouping to which an individual belongs. The hidden name has power and magic if we know what it is and learn how to "pronounce or express" it correctly (live it). Even though this name is hidden, it is not secret. Once we know where to look for it, it becomes obvious. God, too has a hidden name. The secret to knowing the hidden name of God lies in a passage in the Gospel according to Matthew.

In Matthew 25 beginning at verse 31, we read about The Judgment of the Nations:

> *"When the Son of Man comes in his glory, and all the angels with him, then he will sit on the throne of his glory. All the nations will be gathered before him, and he will separate people one from another as a shepherd separates the sheep from the goats, and he will put the sheep at his right hand and the goats at the left. Then the king will say to those at his right hand, 'Come, you that are blessed by my Father, inherit the kingdom prepared for you from the foundation of the world; for I was hungry and you gave me food, I was thirsty and you gave me something to drink, I was a stranger and you welcomed me, I was naked and you gave me clothing, I was sick and you took care of me, I was in prison and you visited me.' Then the righteous will answer him, 'Lord, when was it that we saw you hungry and gave you food, or thirsty and gave you something to drink? And when was it that we saw you a stranger and welcomed you, or naked and gave you clothing? And when was it that we saw you sick or in prison and visited you?' And the king will answer them, 'Truly I tell you, just as you did it to one of the least of these who are members of my family, you did it to me.' Then he will say to those at his left hand, 'You that are accursed, depart from me into the eternal fire prepared for the devil and his angels; for I was hungry and you gave me no food, I was thirsty and you gave me nothing to drink, I was a stranger and you did not welcome me, naked and you did not give me clothing, sick and in prison and you did not visit me.' Then they also will answer, 'Lord, when was it that we saw you hungry or thirsty or a stranger or naked or sick or in prison, and did not take care of you?' Then he will*

> answer them, 'Truly I tell you, just as you did not do it to one of the least of these, you did not do it to me.' And these will go away into eternal punishment, but the righteous into eternal life."

What we learn from this passage is that **we can only know God's hidden name by proxy, as each other. In other words, each being is one of God's hidden names.** To utter the hidden name of God, we must hallow and honor each other. Hence, God's expressions are written everywhere as you, as me and as nature.

## The Secret Name

The God of the ancient Hebrews had an ineffable name, that is a name that cannot be expressed, described, or uttered. This name is known as the *tetragrammaton* consisting of the four Hebrew letters *yod, he, vau, he (YHWH).* This name was so secret and holy that it could not be pronounced, except once a year, and only by the high priest.

It is interesting that DNA also has 4 nucleotides, "letters" out of which all proteins are synthesized. A (Adenine), T (Thymine), C (Cytosine), and G (Guanine). Even RNA has 4 letters as well, A (Adenine), U (Uracil), C (Cytosine), and G (Guanine)..

These four Hebrew letters, usually transliterated as YHWH or JHVH (Yahweh or Jehovah), are used as a biblical proper name for God. YHWH or JHVH is identical to the Aramaic (Syriac) Yehweh, which means **to be** or **being**, and EHWEH meaning I **Am**.

What is so secret about YHWH, JEHOVA or *being,* and *I Am*?

The secret lies, not in the name, as much as knowing how to utter the unutterable.

## How to Utter the 3 Names of God

1. It is easy to utter the obvious name of God. All we have to do is say the word God, Allah, Brahma, Elohim, El Shaddai, Adoni, Ahura Mazda, and so forth. This is exactly what most do. Uttering this name or hallowing God by simply saying God, or "Hallowed be Thy Name", is empty, sterile and has no power to move or impact anything. Most people use the obvious name of God out of habit and without giving it much thought. Many even use this name in vain or as a curse.

2. It is more difficult to utter the hidden name of God. To do this, we must become aware of others. We must go beyond our self and care for others including animals and nature. To utter this name, we must feel love and compassion. We must see our inter-relatedness and our ultimate unity, not only as people, but also as a unified, harmoniously co-existing planet. Uttering the hidden name of God by honoring the God in another is a powerful way of hallowing the name of God. It can transform all involved. Namaste! The God in me greets the God in you. We are one.

3. The most powerful way to utter the name of God is to use God's secret name. To do this, we must realize that while we cannot utter this secret name, we can assume it. With God's secret name, we do not do, but become and this is why the name of God as YEHWH or BEING and JEHOVA or **I Am** is so secret. To be is not to do. It is to assume and to become. It is to obliterate the boundary between us and others. It is to become one with. By uttering the secret name of God, we do not honor another; we ARE the other. We do not love; we ARE love. We do not see; we ARE that which we see. We do not touch; we ARE unity. In this state there is

no other or anything beyond the Self. All are the same Self, our Self and the Self.

We utter the secret name of God when we express the nature of God within us – our I Am as Love, Beauty and Joy. Discarding our identification with our changing bodies, we sacrifice nothing. Identifying with our changeless I Am, we gain everything. Becoming Love, Beauty and Joy, we lose our sense of the small self and in losing it, we find our ultimate SELF.

> *Those who find their life will lose it, and those who lose their life for my sake will find it. Matt 10:39*

I Am You. You are Me. I Am Nature, Nature is Me.

# HOW CAN WE KNOW
# FOR CERTAIN?

*Uncertainty will always be part of the taking
charge process.* — Harold Geneen

There are very few things we know for certain. We know we exist. We know we breathe, eat, drink and need to rest. We know we have a physical body, but we are not sure if we have an astral or a spiritual body. The vast majority of what we think we know is belief, conjecture or circumstantial. How can we know for sure that we have souls and whether or not reincarnation is fact or fiction. Science gives us facts. What if what we need is spiritual truth? Can we know anything for certain?

Religion advocates God as the answer to all mysteries. If we make the effort to study the tenants of religion, we soon realize the gaping holes within these doctrines. We are asked to simply believe, accept in faith, obey and follow. Besides, whose version of religion are we supposed to accept? There are so many of them.

If God created us and we are in God's image, why are we so frail and subject to disease, pain, suffering, aging and death? How can we explain evil? Why do children die? Why are we imperfect and handicapped?

While science provides answers and great tools to enhance the quality of our lives, it has yanked the carpet out from under our feet. It denies the existence of our souls and postulates that we are the result of random forces of nature. Thus, while we are living "longer and better", we have lost our sense of value and meaning.

Science postulates that matter and energy are the ultimate reality. Even fields are forms of energy. Yet, no one knows what matter or energy are other than vibrations. But what is vibrating? The deeper we look into the nature of matter, the more "emptiness" we find. And even though science asserts that the laws of physics shape the universe, they ignore that these laws, even though they are in matter, are nowhere to be seen since they are intangible. If we can assert the existence of these intangible laws, we can declare the existence of other intangibles such as consciousness and the soul.

Spirituality, in addition to emphasizing the importance of science, religion and philosophy to gain knowledge, considers the value of our experiences as well. We can learn a great deal from systems of knowledge. Yet, personal experiences have a major contribution to make. An unusual aspect of personal experiences are synchronicities. Synchronicities in my life have been an eye-opener. I gleaned answers that I could not have had any other way.

There are two ways to know for sure. The first way is to follow Christ's advice:

> Ask, and it will be given to you; seek, and you will find; knock, and it will be opened to you. For everyone who asks receives, and the one who seeks finds, and to the one who knocks it will be opened. Matt 7:7-8

We can know for certain if we desperately want it. If we insist, persist and continue to seek, it is a matter of time before we have the answer. The asking must be earnest, persistent and passionate. The knocking must be loud, insistent and desperate. The answer will come. It can come as an inspiration, in a dream or as a personal experience. When it comes, we will know for sure and there will be no doubt. The answer will come at its own opportune time. When I asked, knocked and desperately wanted to know if I had a soul, I had a near-death experience. Then I knew.

The second way to know for certain is that of the Saints, Yogis, Gurus, Sufis, Shamans and Mystics. Through incessant prayer, meditation, contemplation, visualization, assumption, union and communion with what we seek, we will have a revelation. The answer we are searching for will appear. During fervent prayer or deep meditation, we transcend the physical and the astral and enter the spiritual realm. Our consciousness rises to that of Christ Consciousness or Super Consciousness. Here we find the answers to all the questions we have through revelation.

A perfect example of this would be Gautama Buddha. Buddha wanted to know why we suffer. He was not a scientist. He did not go to a laboratory to run experiments. He did not conduct surveys to find out why people suffer. He did not even consult experts. He became obsessed with the question. He isolated himself in the woods, meditated day and night until he had the answer. The answer came as a flash. He had a revelation. The cause of suffering is attachment.

Where did the answer come from? From the Christ Consciousness through his Higher Self. Where else? This is how many get their answers, including me.

Revelation could come invited or uninvited. It appears as a deep-seated knowing, a calling or an urgent desire to fulfill a mission. This is what happened to Florence Nightingale. She claims that at 17, she heard the voice of God as a calling for her to tend the sick and the infirm. She could have ignored it, instead she forsook marriage and an easy affluent life for hardship pursuing her calling. Her decision to nurse changed the world. This is also what happened to Harriet Tubman, Joan of Arc and many others.

When we have a gnosis, we know, not because we have been told or read it in a book, but because we glimpsed the answer, had an intuition or a revelation. With firsthand experience, there is no doubt. To have satisfying answers, we require fearlessness, a passionate desire to know and persistence. We must want it bad enough. Instead of belief and speculation we can have knowledge.

◆ ◆ ◆

Reincarnation is a widely held belief the world over. It is in Hinduism, Buddhism, Judaism, Christianity and Islam. Where did the original knowledge regarding reincarnation come from? Ancient Yogis, Saints, Prophets and Mystics must have received it as an inspiration, a revelation or even in a dream. This can happen while under the influence of hallucinogens, drugs, rituals, meditation or fervent prayer. Once we contact the superconscious (Christ Consciousness), we receive the knowledge we need. When we know, there is no doubt. When the light appears, darkness disappears.

We do not need to know for certain that reincarnation is a fact. Yet, for those who remember their past lives and those who cannot explain personal proclivities in any other way, for them reincarnation is a fact.

We do not need to know for certain that we have an astral body. Yet for those who leave their physical body behind and become aware of themselves out of the body looking down at their physical body, the astral body is a fact.

We do not need to know for certain that we have a spiritual body. Yet, for those who have contact with spiritual beings or have spiritual experiences, the spiritual body is a fact. In most, the spiritual body is rudimentary. It must be nurtured and developed by embodying spiritual qualities such as love, compassion, empathy and service. It requires us to build our body of light by increasing the rate of our vibration and by embodying and expressing the virtues. We will know that we have a spiritual body when we begin to express spiritual powers such as healing, intuition and inspiration. We know that Christ and a few others had well developed spiritual bodies. This was apparent for their contemporaries. The vibration of the spiritual body is so powerful that it outshines the entire physical and astral bodies. People see it as a halo surrounding the body, usually around the head. The spiritual body in such individuals is so magnetic that anyone coming in contact with it will feel it and even be healed.

What we know for certain depends where we dwell. If we are trapped in the physical, then external sources are where we get our knowledge from. We believe that we know much and we go around convincing others of our point of view. If the astral is where we dwell, then whatever we can mentally comprehend and emotionally feel is truth for us.

Spiritually minded individuals do not need to know many things. They know that they are a living soul. They know that the world is a transient school and a proving ground. They know who they are. They know why they are here and what they need to do. They live simple, peaceful, and exemplary lives.

Knowing something for sure does not mean that we can convince others of its validity. If we ever had an experience that was out of the ordinary, we know the absolute truth of that experience. Yet if someone asked us, how do we know it really happened? We would be stumped and perhaps unable to explain. These experiences are rare and when they happen, are for our own edification, not necessarily to be shared or to convince others of their validity.

We need to know who we are, how to unconditionally love ourselves and how to fearlessly express ourselves. We are a seedling on a journey. Our source and destiny are divinity. This knowledge must be intimate, certain, unshakeable and absolute. It is truth. What we believe and how we act, is a different story.

> *I said, "You are gods, sons of the Most High, all of you;.."* Ps 82:6

In the Gnostic Gospel of Thomas, there is the following statement:

> Jesus said, "If those who lead you say to you, 'Look, the Kingdom is in the sky,' then the birds of the sky will get there first. If they say 'It is in the sea,' then the fish will get there first. Rather, the Kingdom is inside of you, and it is outside of you. When you come to know yourselves, then you will become known, and you will realize that it is you who are the children of the living Father. But if you will not know yourselves, then you dwell in poverty, and it is you who are that poverty." *John Dart and Ray Riegert*

Our prime directive and our primary responsibility are to know ourself intimately, to love ourself unconditionally and to express ourself fearlessly. When we do, everything will fall into its proper place.

# PART III

## Love Yourself Unconditionally

1. Concepts of Self
2. Accept Yourself
3. Forgive Yourself
4. Love Yourself
5. Love Others
6. The Nature of Love
7. The Quest for Happiness

# CONCEPTS OF SELF

*There are three things extremely hard: steel, a diamond, and to know one's self. —Benjamin Franklin*

What is the Self?

Views as to what the self is vary greatly among scientists, philosophers and religious leaders. For some, the self is the soul. For others, it is the center of all the phenomena we experience be it social, psychological, neurological or molecular. Some even deny the existence of the self outright.

To love ourself, we must know what the self is. Is it the body? Is it a concept? Is it all of our parts coming together? Is there a real self somewhere within us?

A car can be the sum of its parts.
A house can be the mortar, bricks, HVAC and the other components.
A human can be its cells, tissues, organs and systems.
In a purely material world, all of the above would be true.
1+1+1=3.
A car, a house and a human, however, are much more than their component parts.

A car transports us to places we would not be able to visit otherwise. A car provides shelter from the elements, transports goods, is an investment and is an extension of a person's self-image.

A house is much more than its components. A house is a home where children are raised, pets are kept, families are nurtured and memories are made.

Similarly, a human is far more than its cells, tissues, organs and systems. A human can imagine, believe, sing, dance, cook, paint, compose, dream and love. These intangibles are not part of the makeup of a car, a house or a human. Yet, they are the most important aspects. These are manifestations of a higher order – intangible benefits that did not exist prior to the parts coming together. One of the most obvious intangibles of a human is the reality of the self.

## The Self

There is no self when we allow our appetites to rule our lives.
There is no self when we react as in "an eye for an eye".
There is no self when emotions such as hate, anger and rage consume us.
There is no self when others can push our buttons.
There is no self when we are taken over by mindless rites, rituals, customs and traditions.
There is no self when nationalism blinds us.
There is no self when we do not think, reason and use our freedom of choice.

We all have a self. Having something without using it is as good as not having it.

How do we know if we have a self?

1. We experience external realities through our senses which receive electromagnetic waves that stimulate the nerves. Nerve impulses travel along nerve fibers from the sense organs to the brain causing the brain cells to fire certain patterns. Somehow,

the brain converts these mental impressions into representations of the external world. We see colorful objects, hear melodies, smell, taste and feel what we believe to be real things. In reality, all are creations of our mind. All external things are experienced internally in the mind. We can never know exactly what is out there. All we know is what is in our mind. Does the brain know what reality looks like in order to reconstruct it? Or, is it the self that carries out the magical transformation of electrical impulses into experiential realities?

2. We know that we have a self when a simple telephone call from a loved one can transport us to the stratosphere. Conversely horrific news about a loved one can pummel us into a hellhole.

3. We know that we have a self when, after a period of thinking and reasoning, we decide. It is the self that decides.

4. We know that we have a self when we observe. Observing impacts how atoms behave. It is the conscious self that observes and impacts everything.

5. We know that we have a self when we recognize people and objects. Recognizing, we transcend. It is the self that recognizes and transcends.

6. We know that we have a self when we look at a picture of our child or grandchild and see, not pixels, but the self of our beloved. It is the self that transcends the picture and connects with the self of that person.

7. When we read a book, we transcend the words into the ideas. We visualize, imagine and connect with what the author has in mind. This is the handiwork

of the self.

8. Hugging a loved one is not simply body-to-body contact. Our self merges with the self of our beloved. When two lovers kiss, who is doing the kissing? Is it the lips, or is it two selves intertwined?

9. When we talk, who is talking? When we listen, who is listening? Is it the vocal cords? Is it the brain? Or, is it the self? Does the brain have the know-how to create the words and string them together to make perfect sense? Does the brain understand the meaning of words and the intent of the speaker?

10. Are we like a vehicle on auto-pilot? Or is there a driver in the vehicle? Some believe that we have no self or free will because the subconscious decides for us. The subconscious, however, is an aspect of our being formed and updated by us. We are not only our conscious self, but the subconscious and the superconscious as well.

11. Can elements have an ego, emotions, hopes and dreams? Can they have pride and hurt feelings?

12. When someone writes a book, composes a poem or creates a work of art, are these the works of the brain? Or a sign of the creativity of the self?

13. When we hear a touching song, is it just air vibrations interpreted by the brain as words? Or are we feeling the soul, the self of the singer?

14. When we say "my foot", "my arm", "my head", "my idea" or "my house", what are we referring to if not the self?

15. Because we have the ability to plan, set goals, dream, imagine, visualize and create, there must be a doer.

This doer is the driver, the self.

16. Imagine you are in bed. Suddenly you hear a noise. You focus all your attention on that noise. Who is doing the focusing? Does it happen on its own? Since you can choose to focus at will, on any part of your body, there must be a self that is the decider, the doer, the director.

We have two selves. One is in the body focused on the here and now. The other, a Higher Self, is not confined to the body, to space or to time.[2] We are both selves. There are at least four levels from which we can view and identify with the self.

## 1.   Circumstantial

The circumstantial aspects of self are associated with the physical body. They include our social status, employment history, race, nationality, religion, sex, physical features, family and the various roles we play in society. This varies greatly, for some have lived in several countries, assumed diverse roles and even changed nationalities. Identifying with our circumstantial self one would say: I am an American, of Italian descent, working as a mechanic, living in Connecticut and am married with two daughters.

## 2.   Cultivated

The cultivated aspects of self are associated with the astral body. They include our emotional and mental aspects such as our education, habits, attitudes, expectations, beliefs, fears, hopes, dreams, goals and values. Identifying with our cultivated self one would say: I am a college graduate, Christian, industrious and hope to buy a home someday.

### 3. Willed

The willed aspects of self are associated with the spiritual body. Self here is determined by us. It is willed and created. We manage our circumstantial and cultivated aspects for best outcomes. We use them as we see fit. Identifying with our willed self, one would say: I am a creative being capable of anything I determine to undertake. I am free to change directions at any time for I am not limited to one and only one identity.

### 4. Pure

Our pure self is our soul, the I Am that is the core of our being. This is **who** we are rather than **what** we are. Identifying with our core, one would say: I am a living soul, an inseparable aspect of the divine. I was, am and will always be Love, Beauty and Joy.

From the above, it is easy to see that what we believe matters for we act accordingly. If we believe that we can do something, then we do it. If we believe that we cannot do something, then we do not undertake it. Regardless of which aspect of self we identify with, it matters how we see ourselves, how much we esteem ourselves and what we believe our potential is. These constitute our self-image, our self-esteem and our ideal self.

## Self-Image

Looking in the mirror, what do we see? Who do we reflect? Which aspect of ourselves do we identify with? In whose image are we? What thoughts come to our minds when we look in the mirror? What kind of a person are we? What type of a friend, parent, sibling, employer or employee are we?

Our self-image is our present reality – our current station in life. The picture we have of ourselves does not have to be based on facts. We can look at ourselves with colored glasses (biases, prejudices, and ignorance) and we can accept falsehoods about ourselves as true. We might believe that we are fat and ugly when we are not. We might believe that we are victims when we are not. We might be convinced that we are powerless when, in fact, we might be capable of a great deal. Regardless of reality, our actions are based on how we perceive ourselves. Often, we see ourselves based on how we compare ourselves to others. Comparing, we judge. This leads us to see ourselves either as inferior or superior.

Our self-image directs our activities and limits how far we can go. To accomplish more, we must change our self-image, expand it and continuously polish it so it reflects more of our true capabilities. We must learn to see ourselves not as we are, but rather as we want to be. By living what we aspire to be, we will surely attract the circumstances that we need to achieve what we desire.

What we believe and accept about ourselves makes a profound difference in our self-image and the quality of our lives. To move forward, we must free ourselves from past traumas and stop heaping blame on others or circumstances. Our focus must be on the rich and abundant reality that is before us right now and act decisively. We must project into the future what we want to achieve without focusing too much on the details. The details will work themselves out as we take one step at a time.

## Self-Esteem

Self-esteem is the way we feel about ourselves. It determines how happy and content we are with who we are. Accepting ourselves as a package of strengths and weaknesses is a reflection of our self-esteem and psychological maturity. If we have high self-esteem, we unconditionally accept ourselves physically, emotionally, and mentally. We harbor no resentments, shame, fear, or hate. We treat ourselves gently, with appreciation and affection. We even pamper ourselves once in a while. Our enjoyments should be without guilt, shame, or remorse. Our self-esteem impacts our emotions, affects our health and shapes our attitudes.

Low self-esteem is the root cause of many of society's ills. It can lead to failure, crime, conflict, abusive behavior, hate and murder. Individuals with low self-esteem are easily controlled and manipulated by their own emotions and by external factors.

The impact of our self-esteem is profound because it is emotion-based. The way we feel determines how we think and act. Since how we feel about ourselves changes frequently, our self-esteem is more like a barometer than a stable indicator. Our current sense of identity is the pointer on the barometer. This indicator rises and falls based on how much we esteem ourselves.

We can enhance our self-esteem by being true to ourselves, doing only what we want and doing it as well as we can. We should only make commitments we want to keep, eat the food we desire to eat, wear the clothes we prefer to wear, and work at a job we value, if possible. We should never go against our inner feelings, always being genuine, honest, and truthful. We should treat ourselves kindly, patiently and admiringly. To increase our self-esteem, we should get involved, contribute, play, laugh, and have fun.

Keep in mind that how we feel about ourselves is at the core of how we behave. Thinking, feeling and action are our greatest tools. We can use these to reinterpret our past and create the future we desire. To the degree that we like and accept ourselves, to that degree we magnetize ourselves. We attract to ourselves in accordance with who we are.

## Ideal Self

The ideal self is who we are at our core – pure love, sheer beauty and ineffable joy. It is our possible self. It is who we are becoming. How fast we reflect our ideal self depends on us. We are like a *seed* anchored in the soil. It is up to us to nurture this seed and help it grow, unfold, and mature. What a seed can be is a magnificent tree. We can be whatever we decide to be based on our abilities and passions. Each step we take in the right direction, opens up more possibilities for us to take advantage of. Slowly, we are shaping our future.

To better reflect our ideal self, we must learn to listen to the still small voice within, be guided by our ideals and have a clear vision for the future we aspire to. We create the conditions for our ideal self to express itself by nurturing our bodies, purifying our emotions, and cultivating our minds. Equally, through creativity, imagination and pure intention, we open up the line of communication between our self-image (our current reality) and our ideal self (our limitless possibilities). We become intuitive and live inspired lives.

# ACCEPT YOURSELF

*Acceptance is such an important commodity; some have called it "the first law of personal growth."*
— *Peter McWilliams*

A ccepting ourselves is an unconditional embrace of who and what we are. Even though who we are never changes, what we are varies greatly from one person to the next. While some are tall, others are short. While some are fat, others are skinny. Many are self-assured, others lack confidence. We could be male or female, white or black, wealthy or poor, exceptional or average. We could even be handicapped in more ways than one.

Accepting ourselves is acknowledging our starting line. It is taking an inventory of ourselves – what we have to work with. It is knowing what is in our package – our weaknesses and our strengths, our special traits and unique circumstances.

## We Are a Package

Each individual is a package of blessings and challenges. Blessings are strengths if they are put to good use. Challenges are to face, overcome and triumph over. We are in a physical body to face our challenges head-on and push beyond them.

Accepting ourselves as a package, we function from our reality. It is much easier to accept ourselves if we are honest with ourselves – admitting our challenges and recognizing our blessings. Accepting ourselves means being comfortable with who and what we are. We have a choice between accepting reality and doing our best or complaining and remaining stuck. The good news is that while our challenges are limited, we can add to our list of blessings at any time.

There is more to us than what is apparent. We do not know what we are capable of until we try. Our abilities are not evident until we are challenged or under duress. Mothers are known to perform great feats to protect their children. Circumstances are known to bring forth the heroes in us. We are never a finished product and that is a blessing. We can always be more and be better. All it takes is interest, motivation and intelligent action.

The question we must ask ourselves is: "What is the best use of the package that we are?" Obviously, the makeup of our package changes over time as we become more educated, acquire experience and add to our skillset. The most important factor in our packaging is to discover what makes us unique. Even though everyone is unique, not everyone acts on their uniqueness and uses it as an advantage to excel. We distinguish ourselves to the extent that we utilize our uniqueness. Highlighting our uniqueness and discovering what we are passionate about goes a long way toward ensuring our success and happiness. It is our differences that set us apart. We are unique because of them. As we become more proficient in distinguishing ourselves, our self-esteem grows. We reflect more of our potential. Liking, appreciating and accepting ourselves is imperative since the alternative is misery.

Our individual packages vary. Each has their own collection of blessings and challenges. To have a more complete picture of what our packages include, we must highlight our strengths and weaknesses, our special traits and unique circumstances.

It is a good idea to make a list of our strengths and be familiar with them. Our strengths could be physical, emotional, mental or spiritual. This could include: decisiveness, timeliness, being organized, determined, easy to get along with, confident with the ability to multitask.

It is also a good idea to make a list of our weaknesses and be familiar with them in order to work on them. Our weaknesses could be physical, emotional, mental or spiritual. This could include: poor time management, lack of motivation, procrastination, being a perfectionist and lack of faith in ourselves.

Our list of special traits and unique circumstances could include: being bi- or multi-lingual, having lived in a foreign country, having a unique heritage and specific inclinations such as a proclivity for electrical, mechanical or computer skills.

We should also make a list of what we can work on to become better. This could include: body weight, health, exercise, habits, attitudes, expectations, beliefs, acting instead of reacting and being more patient.

Once we have our lists, we should reflect on them daily. It is human nature not to fully appreciate what we have until we lose them. We can do better. The more we appreciate what we have, more blessings will come into our lives. What follows are general lists of blessings and challenges. We should have our own lists to dwell on.

## List of Blessings

1. We live on a beautiful planet. This is a wondrous time where we can easily live better than most ancient royals. We have dwelling places that are heated and air-conditioned with plumbing, water and electricity. We have modern gadgets to make

our lives easier. We can purchase food anytime. We have medicine that keeps us healthy and enables us to live longer.

2. We have a multiplicity of senses to enhance our experiences. In addition to sight, hearing, smell, taste and touch, we have a sense of humor, location, balance, direction, appreciation of the fine arts and many others. We can even have common sense.

3. We are loved. There is no doubt that someone loves us. It could be a parent, sibling, spouse, or friend. It is a blessing indeed to love and be loved.

4. We are endowed with consciousness and freedom of choice. This is a privilege indeed if we take full advantage of this precious gift.

5. We have a powerful mind through which we can reason, plan, imagine, visualize and create a better future for ourselves and our loved ones. We can cultivate new skills and add to our enjoyment by adopting new hobbies at any time.

6. We have the ability to learn and to continuously improve our station in life by cultivating our minds, refining our emotions and by making better choices.

7. We are social beings. We can choose to relate to others intimately, deeply and profoundly. We can experience love, appreciate beauty and know joy.

8. Nature is amazing. It is diverse, intricate and beautiful. We can be alone in nature and experience calmness and serenity.

9. To experience children and grandchildren is a

wonder indeed.

10. Diversity. The incredible abundance and diversity of people, plants, animals, fruit and vegetables is a gift beyond measure.

After reviewing our list of blessings, how about creating a new mantra for ourself that expresses our appreciation for these blessings. A mantra such as: "I am fortunate to be alive at this time."

## List of Challenges

1. Disease is a major challenge that all of us must face. How often and for how long depends on how healthy we manage to stay.

2. Loneliness could be a problem for many. Contemporary people tend to live more isolated lives.

3. Lack of purpose and direction can also be a challenge because no one is born with a manual for living. We have no clue as to why we are here or what we are supposed to do with our lives. We may even harbor fear of the unknown, especially fear of death.

4. Ignorance is a major challenge for we are seldom aware of our ignorance and we rarely acknowledge it. We live as if we have all the answers. It is only after enlightenment that we realize we have been in the dark.

5. Poverty. Many do not have adequate food, clean water and shelter. It is easy to be poor amidst plenty.

6. Pain and suffering are a human calamity that

everyone experiences at some point.

7. Loss of loved ones can be devastating, especially the loss of a child.

# FORGIVE YOURSELF

*Holding on to anger, resentment and hurt only gives you tense muscles, a headache and a sore jaw from clenching your teeth. Forgiveness gives you back the laughter and the lightness in your life. – Joan Lunden*

Being human implies that we are not perfect; we will make mistakes. That, however, is not a license to continue making mistakes. When we err, we must reflect on our act. We must undergo an intentional psychological review of what took place and why. Once we understand the causes of our action, we can forgive ourselves. There are 4 steps we must consider in forgiving ourselves. We must:

1. Clarify what lessons we learned;
2. Resolve to make amends;
3. Resolve to be more tolerant and understanding of others who are prone to making mistakes as well;
4. Determine never to repeat the mistake.

To forgive is to let go. It is to move on. By forgiving ourselves, we do not have to carry the burden of guilt. We do not have to be tormented. We are free. Before we let go, we must relive our transgression and understand the impact it had on the victim. We must feel their pain. We must regret and resolve to make amends.

In the days of Christ, forgiveness was often associated with sin.

> *And behold, some people brought to him a paralytic, lying on a bed. And when Jesus saw their faith, he said to the paralytic, "Take heart, my son; your sins are forgiven." And behold, some of the scribes said to themselves, "This man is blaspheming." But Jesus, knowing their thoughts, said, "Why do you think evil in your hearts? For which is easier, to say, 'Your sins are forgiven,' or to say, 'Rise and walk'? Matt 9:2-5*

It is possible that the guilt from some of our more egregious mistakes weighs heavy on our conscience and after some time, the emotional impact may cause disease. That is why, in order to heal, Christ had to let the person know that their sins were forgiven. Pent-up emotions can cause sickness, while letting go through forgiveness leads to healing. Forgiving is releasing a burden.

We must not only forgive ourselves for our transgressions, but also forgive those who transgress against us. This is made clear in the Lord's Prayer:

> *Pray then like this:*
>
> *Our Father in heaven, hallowed be your name.*
> *Your kingdom come, your will be done, on earth as it is in heaven.*
> *Give us this day our daily bread, and forgive us our debts, as we also have forgiven our debtors. Matt 6:9-12*

Christ has made it clear that if we do not forgive others their sins, our sins will not be forgiven.

> *For if you forgive others their trespasses, your heavenly Father will also forgive you, but if you do not forgive others their trespasses, neither will your Father forgive your trespasses. Matt 6:14-15*

When Peter asked Christ how many times should we forgive others, His reply was 77 times.

> *Then Peter came up and said to him, "Lord, how often will my brother sin against me, and I forgive him? As many as seven times?" Jesus said to him, "I do not say to you seven times, but seventy-seven times. Matt 18:21-22*

The 77 times of forgiveness is not literal. It simply means that we should forgive as many times as it takes. It is important to realize that this does not mean we should tolerate abuse and keep on forgiving. If there is no genuine regret, we should still forgive, but at the same time, move away from that environment and cut loose all associations.

Most transgressions are unintentional, due to ignorance with no malice intended. These are easy to forgive. This is how Christ viewed what we did to Him.

> *And Jesus said, "Father, forgive them, for they know not what they do." And they cast lots to divide his garments. Luke 23:34*

It is harder to forgive transgressions with intentional malice, but we must forgive regardless. It is difficult to imagine a transgression that is unforgivable, yet there are several of these in the Old Testament where the Lord God was not willing to forgive.

> *The LORD will not be willing to forgive him, but rather the anger of the LORD and his jealousy will smoke against that man, and the curses written in this book will settle upon him, and the LORD will blot out his name from under heaven. Deut 29:20*

> *But Joshua said to the people, "You are not able to serve the LORD, for he is a holy God. He is a jealous God; he*

*will not forgive your transgressions or your sins. If you forsake the LORD and serve foreign gods, then he will turn and do you harm and consume you, after having done you good." Josh 24:19-20*

The New Testament mentions only one unforgivable transgression:

*Therefore I tell you, every sin and blasphemy will be forgiven people, but the blasphemy against the Spirit will not be forgiven. And whoever speaks a word against the Son of Man will be forgiven, but whoever speaks against the Holy Spirit will not be forgiven, either in this age or in the age to come. Matt 12: 31-32*

What does *"blasphemy against the Spirit"* mean?

No one can commit a sin against God because God is Spirit. However, within us is a spark of this Spirit as the Holy Spirit. Sinning against the Spirit can only happen if we do it against the spirit of God within us.

The *"blasphemy against the Spirit"* in this case is our spirit, not God's spirit. While we can never blaspheme against God, we can do it against the spirit of God within us. This happens when:

- We intentionally, knowingly and willingly harden our hearts and refuse to see or hear the truth being revealed to us;
- We continuously refuse to hear The Voice Within and act accordingly;
- We knowingly, intentionally and repeatedly choose evil.

By sinning against the spirit within us, we shut the door of forgiveness against ourselves. Acting contrary to the nature of our spirit is a transgression against the Holy Spirit within us.

It is unforgiveable, but it is not forever. If we make an about face and change our ways, then we forgive ourselves. When we do, we are automatically forgiven. The power to forgive resides within us.

## Cardinal Sins

The seven deadly sins are pride, envy, gluttony, lust, anger, greed and sloth. If sin is a transgression against divine law, how could these be sins? These are human shortfalls that we need to work on. They are not something that God is concerned with. Karma will ensure that every act has its consequences. If we are proud, envious and gluttonous, we mostly hurt ourselves. If we lust and commit adultery, then we must bear the consequences. Anger, greed and sloth are easily curable. In fact, the cure for the cardinal sins is to convert them into cardinal virtues. In addition to the seven heavenly virtues of faith, hope, charity, fortitude, justice, temperance and prudence, we can have the seven cardinal virtues of humility, praise, moderation, empathy, patience, generosity and industry. All sins can be transformed into virtues. The more virtues we embody, the fewer sins we will have.

## Original Sin

The idea that we are born in sin and that Christ came to die for our sins as atonement is primitive and based on ignorance. It is a demeaning and degrading belief. It is a sure recipe for low self-esteem. We are not born in sin unless by sin we mean ignorance. We are made in the image of God and are His children.

Blood sacrifice for atonement is a primitive belief. God needing a blood sacrifice in order to forgive is juvenile at best. God is Love, whole, complete and lacks nothing. God is the source of all. The idea that God wants or needs a blood sacrifice to be pleased is a human myth. It is intended to instill fear in our hearts, keep us ignorant, obey and follow. We have been controlled too long. It is time to wake up, know the truth about our relationship to God and set ourselves free. Relationships are best when founded on love rather than fear.

God is the creator of all the universes. Christ came to show us the abundant and possible life. He was killed because, as He said several times – we have eyes, but cannot see; we have ears, but cannot hear; and hearts hard like a rock. No human needs to carry the guilt of needing the blood sacrifice of Christ, the Son of God, to be saved.

We are already saved, but do not realize it. We are forever the children of God regardless of what we have done or what we do. The truth is the opposite. God, our Father, would gladly sacrifice the fatted calf for us in celebration, if only we wake up and realize who we are and return home. Return to our Heavenly Father in love, in joy and in celebration.

## Forgiving Others and the Past

Many have lived through childhood traumas where neglect and abuse were prevalent. Yet, we do not have to be victimized by our past. We can let go and move on. Even though we cannot forget the past, we can revisit it, reimagine it and view it from a higher perspective. Our parents might not have been the best, but they did the best they knew how given their circumstances. We can use our pain as lessons learned and resolve to do better. We must forgive the past so it no longer has any hold on us. We must let go of the negativity of the past.

We can look at our past as "where we came from" and not as our dwelling place, the now. Now is where we are at. From here we can go in any direction we choose. By letting go and forgiving those who wronged us, we become lighter, freer and unencumbered. We can move forward at a faster pace.

While young, we were in the care of others – our parents and society. We were indoctrinated with certain beliefs that no longer serve a positive purpose. People function from where they are at and do the best they know how. Blaming anyone for past deeds does not help. Perhaps, it was the best they had to offer. As adults, we must examine our beliefs, habits, attitudes, biases and prejudices keeping what is noble and discarding the rest. We do not owe the past any debts.

We must let go and forgive the past if it no longer serves a good purpose. Forgiveness is a powerful catharsis. Our focus should be teaching the next generation a better truth based on the example of our lives. Each generation must do better than the previous one. We must move the guidepost forward. We must do our part.

# LOVE YOURSELF

*Learning to love yourself is the greatest love of all.*
*– Michael Masser and Linda Creed*

Now that we have accepted and forgiven ourself, the next step is to love ourself. To do that, we must look at ourself with loving eyes – the way we look at a beloved.

It is miraculous that we can love. Falling in love is a blessing indeed. Loving is appreciating the beauty of the beloved; it is exuding joy. Overflowing with love is manifesting God. And why should we love ourself? Because we are alive at this time and in this place, and we are conscious. There is no one like us. There never was and there never will be.

We do not know if any other creature is capable of love the way we are. Next to freedom of choice, the best gift we have is the gift of love. To love is to express our deepest nature for at our core, we are love, beauty and joy.

We crave love, seek beauty and look for joy because our essence is of God who is love, beauty and joy. It is natural and instinctive to reflect our nature and to love. If we cannot love, then we have hearts of stone. Intentionally suppressing our love is going against our nature. As children of God, we are deserving of love. We are loved by God and if God loves us, why shouldn't we do the same – love ourselves as an appreciation of the wonder that we are?

Loving is the most natural thing we can do. It is effortless. Our love for ourself is not narcissistic. It is not love that compares one to another. It is a celebration of the divinity dwelling within us. It is allowing our innate nature to express itself.

When we know ourselves as unique expressions of divinity, then loving ourselves is genuine and automatic. It is a celebration of individuality, an outflow of joy and is a direct result of feeling the marvel of being an aspect of God. Each is a miracle beyond comprehension, a wonder to behold. Talking, walking, singing, touching and dancing, kissing and communicating – aren't these miraculous? They would be if we lost our ability to perform them. We would definitely know how miraculous these are if we were engineers and had to design and build machines to express these capabilities. Our skills, abilities and expressions are miraculous. They are not easy fetes. We take them for granted because we are used to having them. Yet nothing is ordinary in us.

Loving ourselves requires caring for ourselves, being gentle and appreciative. When we love ourselves, we will have high self-esteem and will not abuse ourselves with addictive behavior. We will not allow ourselves to deteriorate unnecessarily. We will not torment our organs by taking in tobacco or alcohol in excess. We will express gratitude to our cells, tissues and organs every day for enabling us to function, for healing us, and for giving us the energy we need to express our uniqueness. Our bodies enable us to rejoice, to love and to celebrate. They deserve gratitude.

To love ourselves is to take it easy and to enjoy ourselves.

Here is a pertinent quote from my book, **A Passion for Living**, *a path to meaning and joy*:

> *"To enjoy life, we must enjoy ourselves for that is all we can enjoy. We must greet each day with enthusiasm if we*

*want to live life abundantly. If you are a woman, revel in being a woman. If you are a man, celebrate being a man. Savor every stage in your life and every role you get to play. When you are a spouse, a parent, a student, or a laborer, be the best you can be for this is your moment in history to demonstrate what you can do in each situation. We are actors and actresses in our current role. This is our opportunity to stamp the event with our uniqueness. We go through each stage of our lives once and for a short duration. If we learn to appreciate whatever comes our way and take full advantage of our opportunities to make a positive contribution, then what we can enjoy and cherish is limited only by our imagination.*

*Everyone and everything is a perfect expression of the Cosmic Intelligence. No one can play our role of being who we are better than ourselves. Just as a flower is the perfect flower it can be and a cloud is the perfect cloud it can be, we are also perfect as an expression of the Cosmic Intelligence. There is nothing commonplace in life. There are only common eyes. Even a "common" activity such as talking, walking, or cooking is magical. When we see and experience magic everywhere, we carry that sense of wonder with us. We become transformed and our lives become filled with peace, joy and gratitude. Living becomes sacred."*

There is a great deal we can love about ourselves. We have miraculous bodies. We can think and feel. We have brains and minds that are among the most sophisticated in the universe. We have astral bodies of light that can traverse walls and appear anywhere instantly. We have spiritual bodies that when well-developed can perform miracles as normal activities.

We are reminded that our bodies are holy temples where God, in the local form of our I Am, lives.

*Do you not know that you are God's temple and that God's Spirit dwells in you? If anyone destroys God's temple, God will destroy him. For God's temple is holy, and you are that temple. 1 Cor 3:16-17*

It is much easier to love ourselves if we have high self-esteem. We can raise our self-esteem by undertaking activities we can be proud of. By being helpful to others and by embodying ideals we value, our self-esteem will blossom. Once we like ourselves, we can easily move on to loving ourselves. Loving ourselves transforms us. It opens our hearts and minds. We feel lighter and we live healthier lives.

We were conceived and we were born in love. Sex can never be a sin. Enjoying the body is a gift of our physicality. It is a gift from God. Sex is great when shared. We should never manipulate or take advantage of anyone. Forcing ourselves on another is a crime. Sharing ourselves with another is a joy.

Doing what we love increases our love for ourselves. Making a list of things we love to do and following through in action is a great way to feel good about ourselves. Here is a sample list:

## List of 10 "To Dos"

1. Going on a cruise. Visiting a foreign country;
2. Attending concerts, operas, or plays at a performing arts center;
3. Going to a live game;
4. Reading uplifting books;
5. Calling a dear friend;
6. Celebrating family;
7. Going to a fancy restaurant;
8. Making a bucket list and acting on them;
9. Being in nature;
10. Having alone time to pray, meditate, reflect and contemplate.

Remembering the loving feeling we get when we engage in certain activities also enhances our feelings of love.

## List of 10 "I love it when,..."

1. I feel tremendous love when I am holding a baby in my arms;
2. I love it when my spouse falls asleep in my arms;
3. I love it when I attend a musical;
4. I am bathed in love when I encounter beauty in any form;
5. I am buoyed with love when I am inspired;
6. I feel thrilled when I finish a great novel;
7. I love it when I enjoy a delicious meal, or perfectly ripe fruit;
8. I love it when it rains or snows;
9. I jump with love when I hear my favorite song;
10. I am overwhelmed with love when I hear children laughing.

Loving ourselves is not as difficult as it seems. It is natural if we choose to dwell on the positive aspects of our being rather than focusing on the negative. By loving ourselves every day, we will establish the habit of being in love with ourselves, not as a narcissist, but as recognition of our uniqueness and as an appreciation of the gift that we are.

# LOVE OTHERS

*That best portion of a good man's life, His little, nameless, unremembered acts of kindness and of love.*

*— William Wordsworth*

Once we learn to love ourselves, then loving others becomes easy. With time and the proper understanding, we soon realize that the "other" we are referring to is not a stranger. For the same spirit that confers life, awareness, and consciousness to us, does the same to everyone else. All share the same spirit. Each is a unique expression of the one and same essence – divinity.

Keeping in mind that we are on the stage of life to play a role, learn, grow and contribute makes it easy to realize the role others play on the same stage of life. Without the contribution of each actor, there is no play, drama or musical. It requires the contribution of everyone to manifest the purpose of our life on Earth.

The people we encounter in life are exactly who we need. They are placed in our path for the benefit of all concerned. When Christ admonished us to love others as ourselves and to even love our enemies, what He meant was that others are essential for our growth and maturation. They provide us the opportunities we need and in return, we do the same for them. We are in the same drama, playing different parts, even adversarial at times, just to provide the opportunities each needs. Once the play is over and we are on the other side, we get together to congratulate each other for the roles we played. Enemies are friends in disguise and only for the duration of the play. Our perceived enemies could be our siblings, parents and best friends from this lifetime or from previous lives. Unfortunately, we do not realize this until after we die and are on the other side. Then we recognize the role each played to give us the opportunities we needed. This is exactly why Christ admonished us to love our enemies.

> *You have heard that it was said, 'You shall love your neighbor and hate your enemy.' But I say to you, Love your enemies and pray for those who persecute you, so that you may be sons of your Father who is in heaven. For he makes his sun rise on the evil and on the good, and sends rain on the just and on the unjust. Matt 5:43-45*

The sun shines on everyone equally without judgment. We should do the same. We should not be influenced by how we are treated and reciprocate. We should maintain our equanimity, treat everyone with respect and contribute our best. We should do our part and move on, not expecting any recognition or reward in return.

If we are happy and content when we look in the mirror, we see a happy and content reflection. If we are miserable, we see a different reflection. People and circumstances in life are mirrors reflecting back to us where we are on our journey of learning and growth. If we react, tit for tat, then we have a long way to go. If we recognize events as opportunities to learn from and to contribute our best, then we act with compassion, demonstrate maturity and have a positive impact. Our purpose is to learn, to grow and to contribute, regardless of circumstance. Once we demonstrate mastery of a situation, we graduate from those circumstances and move on to the next challenge.

Christ gave us only two commandments which are in fact just one – love.

*The Great Commandment*

*And one of the scribes came up and heard them disputing with one another, and seeing that he answered them well, asked him, "Which commandment is the most important of all?" Jesus answered, "The most important is, 'Hear, O Israel: The Lord our God, the Lord is one. And you shall love the Lord your God with all your heart and with all your soul and with all your mind and with all your strength.' The second is this: 'You shall love your neighbor as yourself.' There is no other commandment greater than these." And the scribe said to him, "You are right, Teacher. You have truly said that he is one, and there is no other besides him. And to love him with all the heart and with all the understanding and with all the strength, and to love one's neighbor as oneself, is much more than all whole burnt offerings and sacrifices." And when Jesus saw that he answered wisely, he said to him, "You are not far from the kingdom of God." And after that no one dared to ask him any more questions.  Mark 12:28-34*

Can we love anyone with all of our heart, mind and soul?

Fortunate indeed is the one who has someone to love. For once we love the way Christ wants us to love – spiritual love, it is permanent love. Like most things in life, it takes intentional practice to master a skill. To love another, we start by loving someone who is easy to love. This could be our child, parent, sibling, grandchild or a pet, better yet, our spouse.

It is important to fall in love with someone. Some fall in love spontaneously. Even though this can happen, to keep the blaze going, we need to fan the flame by expressing love in thought, word and action on an ongoing basis. It is easier to love others when we dwell on their positive qualities, emphasizing the good and de-emphasizing the not so good. As our love grows, it becomes a mighty river cleansing, recharging and rejuvenating us.

We do not need to love everyone. There is no denying that there are evil people in the world. We do not need to dwell on them. All we need is one good person to love. Once the fire is lit, it is easy for the flame to spread. The person we love should not necessarily be someone who has been good to us. We should not love someone as a reward or as a payback. We should only love them for love's sake.

# THE NATURE OF LOVE

*There are four questions of value in life, Don Octavio. What is sacred? Of what is the spirit made? What is worth living for and what is worth dying for? The answer to each is the same. Only love.*  – Lord Byron

God is love. In other words, the nature of God is a continuous outpouring of love. Love is different from all other emotions. Love is a doorway, that will transport us to a magical land where we will see and know our innate reality. There is no love that is not beautiful. There is no love that does not engender joy. The most important experience we can have as humans is to know love – to love and to be loved.

## Love Reveals our True Nature

In John 8:33 we find the following statement:

*"..and you will know the truth, and the truth will make you free."*

How do we recognize the truth when we see it, read about it, or hear it? There is something deep within us that resonates to the truth when we encounter it. We intuitively know what the truth is and feel it in our gut. There is something in us that we cannot identify or name that acts as our barometer for the truth. Yet, this aspect buried deep within us is what gives us our sense of selfhood, identity, and individuality. It resonates with love, beauty, joy, freedom and truth.

This changeless, ever present and eternal self is our true identity. It reveals itself most readily when we are in love. We forget our little self, the ego, and are aware of ourselves only in the vibration of love.

When we are in love, what are we actually in love with? Is it the body of the beloved? Is it the mind? Is it the voice? Or is it in the kiss of the beloved as the song goes? We love the body, mind, and voice of our beloved. In fact, we love most everything about our beloved. For we are in love with the person and not with his or her body parts. We love the body of the beloved because it is an expression of the beloved. We love the mind, the voice, the kiss of the beloved because, like the perfume of a flower, they are aspects of the beloved. We are in love with the essence, the soul, and the individuality that is our beloved. Our love for the beloved is a love for the eternal self, the soul of the beloved shining forth through every aspect of the beloved.

Physical love based on attraction is not the same as spiritual love. Attraction can fade and, over time, our physical love can even turn to hate. When we are spiritually in love, we will remain in love even if the body, mind, and voice of our beloved changes or are lost. We will keep on loving our beloved even after our beloved dies. And this is how love reveals its nature. Love is the way back home, back to God and to unity. Love, Beauty and Joy are the way to our source – divinity.

Alone, we never feel complete. Joined with our beloved, we are complete. Each of us is half of a being. We are either male or female but in reality, our whole self is both male and female. When we are joined with the one we love, our sense of loneliness, the part of us that was missing, disappears. Together, we are one full, complete being.

## Love and Marriage

When we are in love, we want to be in the company of our beloved. We want to touch, smell, taste and merge into and become one with our beloved. Love is how we lose ourselves in another. We let go and merge our individuality with the essence of our beloved. Once we are joined together and are one, we know ourselves as complete. Our eyes open. We see that we were naked and did not know it. We become wise, knowing good from evil. This knowing is what is referred to when Adam knew Eve or when a woman knows a man. This knowing is recognition of the oneness of the two – the "bride" and the "groom." This union is the true essence of marriage and is the reason why marriage is a sacrament. For when a man and woman know each other, they become one. They are no longer two individuals but one individual in two bodies.

When people get married, hopefully, it is because they love each other. Unfortunately, for most the honeymoon is the peak of their love. The more a couple know each other, their love should grow stronger, richer and become fuller. During the wedding ceremony many use a beautiful passage from Corinthians chapter 13, verses 1-13.

> If I speak in the tongues of mortals and of angels, but do not have love, I am a noisy gong or a clanging cymbal. And if I have prophetic powers, and understand all mysteries and all knowledge, and if I have all faith, so as to remove mountains, but do not have love, I am nothing. If I give away all my possessions, and if I hand over my body so that I may be burned but do not have love, I gain nothing.
>
> Love is patient; love is kind; love is not envious or boastful or arrogant or rude. It does not insist on its own way; it is not irritable or resentful; it does not rejoice in wrongdoing, but rejoices in the truth. It bears all things,

*believes all things, hopes all things, endures all things.
Love never ends. But as for prophecies, they will come to
an end; as for tongues, they will cease; as for knowledge,
it will come to an end. For we know only in part, and
we prophesy only in part; but when the complete comes,
the partial will come to an end. When I was a child, I
spoke like a child, I thought like a child, I reasoned like
a child; when I became an adult, I put an end to childish
ways. For now we see in a mirror, dimly, or in riddle
but then we will see face to face. Now I know only in
part; then I will know fully, even as I have been fully
known. And now faith, hope, and love abide, these three;
and the greatest of these is love.*

When we are in love, we might assume that we love the other
more than we love ourselves. In reality, we love the other
**as** ourselves. When we are in love, we do not hide our love
under the table. We shout it from the mountain top. This love
becomes our light that we shine forth for all to see. For to be in
love, is to radiate love at all times.

Love is a spiritual quality governed by spiritual laws. Spiritual
laws govern the internal forces of our nature and contribute to
our spiritual welfare. Physical laws govern the external forces
of nature such as gravity, electromagnetism, the weak and the
strong interactions. They contribute to our material welfare.
The mastery of physical laws leads to comfort, efficiency, and
abundance. The mastery of spiritual laws leads to happiness,
peace, and contentment.

In the material world, if we have two shirts and we give away
one, we end up with only one. In the spiritual world, what we
give in the spirit of love comes back to us multiplied. When
we give in love, we give of our self. We give gladly without any
expectation for reciprocity, yet we end up richer than before.
As we give of ourselves, we leave a part of ourselves with those
who receive. Thus, we multiply ourselves through giving in the

spirit of love.

## Love As A Vitamin

We are familiar with many forms of love: love between parents and children, siblings, spouses, caregivers and lovers. There is also love of God. These are various gradations of love. The highest vibration of all is spiritual love – the love that Christ proclaimed and exemplified.

Love is an essential vitamin. It is a required ingredient for healthy growth. If newborn babies are denied love, they fail to thrive and they die. That is why nature instilled love in us. We love our babies instantly, instinctually and unconditionally. We transmit love through touch, sight, words, smiles and embraces. The world revolves around love, the lack of it, the desire for it and wanting more of it.

Physical love can be based on need, be one-sided, subside and can even change to hate over time. Spiritual love is forever. It is profound, altruistic and unconditional. Loving others spiritually multiplies our love. When we smile, praise, admire, and serve others lovingly, we are enriched with abundance, energy and vitality.

## Love Is A Miracle

Love is positive energy. It warms hearts and melts resistance. It is transformational and it keeps us healthy, happy and content. Love is liberating, beautiful and joyous. Love shatters our limited self and expands it to include others.

Love links, connects and unites us. In love, we undertake joint ventures. We build together and we prosper. With love, we transform our Earth into Heaven.

**By loving:**

We heal;

We feel complete;

We see value, find meaning and enjoy our earthly journey.

**With love:**

We convert the desert of our lives into a heavenly garden;

We possess the philosopher's stone;

We possess the elixir of life. We have the secret to youth, health and vitality;

We are an outpouring. Our love flows like a mighty river cleansing us all;

With love in our hearts, we become like the sun, shining, giving freely to all without expecting anything in return.

**In love:**

We surpass our humanness;

We express our truest, deepest nature;

The purer and stronger our love, the godlier we are.

**When we love:**

We feel great;

We feel liberated;

We feel expanded;

We feel heroic and capable of wonders;

We know the truth and we are free.

# THE QUEST FOR HAPPINESS

*There is only one happiness in this life, to love and be loved. – George Sand*

The purpose of life is not the pursuit of happiness. Happiness is a byproduct of living purposeful lives, learning, growing and contributing. Happiness is a result, not a goal we can seek. It comes about when we immerse ourselves in joyful activity and are in the company of loved ones.

We are unhappy when we are in pain, suffering, feeling miserable, are taken over by worry, fear and are in undesirable situations. We are happy when we are engaged in meaningful activities, are thankful, content, serene, laughing and enjoying ourselves.

Worry is an endemic problem. It saps our energy. It is normal to be concerned, but too much worrying robs us of peace of mind and denies us happiness. Keeping in mind that most things we worry about never come to fruition should lessen our need to worry. Why worry about what is beyond our control? If we worry about something we did, why not find out what we can do to remedy the situation? Why cry over spilled milk? What is done is done. There is no going back. There is a lot we can do going forward.

The best way to stay happy is to be in love. Anytime we are in love, we are happy. Being in love with another can make us happy for a while, however; we need to learn to be comfortable with ourselves and enjoy our own company as well, for we always have ourselves. Being at home with ourselves is the ultimate form of happiness and the most enduring. Once we are happy with ourselves, it is much easier to be happy with another.

## The Road To Happiness

Being genuinely ourselves is the first step to happiness. Requiring very little to be happy is the next step. We are inundated by trivia. We should focus on what is important, the critical few, and ignore the rest. We should stop getting upset over what matters little or is of no consequence. Why stew over what will soon be forgotten?

Here is a pertinent quote from my book: **A Passion for Living, a path to meaning and joy**

> *"We must not wait for grand events to make us happy. Rather, we should celebrate each moment with a spirit of gratefulness for the gifts of life. Being thankful is a vitamin that aides our health and hastens our blossoming. To assist us in this process, we can make a list of items for which we are grateful, beginning with being alive, having family and friends.*
>
> *If we learn to be happy enjoying ourselves, then we will constantly be happy for we always have ourselves. To enjoy ourselves, we should not take ourselves too seriously. We need to relax, laugh and take it easy. If we practice taking it easy, we will not harbor stress and store negative emotions. If we do not accumulate stress, we live longer, healthier and happier lives. Quite often we already have everything we need to be happy.*
>
> *Once we learn to enjoy ourselves, we must extend outward—determine to enjoy nature, our family,*

*community, country and the world. Just as we can never love anyone more than we can love ourselves, how much we enjoy others is limited by how much we can enjoy ourselves. In a way, to enjoy is the same as to love, for if we love someone, we automatically enjoy that person. Hence, to enjoy nature, family, community and the world is to learn to appreciate and love them.*

*It is easiest to appreciate someone if we can recognize an aspect of ourselves in that person. We can start loving others by noticing common features that we both share. Before we recognize aspects of ourselves in others, we must get to know ourselves—the traits we have, our weaknesses and strengths, our abilities and handicaps, our likes and dislikes. We can only reflect what is within us. If we know what we are and why we are the way we are, we can accept others for being the way they are. The more intimately we know ourselves, the better we can know, appreciate and love others."*

Those who have no money believe that if and when they have money, then they will be happy. Those who are frail and sick believe that once they are well, then they can be happy. Some seek fame, power and influence believing that then they will be happy. The more we chase happiness, the faster it will run away from us. We must learn to be happy with who we are, where we are and with what we have. We can be happy doing the simplest of things. For those who cannot walk, walking is happiness. For those who cannot see, seeing is happiness. We have what we need to be happy right now.

We should seek health, security, and financial independence for without these, it is difficult to be content. However, rather than seeking fame, fortune and influence, we should seek to fall in love, be in love and live in love. For when we are in love, we are free flowing, energetic, creative, and happy.

When we are in love, the happiest place for us to be is in the arms of our beloved. The best food we can eat is when we share it with the ones we love. The best time we have is the time shared with our loved ones. When we are in love, we are content.

According to Henry David Thoreau, "The mass of men lead lives of quiet desperation." Even though, as Thoreau states, the masses lead lives of quiet desperation, we do not have to. We do not have to be one of the masses, doing what the masses do. We can be the exception to the rule. Happiness is a byproduct of how we think, feel and live. The more freely we give to others in loving service, the better we feel and the happier we are. This is a fundamental spiritual law. By giving value to others, we instantly receive value in return. Instead of wanting happiness for ourselves, we should focus on making others happy instead. Our happiness will then be automatic.

# PART IV

## Express Yourself Fearlessly

1. Be Prepared, Always
2. Be Fearless
3. Highlight Your Uniqueness
4. Sharpen Your Toolset
5. Express Yourself

# BE PREPARED, ALWAYS

*The future belongs to those who prepare for it today. —Malcolm X*

It is a good idea to always be prepared, ready to tackle whatever life brings our way. If we are students in the school of life, it is best to be ready for any quiz or test that life may throw at us. Since we must face our challenges from where we are, we should endeavor to be at our best at all times. Since the conditions we face are constantly changing, our preparation must be current. To be prepared and ready, we should:

1. Have the desire, motivation and the willingness to constantly improve ourselves;
2. Continuously educate ourselves to be relevant and effective in facing our challenges;
3. Be ready to take advantage of any opportunity that comes our way;
4. Have the right mental framework – attitude;
5. Be confident, fearless and ready to engage.

We are confident when we are prepared and ready. Preparing ourselves should not be a struggle, or something that is expected of us. Rather, it should be our natural state of being if we want to live full and meaningful lives. Being at our best is important when we have children. They learn by observing and imitating us just as we did when we were young. If we want to raise children who are confident, know, love and express themselves fearlessly, we must have those qualities ourselves. Whether we know it or not, we are always influencing and are being influenced by others at the same time

We are encouraged to excel, to be somebody, and to achieve. These external pressures can cause undue stress. We do not need that. We can live the life we want, reflect who we are if we know what is important for us and do it. Ultimately, we are accountable only to ourselves and if we live in a way that we are content, then we have achieved our goal.

Staying prepared is reflecting the best version of ourselves. Having the proper mindset goes a long way to ensure our preparedness.

## Mindset

Life is full of challenges. Some are major obstacles, others are simple, but necessary tasks that we must do. Tackling major challenges is a test of our resolve. It is our moment of truth. How we deal with these challenges reveals our character. These are our important tests. Like any test, the more prepared we are, the easier it is to overcome them. This is why being ready, always, is so important.

How we face our challenges is something we can control. It is a matter of the proper mindset. Take the simple necessity of having to do household chores as an example. If we must do them, we have two approaches. We can complain and put off tackling them, or we can do them gladly. It is a matter of attitude. We can practice loving what must be done. Doing dishes, cleaning our residence, walking our dog and taking care of our backyard can be fun activities. They can be relaxing and therapeutic. All we have to do is look for a reason to enjoy the activity, then continue to practice it until it becomes second nature.

> *"Not in doing what you like, but in liking what you do is the secret of happiness." James Barrie*

According to W. Clement Stone the amount of energy we have to do things in life is directly related to how much value we place in the activity. The more important it is, the more energy we assign it. Fortunately, we determine the value of everything.

If we must do something, why not see the value in doing it? This will give us energy and makes the activity fun. Being enthusiastic and enjoying what we do releases positive chemicals that rejuvenate the body, while detesting an activity does the reverse. Rather than focusing on what we must do, we can instead dwell on the benefits that will result once the activity is done.

Attitude is important. However, without aptitude, we cannot achieve much. Being ready is having the right attitude and continuously upgrading our skillset – our aptitude. Self-talk can be instrumental. A few simple ones we can practice are:

1. I can handle this;
2. I love doing the dishes;
3. This too shall pass.

## Always Prepared And Ready

By continuously improving ourselves through education, introspection and by guarding what thoughts and feelings we entertain, we stand ready. We can face whatever life throws at us. By learning from our mistakes and from others and by extracting the most value from our experiences, we are prepared. By mentally rehearsing the outcomes we desire and by visualizing ourselves at our best, we perform at our best.

We are told that when the student is ready, the master will appear. Practicing until we gain mastery is how we get ready. And when we are ready, the master does not miraculously appear. What happens instead is that we become the master. Our Higher Self guides our steps.

Being ready is the best way to take advantage of any opportunity. It also improves our odds at success.

> *Then shall the kingdom of heaven be likened unto ten virgins, which took their lamps, and went forth to meet the bridegroom. And five of them were wise, and five were foolish They that were foolish took their lamps, and took no oil with them: But the wise took oil in their vessels with their lamps. While the bridegroom tarried, they all slumbered and slept. And at midnight there was a cry made, Behold, the bridegroom cometh; go ye out to meet him. Then all those virgins arose, and trimmed their lamps. And the foolish said unto the wise, Give us of your oil; for our lamps are gone out. But the wise answered, saying, Not so; lest there be not enough for us and you: but go ye rather to them that sell, and buy for yourselves. And while they went to buy, the bridegroom came; and they that were ready went in with him to the marriage: and the door was shut. Afterward came also the other virgins, saying, Lord, Lord, open to us. But he answered and said, Verily I say unto you, I know you not. Watch therefore, for ye know neither the day nor the hour wherein the Son of man cometh.  Matt 25: 1-13*

**"and they that were ready went in with him to the marriage: and the door was shut."**

*Those who are ready benefit from opportunities that knock. Those who are not ready, are left out in the dark.*

# BE FEARLESS

*What is a fear of living? It's being preeminently afraid of dying. It is not doing what you came here to do, out of timidity and spinelessness. The antidote is to take full responsibility for yourself - for the time you take up and the space you occupy. If you don't know what you're here to do, then just do some good.* — Maya Angelou

Fear is an awareness of an actual or an imagined danger. It is a feeling that something may happen contrary to one's desires. Fear is natural except when it is a continuous state of fright, dread or alarmed concern. To live in fear is debilitating. It paralyzes us and drains our energy. Living under fear is like being held hostage. The terrorists in this case are our own thoughts and feelings.

Fear is natural. It is meant to bring caution into our lives. Without it, we might act like daredevils and take unnecessary risks that can endanger our lives. Phobias, on the other hand, are not normal. They require professional intervention.

According to Penn Medicine: "Everyone is born with the two innate fears of falling and loud sounds. The rest are learned. Our surroundings – parents, siblings, friends, TV – teach us at a young age to be scared of things, like the dark or monsters. Experience shapes our fears as we get older." Our learned fears range from natural anxieties to irrational phobias. They include fear of making decisions, of being alone, of public speaking, of rejection, of looking foolish, of failure, of success, of dying, of snakes, of water, of heights, of God and of the Devil.

The **underlying cause** of all fears is a feeling of helplessness. Helplessness stems from the realization that we cannot handle what life may bring our way. Fears can be unconscious or conscious and can cause nightmares and daymares.

Here are a few factors to keep in mind:

1. **Fear will never go away as long as we continue to grow.** It is normal to experience fear once in a while. For if we are to grow, we must face the unknown and take some risks. This can engender fear. Just as a car in the garage is safe, that is not what a car is made for. So it is with us. We can stay home and avoid all risks, but then we stop growing and that is not in our best interest. Even though fear is part of life, it does not have to dominate us. We can manage it. By evaluating a situation, we can decide if the fear is warranted or not. If it is, we take precautionary measures. If not, then we plunge ahead and give it our best shot.

2. **We are not alone.** We are in good company and are never alone. Everyone, when on unfamiliar ground, experiences some fear. Fear of public speaking, for example, is not a real fear since there is no real danger. What we are experiencing instead is anxiety disguised as fear. This is normal and healthy. We can use our anxiety to prepare well in advance of the event. The more prepared we are, the less anxious we will feel. If we have phobias, we can seek professional help.

3. **Pushing through fear is less frightening** than the underlying fear of helplessness. Our imagination is often worse than the fear itself. Acting boldly, facing

our fear and pushing through it, will vanquish the fear and replace it with the exhilaration of triumph. The more confidence we build, the less fearful we will be. Taylor Swift expressed it best when she said: *"I think fearless is having fears but jumping anyway."*

*"Seize this very minute; what you can do, or dream you can, begin it, boldness has genius, power and magic in it. Only engage and then the mind grows heated. Begin and then the work will be completed." Goethe*

4. **The object of the fear is not the problem. How we hold fear in our mind, is the problem.** Nothing in and of itself is scary. Fear arises as a result of our imagination, interpretation and reaction to what we are witnessing or thinking about. If we manage our thinking, imagination and our reactions, we control our fears. We represent fear in our minds as images, sounds, and movements. Since we control how we represent fear to ourselves, we can diffuse the fear with awareness and self-talk.

5. **Fear can only have an impact on us if we associate some pain or dread with the activity.** It is not things in themselves that cause us fear; rather, it is the results we imagine. Often, it is our attitudes and beliefs that cause us to experience the most fears. Using self-talk, we can counteract fear. We can sing or shout empowering mantras to embolden ourselves. We can imagine positive outcomes.

6. **Fear is of our own creation. It teaches us something about ourselves.** We build fear up through our thoughts and imaginings. If we can create something, we can dismantle it as well. All it takes is a shift in what we focus on. Focusing on the positive, such as benefits, shifts our focus from the fear to

what we might gain. With a shift in our focus, instead of having fear deplete our energy, we receive a new supply of energy as excitement.

Fear is ours. It represents what is going on inside our heads – what we are thinking and feeling. By analyzing our fears, we learn about ourselves.

*Fear is a question: What are you afraid of, and why? Just as the seed of health is in illness, because illness contains information, your fears are a treasure house of self-knowledge if you explore them.  Marilyn Ferguson*

**7. Fear, like worry, is often about things that we may never experience.**

We succumb to fear because of self-doubt and by listening to the chatterbox of fear. We can instead listen to empowering self-talk and dispel the fear. Most fears are a disguised form of helplessness. Since we always have a choice in how we act, why not choose to dwell on what we want to achieve instead of what scares us? Instead of imagining the worst outcomes, we can choose to dwell on what we will gain once we act with boldness and confidence. If we continue to face our fears and act boldly, soon a habit of confidence will engulf our being. We will no longer fear.

# HIGHLIGHT YOUR UNIQUENESS

*There is a vitality, a life force, an energy, a quickening, that is translated through you into action, and because there is only one of you in all time, this expression is unique. And if you block it, it will never exist through any other medium and will be lost.*
*– Martha Graham*

L iving is a delicate dance which requires balance. On the one hand, we must belong, conform and be accepted. On the other hand, unless we set ourselves apart, we cannot excel. We need to stand out and fit in at the same time. We need to balance our needs with the needs of society, our values with the values of others, our individuality with the rest of society. To excel, we must highlight our uniqueness.

## Set Yourself Apart

We are unique in several ways. We have unique personalities, histories, values and perspectives. We have unique circumstances, talents, skills, strengths and weaknesses. Unfortunately, instead of focusing on what makes us different and using it to our advantage, we blend in and give up what sets us apart. We join the crowd and we follow. We become one of the masses and share their fate. At times, we must do this and at other times, we must break away and chart our own course.

Everyone is unique in a special way. Therefore, knowing how we are different and making the most of it is how we set ourselves apart.  As children, we are encouraged to fit in. Obviously, to be accepted is important, but not at the expense of our individuality. We can belong and stand out at the same time.

We are the most evolved life form on the planet. We routinely accomplish miraculous feats. This is because we have more specialists than all other life forms. We have plumbers, electricians, carpenters, engineers, architects, machinists, analysts, programmers, musicians and so forth and each field in turn has sub-specializations. In a way, the ultimate evolution for humanity would be that each individual be a specialist in a unique niche. We start life as generalists but progressively move toward ever increasing specialization.

Our education system is a reflection of this. After high school, we go to college and specialization begins. Our first degree is a Bachelor's followed by a Master's degree and ending with a PH. D or a Dr. of Philosophy. Each higher degree is a higher level of specialization. We are at the top of the evolutionary scale because we are the most specialized.

Specialized individuals have a limited scope of work. They focus on their specialty and are experts at it. Their field of interest is narrow yet they provide the best approach and the most comprehensive understanding of their particular specialty.

Each of us is a unique specialization of God.  Each of us is at the acme of what we and we alone can be and do. Each of us has a particular view. We live under unique circumstances. No one has experienced what we have. We are the ultimate specialists in matters of our lives. Our package of blessings and challenges is specific. It sets us apart and makes us unique.

To know anything in great detail requires specialization. God cannot know details except through us, the specialists. Therefore, what makes us stand out is the unique view that we can contribute and the specific talents and skills that we have mastered from our particular circumstances. We are the ones who have suffered and learned, agonized, had aha(s), lamented and rejoiced. We are the experts in our particular mode of living.

Humanity excels through the specialization of its talented individuals. The human body is miraculous because of the specialization of its cells, tissues and organs. Each of us is God's specialized individual in a unique niche. Each of us is learning and contributing in our specific way. A poor woman living in India in the year 2023, is an expert on being a poor woman living in India in that year. A handicapped person living in Afghanistan is a specialist in that particular arena.

Successful living is not determined by how much money we make. It is by doing what is in our best interest, in accordance with our innate nature, and in harmony with our life plan, reflecting our unique packaging, and based on what we are passionate about.

Success in material possessions is a quest many pursue. Achieving it might not result in contentment, satisfaction and happiness. Meaningful success is more than reaching our goals. It is making sure that we end up where we want to be expressing our uniqueness. Therefore, the best we can do is to pursue that which is in harmony with the plan for our lives based on our innate nature and unique package. Expressing our uniqueness puts us in our element. We are passionate, productive, and content. This is what doing the Will of the Father, or God's will entails.

The ancient Egyptians used the term MAAT to express the concept of right living, truth, or what the ancient Chinese called the Tao. In simpler terms, this is finding our niche and living to express our uniqueness.

When an ancient Egyptian died, his or her soul was weighed against MAAT or the feather of truth. This was done in the Judgment Hall in the presence of Osiris. What is important to realize is that what the deceased was being judged against was whether or not he or she lived their lives expressing themselves as unique entities. MAAT implies that everyone has his or her own place in the scheme of things and that life is a web with everyone forming an important thread in the fabric of life. To live in Truth or according to MAAT is to find our place in life and express ourselves as unique individuals.

It is important that we discover and pursue our passions – doing what we deem important, valuable and meaningful. Our passions along with our unique packaging, should be our rallying point, our focus and guiding light. Led by our passions, we can set goals that we can pursue and achieve.

We were born to be unique. We carry the seeds of greatness within us. If we utilize our passions, highlight our uniqueness and act on the opportunities that we can create or that come our way, we can live a life of power, creativity, and abundance.

## Capitalize On Your Uniqueness

We are formed from an egg and a sperm. But these were not ordinary. The egg and the sperm that formed us came from a long line of evolutionary successes spanning millions or perhaps billions of years. In other words, they were exceptionally adapted and came from an unbroken line of successes. Additionally, this line, having survived for billions of years, is most fit to continue to survive. Out of the millions of sperms competing to fertilize the one egg, we are the result of the one that won the contest. We start life as successes. So, what happens to us to make us feel weak and powerless as we grow older?

If we believe that we are an accident of nature, are here by chance, then we can feel powerless. Instead, if we accept that we are here because we decided to be here and for our own purpose, we feel empowered. We determine the quality of our life. Our current status is the result of our previous decisions. We are reaping in accordance with the seeds we sowed, whether or not we were conscious of the process. We can change course toward a better future at any time by sowing seeds we choose intelligently.

Unless we capitalize on our uniqueness, we will end up lumped with the masses. If that is our choice then that is fine. If, on the other hand, we have a unique contribution to make, then we must stand out and distinguish ourselves. We can allow external forces to determine who we are and how we should live, or we can decide for ourselves.

We are unique to the extent that we highlight and capitalize on our uniqueness. To be clear about what sets us apart, we should make a list of our unique circumstances, capabilities, talents and abilities. Next, we should package these in the most effective way. Finally, we should seek avenues to express our uniqueness in the most effective way.

We are how God experiences our world in a personal and intimate way. This should incentivize us to highlight and express what we have been gifted with, our uniqueness. It is useless to be a unique, individualized expression of God, and live a common mediocre life. We are the microscopes through which God focuses on our limited world for a closer experience of reality. Let us endeavor to give God a most memorable view.

# SHARPEN YOUR TOOLSET

*If I had eight hours to chop down a tree, I'll spend seven hours sharpening my ax. – Abe Lincoln*

We still use axes; however, our use of tools has come a long way. In fact, the use of tools is the measure of advancement for an individual, a society and a nation. What tools we use and how well we use them, makes all the difference in how well we live and how fast we reach our goal and achieve our purpose.

Tools greatly simplify our lives and avail us of free time. There are two types of tools: external – physical, and internal – mental. We are familiar with many physical tools. These are the chain saws, forklifts, knives, hammers, planes, jets, elevators, and computers. We are constantly adding to our toolset, changing and refining them. There are many specialized tools as well. Unless we know of them, we will not use them.

Internal tools are mental. They are limited in number, but unlimited in capability. They are in us and part of our makeup. They are among the most precious tools we have. The more we use our internal tools, the deeper we incorporate them into our makeup and the more effective they become.

## A. External Tools

There are two types of external tools: general and specialized.

236 | KNOW YOURSELF, LOVE YOURSELF, EXPRESS YOURSELF

We are familiar with the general tools. We use these in our everyday life. We are less familiar with the specialized tools that are used in industry. These would be specific tools for precise jobs and incudes robotics and tools using artificial intelligence. The more sophisticated and specialized the tools we use, the higher the level of our technological advancement.

The body itself can be considered a tool. The body can be trained to express particular abilities such as dance, music, painting and sculpture. Individuals can train body parts to b nimbler, flexible, and dexterous. The body can be built and sculpted or it can be allowed to be flaccid and out of shape. It is amazing what some individuals are able to do with their bodies. Some walk tight ropes; others use their fingers and vocal cords in amazing ways playing musical instruments and singing. Some can twist the body in amazing ways.

## B. Internal Tools

The mind is a chest of tools. It contains everything we will ever need to live happy, content and productive lives. It houses thoughts, feelings, habits, attitudes, expectations, beliefs and knowledge. Unlike external tools, we carry our mental tools with us wherever we go.

## 1. Thinking, Feeling, Action And Habit

Og Mandino, in his famous book: **The Greatest Salesman in the World**, explains that the difference between people is the difference of their habits. Yet, what are habits other than mental tools?

How we choose to think, feel and act are the most immediate and readily available tools in our arsenal. The way we think, feel and act determines the organizational structure of our minds. Repeated thinking and feeling in a particular way impels us to act in a certain way. Repeated actions, over time, lead to habits.

Habit is from Latin "Habitus". It is like the clothes we wear. We either dress for success, mediocrity, or failure. Over time, habits become like cables – very difficult to break free from especially if they lead to addiction. We can, however, replace one habit with another, hopefully, a more desirable one.

Forming excellent habits that serve us is one of the most powerful tools we can have. Habits are simple to form, cost nothing and are forever our servants. One such excellent habit is decisiveness, acting without procrastinating.

> *"Whatever thou resolvest to do, do it quickly. Defer not till the evening what the morning may accomplish."*
> *Unto Thee I Grant*

## Processing Power

Our brains are highly sophisticated computers. Computers have input, processing and output. We might not have total control of the input into our brains, but we control some of the processing and most of the output.

Computers use RAM (random access memory) *to process input.* RAM is one of the most fundamental elements of computing. It is a temporary "space" where processing takes place. The greater the RAM, the more processing power a computer has. Unlike computers which have a fixed RAM, we determine the size of our RAM. The more we think, evaluate and contemplate prior to acting, the more RAM is allocated for processing. The more we use our RAM, the greater its size and the more intelligent we are.

Processing inputs prior to acting exercises control of our behavior. It is a measure of our maturity. We can choose how to act. Since 80% of what we encounter is trivia, we can ignore these and remain detached. When we decide to act, we can do so intelligently, decisively and compassionately.

> *The only way you can sustain a permanent change is to create a new way of thinking, acting, and being.*
> Jennifer Hudson

## 2. Attitude

Attitude is the manner in which we act – our disposition. The word is from the Latin "Aptus" meaning fitted or suited. It is the way we fit our various habits together. It is our inclination. Our attitudes affect the endocrine glands. These glands are responsible for building, rejuvenating, repairing and directly controlling the functions of the body. Positive mental attitudes cause positive secretions that help the body. Negative mental attitudes cause negative secretions that hinder the functioning of the body. However, positive attitudes alone are not enough. We require aptitude as well. According to some, accomplishments are based on 85% attitude and 15% aptitude.

Attitude is important in many jobs such as customer service. In fact, it is important in any work environment. How we view our jobs makes a difference. Is work a duty, a drudgery, a responsibility or an exciting opportunity to do our best and to make a difference?

Attitudes are evident when facing a challenge or a life change. While some resist change, others are more open to what life may bring. Similarly, there is a difference between being an optimist or a pessimist. Seeing a bottle as half full is not the same as seeing it as half empty. The expectations and the hormones that are secreted in response are different. Boredom and enthusiasm, interest and curiosity are matters of attitude.

The amount of energy we have is directly related to how much value we place in an activity. The more enthusiasm, interest and curiosity we display, the more energy we have for the activity.

> *Enthusiasm is one of the most powerful engines of success. When you do a thing, do it with all your might. Put your whole soul into it. Stamp it with your own personality. Be active, be energetic, be enthusiastic and faithful and you will achieve your object. Nothing great was ever achieved without enthusiasm.* Ralph Waldo Emerson

## 3. Expectation

Often, we make our own self-fulfilling prophesies. What we expect with confidence becomes our reality. We conduct ourselves based on the expectations we have of ourselves and the outcomes we anticipate.

Expectations can be based on reasonable, outrageous or even wrong assumptions. Reasonable, beneficial assumptions are what we want. Outrageous assumptions can lead to errors in judgment and to disappointment. We can assume wrongly that we are unable to do something when we can. It is far better to expect to succeed than to fail. But we must prepare and be ready. Without preparation, our expectations are hollow.

## 4.  Belief

Beliefs are a collection of mental structures that organize and hold in place our deeply rooted thoughts, perceptions, and memories. Beliefs influence our ideas, experiences, thoughts and feelings. Ultimately, how well we perform depends on our beliefs whether or not they are based in reality. Like the aperture of a camera, beliefs are the windows through which we see the world.

There are positive ennobling beliefs and negative demeaning beliefs. A belief in ourselves and our abilities is self-enhancing. A belief in doomsday, punishment and damnation is negative, unnecessary and degrading. If we believe that we are smart, then we act accordingly. Since beliefs influence our behavior, we should select them carefully and periodically expose them to daylight and examination. We have the mindsets that we do because we have the beliefs that we do.

A collection of beliefs through which we view the world is a paradigm. We have paradigms as to what it means to be an American, a Christian or a patriot. Paradigms can limit us just as any belief would. It is far better to have an open mind than to believe without a basis.

## 5. Skills And Abilities

We have learned skills and abilities and we also have innate ones. We can add to our skills and abilities anytime we take on a new hobby, interest or career.

We have unlimited potential. We are endowed with incredible brains and miraculous minds. We can acquire new skills and continuously cultivate our minds. We can learn to drive, fly and operate sophisticated equipment. We can gain expertise and mastery of anything that excites us and attracts our attention.

We are born with seed talents, abilities and natural proclivities. The worst we could do is have talents and skills and keep these buried within us never allowing them the light of day. We must mine, cultivate and put to good use that which we already have and strive to add new ones. Skills and abilities are how we express ourselves.

## 6. Experiences And Memories

To live is to form memories through experiencing. Memories help us learn, improve and adapt. Some memories are powerful, enduring and consciously recalled. The vast majority of our memories are fleeting and soon forgotten. We have joyous memories. We also have traumatic memories. Negative memories help us decide what to avoid. We have a value system that automatically determines what memories are important to store and what to ignore. Out of the trillions of impressions we receive, we process and consciously remember only a few. These are the ones which aid our survival and contribute to our well-being.

## 7. Goals, Hopes, Aspirations And Dreams

The brain is at its best when challenged. Setting goals challenges the brain and provides an objective to focus on. Our hopes, aspirations and dreams are how we influence the future. They must align with our values. We should strive to express what gives us joy and brings us contentment and happiness. This is always in accordance with our values and passions. It is easy to waste precious time in pursuit of trivia. Focusing only on what is of value, the critical few, is the best investment of our time and energy.

### *Mental and Spiritual Tools to Cultivate*

## 1. Will

Will is not a stubborn force. It must be cultivated and used

242 | KNOW YOURSELF, LOVE YOURSELF, EXPRESS YOURSELF

with discernment. We should use our will to do what we know is right and in accordance with our values.

Will accompanies our intentions. It is dispersed throughout the body and is the force behind our actions. Every move we make is based on our will. Every time we speak, eat or drink, the power of will is behind these acts. When we see birds in flight, we witness intention in action. Will and intention are inseparable companions. They can be conscious or subconscious. Our strongest will is to survive. Our concern for survival extends beyond our individual selves. It is our will to perpetuate our species as well. As long as we have plans for our lives, and a strong enough will to live, we will continue to live. Once our will to live wanes, we begin to die (physical death).

We are never fully free to do as we wish because of the influences in our lives. These are both internal and external, conscious and subconscious. Yet, through intention and will, we can counter any influence and live our lives as we see fit.

Unchecked, our will gravitates toward our greatest desires. These are not necessarily in our best interests. By being attentive and by clarifying our intentions, we can direct our will to serve our best interests.

We can will ourselves to entertain the thoughts, attitudes and expectations that enhance the quality of our lives and speed up our evolution, growth and maturation. We should only focus on what we want and avoid dwelling on what we do not desire. For what we dwell on, we empower.

We can will ourselves to think positive and empowering thoughts.
We can decide to feel confident and be happy.
We can choose to nurture our bodies.
We can slow down, ponder and act with intelligence instead of reacting.

We can decide never to be victims of circumstance.
We can always choose, will and act.
We can use our will to create the life we envision.

## 2. Concentration, Contemplation, Reflection, Visualization, Imagination, Meditation And Prayer

The ability to imagine and to visualize is among the most creative faculties of the mind. We can create the future we desire by first imaging, imagining and visualizing its details in our mind. The power to imagine is potent. It is a double-edged sword. We can imagine the worst and invite havoc, or we can visualize the outcome we want and create a future we desire.  We never stop imaging, imagining and visualizing. Our dreams, hopes and aspirations are extensions of our visualizations. We should master willful, conscious visualization of the outcomes we want. By cultivating vivid imagination, we can mentally create. Releasing the images, we can confidently expect their manifestation.

Visualization takes place in the field of consciousness. What we visualize, we imprint as an image onto this field. These images, based on their magnetism and charge, will seek material manifestation. To visualize effectively, we must concentrate. This requires practice and mastery. We can learn to concentrate by regularly contemplating a subject of interest.

Meditation puts us in touch with the divine within. Prayer, on the other hand, links us to the divine without. Both of these are a means to receive answers, discern the truth and to elevate the consciousness.

It is a human privilege to detach and reflect on our lives. We can examine our thoughts, habits and beliefs. Reflecting on and analyzing our behavior, we can endeavor to be better and to progressively improve. It is up to us to cultivate our mind, care for our body and nurture our soul. If not us, then who?

We can also use visualization and imagination to heal ourselves from traumas.

> *"Therapy is more about building new associations, making new, healthier default pathways. It is almost as if therapy is taking your two-lane dirt road and building a four-lane freeway alongside it. The old road stays, but you don't use it much anymore. Therapy is building a better alternative, a new default. And it takes repetition, and time; honestly, it works best if someone understands how the brain changes."* **What Happened To You?** *Bruce Perry and Oprah Winfrey*

We can change the past by reimagining it. What has happened is in the past. Yet, we can reinterpret its significance and derive new understanding from it anytime we like. We can revisit an incident, detach and view it in a new and empowering way. We can release blame and guilt. We can visualize alternative outcomes. We can understand motives, release and forgive. We can see the bigger picture. Repeating our new visualization and assigning the incident fresh meaning will build a new highway in the mind over time. We change the brain default. We create new connections and networks. We heal.

## 3. Intuition

Intuition is insight from our Higher Self. It appears unexpectedly after we exhaust the use of reasoning and logic. It is easy to confuse intuition with the power of suggestion. Suggestions from others and our desires could be the force behind what we term intuition. True intuitions however, are insights from our Higher Self.

To cultivate intuition, we must be quiet, clear our minds and be receptive. We must be open to The Voice Within and the promptings of our Higher Self. Once we seek, knock and ask we let go and wait trusting that the answer will come.

Earlier in our evolution, intuition was our most important tool to survive. Our survival depended on intuition. As we evolved, we began to shift from relying on intuition to using our reasoning. Both reason and intuition must be cultivated and used together. Adding intuition to our arsenal of tools gives us a powerful advantage.

## 4. Knowledge

Our knowledge is an interwoven system of all that we have accumulated so far as facts, information, beliefs, memories and personal experiences. What we know is determined by our education, experiences and personal initiative to acquire knowledge. The good news is that we can continue to learn and constantly improve. Since we act according to what we know, it makes sense to add to our storehouse of knowledge by a lifelong pursuit of education.

Paradigms are based on belief or knowledge. What we know, or believe we know, determines how we view the world. Our knowledge can trap us into a cell if limiting, or it can place us in a mansion if liberating. We set our own limits based on what we know. Knowledge is the light through which we see, understand and function. May this light shine purely and clearly, unobstructed by the veils of fear, ignorance and debilitating biases and beliefs.

## 5. Connections

Our connections and networks are a potent tool. We must maintain and nurture our connections. We have connections to our family, friends and acquaintances. Our most important connection, however, is to our Higher Self and to the God within. While we can disconnect from our physical bonds by moving away, we can never detach from our spiritual connections.

We are never alone. The more connected we feel, the more powerful we are. The more grounded in our self we are, the deeper our foundation. The more people we share deep, intimate, and abiding relationships with, the more connected we feel, the larger our sense of self and the wider our sphere of influence. Our connections are open doors to opportunity, social outlets, comradery and a sense of belonging.

## 6. The Higher Self

We are always connected to our Higher Self and the God within. We can strengthen these connections via meditation, prayer and visualization. If we maintain an open door to our Higher Self, then it will whisper to us as The Voice Within. At times, it will even thunder through. What we do with the inspiration we receive is up to us. The best way to live a purposeful life is to be guided by the Higher Self. This happens when we subjugate our will to the Higher Will, our self to the Higher Self.

Living is being in a maize. It can be very difficult to navigate from the ground level. Fortunately, the Higher Self is above and can see the entire maize. Seeking the guidance of our Higher Self, we can easily find the best path forward.

## 7. Love And Compassion

Love and compassion are among the greatest tools to relate to others and to invite peace into our lives and the world. Love and compassion are potent tools of transformation. They are agents of harmony, goodness, health and happiness. Cultivating love and compassion for others breaks the barrier of our small self to expand and include others. With love and compassion, we transmute evil into good, hate into love and violence into harmony. Love is a powerful shield that we can surround ourselves with to protect us from any harm.

# EXPRESS YOURSELF

*Wisdom is knowing what to do next; virtue*
*is doing it.*        *—David Starr Jordan*

I t is impossible not to express ourselves. To exist, is to occupy space. Occupying space, we distort it to reflect the nature of our being. How far this distortion extends, depends on how developed our spiritual body is. This is known as our magnetic field, the aura.

Just as nature simply expresses itself, so do we. Just as a flower expresses its wonder and magic for all to see, so do we. However, unlike a flower that has no choice as to what it expresses, we have a choice. We can express our superficial ego-based lower self, or we can express our Higher Self. Since what we express is based on who we are, knowing and loving ourselves is paramount.

## Be A Tool User

Adept tool users excel. Since we carry our internal tools within us, they are readily available for use. Why not use them habitually to make our lives the best they can be – effective, efficient and creative? Why settle for a mediocre life when we can live exceptional and impactful lives?

We can use our bodies, emotions and minds to be healthy, content and productive.

We can use our skills and abilities to make a positive contribution to society and the world.

We can leverage our memories and experiences to gain wisdom and understanding.

We can create habits that serve us, attitudes that uplift us, positive expectations that guide us and ennobling beliefs that light our way.

We can set goals that align with our passions, hopes and aspirations. We can have dreams that energize and propel us to a better future.

We can choose to speak our truth gently and convincingly without trepidation. We can employ our intuition and knowledge to contribute to the welfare of others.

We can imagine and realize a future that is bright, peaceful and abundant for all.

## Be Creative

We are in the image of God in that we are creative. Let us live creative lives.

Our nature is Love, Beauty and Joy. Let us radiate Love, Beauty and Joy.

Let us endeavor to elevate our expressions to reflect our maturing nature.

As we assume various roles in life, let us express the ideal in each situation. As adults, students, teachers, parents, patients and citizens, let us put our best foot forward. As students, let us excel; as teachers, let us be patient, understanding and encouraging; as patients, let us cooperate; as citizens, let us be civic minded. In each stage of our lives, let us express our finest qualities. We do this not to impress anyone, but as a natural reflection of who we are.

Let us enjoy our temporary stay on Earth as much as we can and, at the same time, act compassionately and responsibly towards others.

## Be Like A Garden

Earth is the proverbial Garden of Eden. Locally, the physical body is our Garden of Eden. A garden is an outstanding symbol for our lives. It is the harmonious coexistence of all of its elements. It is a place of retreat where we find shelter, soak in beauty and are revitalized.

Gardens must be maintained. A garden full of weeds and trash is a junkyard. We are the gardeners of our lives. We must pluck out the undesirable weeds and, at the same time, nourish the desirable plants. The "soil" of our garden is our mind and it is especially fertile. We must erect a gatekeeper, a guardian with a flaming sword, to prevent weeds (negative thoughts) from entering, and at the same time, encourage the seedlings of positive thoughts to enter, settle in and grow.

Our garden has the two main trees in it, the tree of life – the heart and the tree of knowing – the mind. These two trees are the source of both good and weed seeds. The heart is the source of both positive and negative emotions. The mind is the source of positive and negative thoughts. Allowed to take root and grow, weeds eventually will suffocate the good plants and destroy the garden. We are the guardians of what grows in our garden. If we do not watch our thoughts and emotions, they become rampant and grow unchecked. If we only dwell on the positive, then our garden will be vibrant, healthy and worthy as a refuge.

If we assume responsibility and guard our garden, our lives will flourish. Else, we will end up with a garden full of weeds, a jungle where we can easily flounder and be lost.

We start life as a grain of mustard seed. By expressing our positive attributes, we grow and become magnificent trees that others take shelter under, enjoy its shade and savor its fruit.

> And he said, "With what can we compare the kingdom of God, or what parable shall we use for it? It is like a grain of mustard seed, which, when sown on the ground, is the smallest of all the seeds on earth, yet when it is sown it grows up and becomes larger than all the garden plants and puts out large branches, so that the birds of the air can make nests in its shade." Mark 4:30-32

## Afflictions

It is difficult to express our best selves while afflicted. We are burdened with physical, mental and spiritual afflictions. Getting rid of our afflictions, we radiate health, energy and optimism.

Physical afflictions are obvious and we can easily seek help to remedy them. When we suffer from infections, parasites, toxins, injuries or are sick, we consult physicians, take medications, and rest until we recuperate.

Emotional afflictions are less obvious. They can hide undetected. We are emotionally afflicted when we have experienced trauma, are gripped with unreasonable fear, incessant worry, uncontrolled anger, excessive greed, unchecked jealousy, venomous hate and succumb to addiction. Since these can evade detection by others, we seldom take them seriously. We do not consider ourselves sick and seek help. The remedy for these is to manage our thoughts and live simple, clean lives. Instead of focusing on what we lack, or what others have, we can choose to be thankful for our blessings. We can forgive, let go, and we can love. Vices are a heavy load to carry around. We do much better without them.

Deciding to think positive thoughts and live virtuous lives is a sure cure for our emotional afflictions.

Spiritual afflictions are few. They include lust, pride, prejudice and ignorance. Fortunately, all afflictions have cures. We never need to fight vices. We do not oppose evil. Instead, we should wholeheartedly seek the virtues. By adopting a virtuous life, seeking wisdom and understanding through progressive improvement, we can rid ourselves of all afflictions. We can be free, creative and express our highest potential.

## Expressing Our Ego – The Lower Self

When we seek ego gratification, we are expressing our superficial lower self. When we compare ourselves to others with pride, we are expressing our lower self. When we fight, try to dominate, bully and force our way on others, we are expressing our lower self. When we are taken over by rage, we are expressing our lower self. Being mean, nasty or selfish is expressing our lower self. Displaying any of the vices such as arrogance, envy or jealousy, is expressing our lower self.

What we express is always a reflection of who we believe we are. Instead of expressing our lower self as a response to situations, we can endeavor to express our highest qualities as often as we can. By constantly refining our expressions through awareness and reflection, we can allow our true Higher Self to shine through and express itself.

## Expressing Our Higher Self

The self that we need to know, love, and express is our Higher Self. This is our light within. It is of no use to know and love Self and keep it hidden within us. It does no one any good. Did not Christ admonish us to shine our light instead of hiding it?

> *You are the light of the world. A city built on a hill*
> *cannot be hid. No one after lighting a lamp puts it*
> *under the bushel basket, but on the lampstand, and it*
> *gives light to all in the house. In the same way, let your*
> *light shine before others, so that they may see your good*
> *works and give glory to your Father in heaven.* Matt
> *5:14-16*

We are the light of the world. Let our light shine. Our light shines as our aura. Let us express our unique individuality with gratitude and joy. A flower does not try to convince anyone of its beauty. It simply reflects its essence. So must we. Each day is a new opportunity to express our light a bit brighter than the day before. Our role ends with our thoughts, feelings and actions. We should always put our best forward and detach from outcomes. Outcomes are not for us to control. Just as the sun shines on everyone, we should shower our best qualities on everyone. Just as the sun expects nothing in return, so should we. Ancient systems of thought such as the Bhagavad Gita forewarn us against attachment to outcomes. Let us do our good and let go, expecting nothing in return or any favored outcome.

Let us be spiritual alchemists replacing pride with humility, fear with courage. Let us stop worrying and figure out what actions we can take instead. Let us decide to be happy, radiating our beauty. Let us be unflappable, functioning from confidence, doing the most with what we have.

Since only humans can laugh, let us laugh more often. It improves digestion, lightens burdens and lengthens lives. Since only humans have arts, sciences, philosophy, literature and music, let us engage in these and enjoy them more often. Since only humans can sing, dance, appreciate, enjoy and celebrate, let us participate in these frequently.

Let us outgrow being parochial, identifying with our race, religion, or nationality. If these bring us closer to others, then we can employ them temporarily. We do not need them if they separate us from each other. Foremost, we are one large family occupying an incredibly beautiful planet – Earth.

Let us bestow upon others genuine praise, admiration, smiles, words of encouragement, help and assistance. Let us do all we can to enrich their lives. Let us even hold back and allow others to take center stage and express themselves. It is wonderful to celebrate their achievements.

# PART V

## Lifting the Veil

1. Secret of Christianity
2. Secret of the Mustard Seed
3. Secret of Prayer
4. Secret of Sleep and Dreams
5. Secret of the Breath
6. Secret of the Alchemists
7. Secret of the Millennium

# THE SECRET OF CHRISTIANITY

*He who begins by loving Christianity more than Truth, will proceed by loving his sect or church better than Christianity, and end in loving himself better than all.*
*—Samuel Taylor Coleridge*

Quagmire.
Misunderstandings of scripture abound. This is because we are spoon fed our religious teachings. We seldom do the work ourselves, digging, inquiring, questioning and seeking true answers. We relinquish our responsibility to find out and rely on others to interpret Holy Books for us. Since scripture is not history and can be interpreted in several ways, this has led us into quagmires difficult to get out of. Spiritual writings are not meant to be literal. They have deeper meanings that must be brought to light. Christ said so on several occasions.

> *And the disciples came, and said unto him, Why speakest thou unto them in parables? He answered and said unto them, Because it is given unto you to know the mysteries of the kingdom of heaven, but to them it is not given.* Matt 13:10-11

In other words, unless we become disciples of Christ, we will not understand the teachings of Christ, why He came and what His life was about. Concepts such as sin, salvation, baptism,

Son-of Man and Son-of God will remain enigmas. If we accept them literally, we find ourselves in quicksand we cannot get out of. Take the Book of Revelation for example. It is purely symbolic. Surface reading would confound anyone. At this level, it has nothing to do with Christianity. We wonder why it is even included in the Bible. Even its name is misleading. Nothing is revealed in the book of "Revelation." It is a jumble of mythical creatures, incredulous events and preposterous speculations. Dragons in the sky, God on a throne surrounded by beasts full of eyes both in front and behind them, a book with 7 seals, a woman clothed with the sun travails, a great red dragon stands before her, ready to devour her child. This book is someone's dream and should be considered as such and if no one can unravel its mysteries, it should be removed from the Bible.

Another example of a quagmire is the belief in Armageddon and the physical Second Coming of Christ. Here again we are confusing religion with spirituality. Religion advocates a literal Second Coming of Jesus to rule the Earth, perhaps for 1000 years. This will never happen because the second coming is a spiritual reference to the Christ Consciousness being born in the hearts of individuals. When enough of us live Christianity spiritually, expressing the Christ Consciousness in our daily lives, then the second coming takes place. In other words, it does not happen on its own. Unless we evolve, grow and mature and express the Christ Consciousness in our everyday lives, it will not come to pass. Some absurdly believe that we can hasten the second coming of Christ by aiding a specific country and supporting it in every way possible to ensure that Jesus comes back. This is misguided at best. Armageddon is not happening and will never happen unless, through our stupidity, we bring it about. Our world is not destined to be destroyed. It is given to us as an opportunity to transform it into a heaven. When we transmute our physicality into spirituality, Christ will be among us in our hearts.

## Christianity Is Spirituality

There is the Old and there is the New. There is Law and there is Grace. Until the birth of Christ, humanity was in the old age and under the Law. Christ came to move us from being in the old and under the Law to the new and into Grace. The birth of Christ fulfills the Law, completes it and puts an end to it. He wanted a clear separation from the Law and a fresh move into Grace. He made this perfectly clear when, in the Sermon on the Mount, He said:

> *You have heard that it was said to those of old, 'You shall not murder; and whoever murders will be liable to judgment.' But I say to you that everyone who is angry with his brother will be liable to judgment; whoever insults his brother will be liable to the council; and whoever says, 'You fool!' will be liable to the hell of fire.* Matt 5:21-22

> *You have heard that it was said, 'You shall not commit adultery.' But I say to you that everyone who looks at a woman with lustful intent has already committed adultery with her in his heart.* Matt 5:27-28

> *Again you have heard that it was said to those of old, 'You shall not swear falsely, but shall perform to the Lord what you have sworn.' But I say to you, Do not take an oath at all, either by heaven, for it is the throne of God, or by the earth, for it is his footstool, or by Jerusalem, for it is the city of the great King. And do not take an oath by your head, for you cannot make one hair white or black. Let what you say be simply 'Yes' or 'No'; anything more than this comes from evil.* Matt 5:33-37

*You have heard that it was said, 'An eye for an eye and a tooth for a tooth.' But I say to you, Do not resist the one who is evil. But if anyone slaps you on the right cheek, turn to him the other also.   Matt 5:38-39*

*You have heard that it was said, 'You shall love your neighbor and hate your enemy.' But I say to you, Love your enemies and pray for those who persecute you, Matt 5:43-44*

In other words, you have been told all these things while under the law, but now that you are in grace, I am telling you to leave all that behind and do instead what I am telling you; the exact opposite.

Christ was not a slave to the law. He lived in tune with the dictates of His conscious and the will of the Father within. For Him, the law was made for our convenience, and not the other way around.

*And he said to them, "The Sabbath was made for man, not man for the Sabbath. So the Son of Man is lord even of the Sabbath." Mark 2:27-28*

He wanted the separation to be clean. The old and the new must not be mixed up, else neither will remain pure.

*No one puts a piece of unshrunk cloth on an old garment, for the patch tears away from the garment, and a worse tear is made. Neither is new wine put into old wineskins. If it is, the skins burst and the wine is spilled and the skins are destroyed. But new wine is put into fresh wineskins, and so both are preserved.        Matt 9:16-17*

The old is religion and laws. The new is spirituality and grace. Religion demands following, obeying, worshiping and has intermediaries between us and God. Spirituality asks us to love, to accept everyone as a child of God, to look for the kingdom of God within and to have no intermediaries between us and God for He is our father, always accessible.

The evidence that Christianity is spirituality is clear. The following few passages should suffice to prove the point.

Christ had a special understanding of what the living and the dead were. Physical beings, even though they are alive in a body, can be spiritually dead. Unless we are spiritually alive, we have no abiding life.

> And another of his disciples said unto him, Lord, suffer me first to go and bury my father. But Jesus said unto him, Follow me; and let the dead bury their dead. Matt 8:21-22

In the Lord's Prayer Jesus teaches us to ask for our daily bread.

> Give us this day our daily bread,   Matt 6:11

He does not mean physical bread since He makes it clear that He is the bread of life.

> Jesus said to them, "I am the bread of life; whoever comes to me shall not hunger, and whoever believes in me shall never thirst." John 6:35

He is not only the bread of life, but the water as well. These are spiritual terms.

> Jesus said to her, "Everyone who drinks of this water will be thirsty again, but whoever drinks of the water that I will give him will never be thirsty again. The water that I will give him will become in him a spring of water welling up to eternal life." John4:13-14

The Eucharist makes it amply clear that His statements were never meant to be taken literally.

> Now as they were eating, Jesus took bread, and after blessing it broke it and gave it to the disciples, and said,

*"Take, eat; this is my body." And he took a cup, and when he had given thanks he gave it to them, saying, "Drink of it, all of you, for this is my blood of the covenant, which is poured out for many for the forgiveness of sins." Matt 26:26-28*

If we take the words of Christ literally, and through transubstantiation the wafer or the bread turns into the actual body of Christ and the wine into the actual blood of Christ, then we are cannibals. The body of Christ is His spiritual body, His teachings. His blood is His essence – love, forgiveness, service and acceptance of everyone.

## The Secret Of Christianity

There is a secret to Christianity few are aware of. This secret is in plain view, yet unless it is pointed out, it remains hidden, undetected and unknown.

Did Christ physically rise from the tomb?

Did He ascend to heaven in a physical body?

What happened at Pentecost?

Easter is the most important holiday in Christianity because of the resurrection. We are accustomed to believe that Christ physically rose from the dead. The good news is that the resurrection did, in fact, happen. However, it was not Christ's physical body. It was His spiritual body that rose. Eventually, Christ ascended to heaven as a spiritual body.

Physical bodies can never ascend to heaven. Spiritual bodies can; for heaven is the abode of spirit. God is in heaven and God is spirit and only spiritual beings can be in heaven. This is evident from the following passage:

*Jesus answered and said unto them, Ye do err, not*

*knowing the scriptures, nor the power of God. For in the resurrection, they neither marry, nor are given in marriage, but are as the angels of God in heaven. Matt 22:29-30*

Those resurrected **are as angels of God in heaven**. Angels are spiritual beings. They have no physical bodies.

Another passage makes it clear that only spiritual beings can be resurrected.

*Jesus, when he had cried again with a loud voice, yielded up the ghost. And, behold, the veil of the temple was rent in twain from the top to the bottom; and the earth did quake, and the rocks rent; And the graves were opened; and many bodies of the saints which slept arose, And came out of the graves after his resurrection, and went into the holy city, and appeared unto many. Matt 27:50-53*

And many **bodies of saints** which slept arose, and came out of the grave after his resurrection. Humans who become saints, can do so only after they die. All saints are spiritual beings. Prophets, on the other hand, are not saintly. Saints, being spiritual, have highly developed spiritual bodies that can be resurrected. While physical bodies decompose in graves, spiritual bodies reside in the spiritual realm and can rise.

Here is another allusion that not everyone is resurrected, only the just, meaning the good, the saintly.

*But when thou makest a feast, call the poor, the maimed, the lame, the blind: And thou shalt be blessed; for they cannot recompense thee: for thou shalt be recompensed at the resurrection of the just.     Luke 14:13-14*

Resurrection of the **just**.

When Christ rose from the dead, it is evident that He was not in a physical body. Those who knew Him, did not recognize Him. He was in His spiritual body.

### Jesus appears to Mary Magdalene

> But Mary stood without at the sepulchre weeping: and as she wept, she stooped down, and looked into the sepulchre, And seeth two angels in white sitting, the one at the head, and the other at the feet, where the body of Jesus had lain. And they say unto her, Woman, why weepest thou? She saith unto them, Because they have taken away my Lord, and I know not where they have laid him. And when she had thus said, she turned herself back, and saw Jesus standing, and knew not that it was Jesus. Jesus saith unto her, Woman, why weepest thou? whom seekest thou? She, supposing him to be the gardener, saith unto him, Sir, if thou have borne him hence, tell me where thou hast laid him, and I will take him away. Jesus saith unto her, Mary. She turned herself, and saith unto him, Rabboni; which is to say, Master. Jesus saith unto her, Touch me not; for I am not yet ascended to my Father: but go to my brethren, and say unto them, I ascend unto my Father, and your Father; and to my God, and your God. Mary Magdalene came and told the disciples that she had seen the Lord, and that he had spoken these things unto her. John 20:11-18

**Mary knew not that it was Jesus**. She could not touch Him, because He was in His spiritual body, if He were physical, she would have known him and been able to touch Him.

What happened to His physical body?

Christ's vibrations were so high that He completely spiritualized His physical body and turned it into a spiritual body. He transmuted the physical into the spiritual. It no longer existed as matter. It turned into conscious, spiritual light energy, His new body of light.

In the above passage, it was only Mary Magdalene who witnessed the resurrection. In Luke, it was a group of women.

***Christ's resurrection is declared by two angels to the women that come to the sepulcher.***

> *And they entered in, and found not the body of the Lord Jesus. And it came to pass, as they were much perplexed thereabout, behold, two men stood by them in shining garments: And as they were afraid, and bowed down their faces to the earth, they said unto them, Why seek ye the living among the dead? He is not here, but is risen: remember how he spake unto you when he was yet in Galilee, Saying, The Son of man must be delivered into the hands of sinful men, and be crucified, and the third day rise again. And they remembered his words,* Luke 24:3-8

These women were:

> *It was Mary Magdalene, and Joanna, and Mary the mother of James, and other women that were with them, which told these things unto the apostles.* Luke 24:10

Mary Magdalene sees two **angels in white**, while the group of women see **two men**. This is because spiritual beings can assume the shape of a man or anything else they like. They can even go through walls, appear and disappear at will. Physical bodies can never do these; only spiritual beings can.

***Christ himself appears to the two disciples that went to Emmaus***

> *So they drew near to the village to which they were going. He acted as if he were going farther, but they urged him strongly, saying, "Stay with us, for it is toward evening and the day is now far spent." So he went in to stay*

*with them. When he was at table with them, he took the*
*bread and blessed and broke it and gave it to them. And*
*their eyes were opened, and they recognized him. And he*
*vanished from their sight. Luke 24:28-31*

**Only spiritual beings can vanish from sight.**

**While physical beings marry and beget children, spiritual**
**beings never marry.**

*And Jesus answering said unto them, The children of this*
*world marry, and are given in marriage: But they which*
*shall be accounted worthy to obtain that world, and the*
*resurrection from the dead, neither marry, nor are given*
*in marriage: Neither can they die any more: for they are*
*equal unto the angels; and are the children of God, being*
*the children of the resurrection. Luke 20:34-36*

Those who are resurrected never marry, never die and are
equal to angels. This is a perfect description of spiritual beings.

Christ made a clear distinction between His physical body and
His spiritual body. When referring to his physical, He used the
term: The Son of Man. When referring to His spiritual body, He
used the term: I Am.

*Jesus said unto her, I am the resurrection, and the life:*
*he that believeth in me, though he were dead, yet shall*
*he live: And whosoever liveth and believeth in me shall*
*never die. Believest thou this? John 11:25-26*

I Am the resurrection. I Am life. I Am the way. I Am light. I
Am the bread of life. These references can have meaning only
in relation to His spiritual body which is imbued with the Holy
Spirit – the Christ Consciousness.

It is easy to understand Christianity as spiritual teaching but
not as a religion. Christ was not religious. He did not come
to establish an institution. He came to be an example of the

possible life so we may have life and have it abundantly. He is misunderstood. While He came to lead us away from violence, "an eye for an eye", away from judgment, revenge, selfishness and the pursuit of worldly treasures; we looked the other way and continued in our old, habitual ways. While He came to put an end to the Old, life under the Law, we refused to budge. He ushered in the New Age of Grace. He urged us to leave behind the old and look forward to a world of peace and cooperation founded on love, respect and service.

Many of us have lost our way. By following a religion, we abandoned the essence of Christianity which is spirituality. And herein lies the secret of Christianity. We are the I Am with three enveloping bodies: physical, astral and spiritual.

The physical body is the least permanent. It has a short life span and once dead and decomposed, it is gone forever, never to reappear again.

The astral body is more permanent. It is the one that reincarnates. It is a body that we use for astral travel, energy work and while out-of-the-body. It is much more capable than the physical body, but it is a holding place until we develop our spiritual body.

The spiritual body is the permanent aspect of our being. It is the "body of Christ" within us. It is the crème de la crème, the object of our pursuit. It is light of the highest rate of vibration. It is the purpose of our being on earth undergoing these experiences. We need to develop our spiritual bodies if we want to survive permanently. Only our spiritual body does not die and is eternal. Once fully developed, our spiritual body is Light, Life and Love. It is Beauty, Joy and the Resurrection.

Not everyone has a well-developed spiritual body. These individuals, once they die, will fall asleep and then wake up in a new body not remembering anything. The good news is that we can develop our spiritual body. It takes effort, determination and action. Since the spiritual body is made of the highest mental faculties and the noblest emotions, cultivating these should be our primary objective.

## A Fresh Look at the Purpose of Life

The purpose of life is to grow and to contribute, but to what end?

It is to develop our spiritual body.

How?

By embracing spirituality, by embodying the virtues and by contributing our best.

Without a spiritual body, we have no permanence. We will not endure. We will wither away and be gone. We are here to develop our spiritual body. Our ultimate freedom of choice is to decide what is paramount and pursue it. The spiritual body is the kingdom within. We must forsake all and seek its manifestation. As we develop our own spiritual body, we must help others do the same – our noblest contribution.

◆ ◆ ◆

At the heart of every religion is the mystery of our relationship with God. Almost all religions confess that we are a creation of God. Since God is All, then we must have proceeded from the nature of God. Hence, in essence, we are of the nature of God.

However, we are not like God. We are weak and limited in our knowledge and capabilities. Yet, we are constantly acquiring new knowledge, abilities and power. This progression of a human on the path of evolution and unfoldment was symbolically enacted as the annual procession from the Temple at Karnak to the temple at Luxor. The Pharaoh, representing a human, would begin his procession at Karnak as a human, the king. Once he arrived at Luxor, he would be transformed into a son of God.

Christianity reveals this secret in the life of Christ. Christ was born a human – Jesus, Son of Man who through the baptism of the Holy Spirit was transformed into Christ, the Son of God.

The purpose of life is also revealed in the Last Supper where transubstantiation takes place. Bread becomes the symbol of the body of Christ and wine becomes the symbol of the blood of Christ. This signifies that we are expected to transform the earthly into the heavenly, the physical into the spiritual.

The purpose of life is revealed in spiritual organizations as well. The acolyte, through initiations, progresses from first degree to the twelfth degree, from neophyte to master. Mastery implies the blossoming of our spiritual body with its associated faculties.

## *Creating the Spiritual Body*

There are two creation stories of humans in Genesis.

> *And God said, Let us make man in our image, after our likeness: and let them have dominion over the fish of the sea, and over the fowl of the air, and over the cattle, and over all the earth, and over every creeping thing that creepeth upon the earth. So God created man in his own image, in the image of God created he him; male and female created he them.    Gen 1:26-27*

This is the creation of the **spiritual** body. The spiritual body is in the image of God, both male and female, just as God is.

> *And the LORD God formed man of the dust of the ground, and breathed into his nostrils the breath of life; and man became a living soul.    Gen 2:7*

This is the creation of the **physical** body. The physical body is not in the image of God. It is either male or female. At first Adam, the male, is created and next Eve, the female.

> Then the LORD God said, "It is not good that the man should be alone; I will make him a helper fit for him."
> Gen 2:18

It is not good for man to be alone. Man needs the woman. Neither is it good for the woman to be alone. She needs the man.

> And the LORD God caused a deep sleep to fall upon Adam, and he slept: and he took one of his ribs, and closed up the flesh instead thereof; And the rib, which the LORD God had taken from man, made he a woman, and brought her unto the man. And Adam said, This is now bone of my bones, and flesh of my flesh: she shall be called Woman, because she was taken out of Man. Therefore shall a man leave his father and his mother, and shall cleave unto his wife: and they shall be one flesh. And they were both naked, the man and his wife, and were not ashamed.        Gen 2:21-25

These two creation stories reveal the nature of our being. Physically, we are either male or female. We are separate, distinct individuals. Spiritually, we must be one being for that is our true nature, both male and female at the same time.

How can this be?

Only our spiritual bodies are in the image of God – male and female. This must refer to masculine and feminine qualities and not to sex. Our masculine qualities are centered in the brain, the mind, while our feminine qualities are centered in the heart. These two must be intentionally united as one. This union is on two levels: internally, as the union of the heart and the mind and externally as the marriage between a male, representing the mind and the masculine qualities and a female representing the heart and the feminine qualities.

If the heart and the mind of an individual are integrated, united and function as one, then the spiritual body is born in that individual. If the union of man and woman is selfless, spiritual, pure, based on love, affection, and admiration then conception takes place, **knowing** results and the spiritual body in both is nurtured and begins to grow and blossom.

## *Developing the Spiritual Body*

There are three steps to developing the spiritual body. These are:

1. Remembering;
2. Activation; and
3. Resurrection.

## 1. Remembering

**We maintain a link to everything we ever experience by creating and leaving behind a "silver thread," that links us to that event, place, or person.** For as long as this thread is intact, memory functions well. Once this connection is severed, overlaid, or obstructed, we cannot remember. In other words, we are like spiders ever weaving connections to all that we experience. Unlike cobwebs, the thickness of what we weave varies based on our emotional attachments and the values we assign to events, places or people we encounter. The stronger the attachment, the greater the value, the stronger and thicker the connection between us and the event, place or person.

We need to remember our permanent nature – who we are. This happens when we develop our spiritual bodies. To adequately do this, we can follow the example of Christ. Christ had 12 disciples, each representing a quality.

To develop the spiritual body, (Christhood), we need to master 12 disciplines. Each individual has their own 12 disciplines to master. Here is a sample of disciplines:

1. Decisiveness based on confidence and faith;
2. Non-attachment to outcome;
3. Fearlessness;
4. Compassion;
5. Love;
6. Non-judgment;
7. Peacemaker;
8. Mastery of the higher faculties of mind (visualization, imagination and mental creation);
9. Mastery of the emotions (expressing only the positive);
10. Mastery of the physical body (optimum health, vitality and vigor);
11. Tapping the superconscious, becoming intuitive; and
12. Meekness and purity of heart.

Practicing one virtue at a time for an entire month will embed that virtue into our subconscious as a second nature – a habit. It will require an entire year to complete this cycle which can be repeated until mastery is achieved. Once these are mastered, we can choose 12 new disciplines to pursue. Mastery of these disciplines transforms us from ordinary humans into spiritual beings. Our spiritual bodies will blossom ensuring our spiritual immortality.

## 2. Activation

Spending one-month on each virtue must be an active, focused and intentional activity. We must put our hearts and minds into it. This awakens our senses, strengthens our neural connections, purifies the body and removes the obstructions between our lower and Higher Self. Intuition will flow freely and the still small voice within will be heard clearly.

To hasten the development of the spiritual body, we cultivate the following emotions (heart): love, empathy, sympathy, forgiveness, tolerance, understanding, compassion, and a spirit of ennobling, empowering service. These are the teachings of Christianity as expounded in the Sermon on the Mount, summed up in two words – Love and Service. Concurrently, we employ the following faculties of the mind: reason, discrimination, imagination, visualization, prayer, meditation, contemplation, concentration, and mental creation.

## 3. Resurrection

The spiritual body is the only body that can be "resurrected." We resurrect the spiritual body out of the physical body by way of the astral. The "physical" body must be made into the spiritual body. "Adam" must become the "Christ".

**Resurrecting the spiritual body out of the physical**

> So also is the resurrection of the dead. It is sown in corruption; it is raised in incorruption: It is sown in dishonor; it is raised in glory: it is sown in weakness; it is raised in power: It is sown a natural body; it is raised a spiritual body. There is a natural body, and there is a spiritual body. And so it is written, The first man Adam was made a living soul; the last Adam was made a quickening spirit. Howbeit that was not first which is spiritual, but that which is natural; and afterward that which is spiritual. The first man is of the earth, earthy: the second man is the Lord from heaven. As is

*the earthy, such are they also that are earthy: and as is the heavenly, such are they also that are heavenly. And as we have borne the image of the earthy, we shall also bear the image of the heavenly. Now this I say, brethren, that flesh and blood cannot inherit the kingdom of God; neither doth corruption inherit incorruption.*     1 *Cor 15:42-50*

Flesh and blood cannot inherit the kingdom. Only the spiritual body can.

We must actively transfigure the physical into the spiritual using our minds and hearts. We must transfigure our base elements – our vices, into noble elements – our virtues. As we do, the material of our body changes from dense matter into radiant spiritual light. That is what Christ demonstrated during His transfiguration, His radiant spiritual body.

## The transfiguration of Christ

*And after six days Jesus took with him Peter and James, and John his brother, and led them up a high mountain by themselves. And he was transfigured before them, and his face shone like the sun, and his clothes became white as light. And behold, there appeared to them Moses and Elijah, talking with him. And Peter said to Jesus, "Lord, it is good that we are here. If you wish, I will make three tents here, one for you and one for Moses and one for Elijah." He was still speaking when, behold, a bright cloud overshadowed them, and a voice from the cloud said, "This is my beloved Son, with whom I am well pleased; listen to him." When the disciples heard this, they fell on their faces and were terrified. But Jesus came and touched them, saying, "Rise, and have no fear." And when they lifted up their eyes, they saw no one but Jesus only.*

*And as they were coming down the mountain, Jesus commanded them, "Tell no one the vision, until the Son of Man is raised from the dead." And the disciples asked him, "Then why do the scribes say that first Elijah must come?" He answered, "Elijah does come, and he will restore all things. But I tell you that Elijah has already come, and they did not recognize him, but did to him whatever they pleased. So also the Son of Man will certainly suffer at their hands." Then the disciples understood that he was speaking to them of John the Baptist. Matt 17:1-13*

Faces that shine like the sun, raiment white like light, Moses and *Elijah* appearing and disappearing at will can only happen with spiritual bodies. *Elijah* being born as John the Baptist can only happen if *Elijah* came back as a spiritual being. While masters come back with their spiritual bodies to serve humanity, we come back in our astral bodies to develop our spiritual bodies. The mystery has been revealed. The purpose of earthly life is clear. What we need to do is obvious. Will we do it?

# SECRET OF THE MUSTARD SEED

*Words are also seeds, and when dropped into the invisible spiritual substance, they grow and bring forth after their kind.* −Charles Fillmore

A seed is the embodiment of the union of the female and male essences. The male essence, (spermatozoan, pollen, ..) and the female essence (ovum, ovule, stigma, ...) both sacrifice their individuality and shed their essence (DNA) to join together. The union is the ultimate sacrifice of individuality to form a new being, both male and female at once.

In the human, somatic cells (body cells) have 46 chromosomes. The germ cells (sperms and eggs), in preparation to carry out their function, shed half their chromosomes. Each sperm and each egg end up with only 23 chromosomes. Each is a half seed, but when united together they become complete once more with 46 chromosomes.

A seed from a tree does not stay a seed. Once immersed in the soil and if nurtured, it will grow into a magnificent tree.

A tree has three main components: a root system, a trunk and branches with leaves. We have three bodies: our root system is the spiritual body; our branches and leaves are the astral body; and our trunk is the physical body. The body, like the Garden of Eden, has two main trees: the brain with mind as the tree of knowing good and evil and the heart as the tree of eternal life. The brain and mind are the male component while the heart is the feminine. These two components must be brought together, united into one to give rise to the spiritual body.

## The Mystery Of The Kingdom Of Heaven

Christ admonishes us to first seek the Kingdom of God.

> But seek ye first the kingdom of God, and his righteousness; and all these things shall be added unto you.    Matt 6:33

He even told us where to look for the Kingdom of God. It is within us.

> Neither shall they say, Lo here! or, lo there! for, behold, the kingdom of God is within you. Luke 17:21

To understand what is within us that is so important, we need to look at some of Christ's other parables.

## And The Kingdom Of Heaven Is Like A ...

> Another parable he put before them, saying, "The kingdom of heaven is like a grain of mustard seed which a man took and sowed in his field; it is the smallest of all seeds, but when it has grown it is the greatest of shrubs and becomes a tree, so that the birds of the air come and make nests in its branches."    Matt 13:31-32

> He told them another parable. "The kingdom of heaven is like leaven which a woman took and hid in three measures of flour, till it was all leavened."    Matt 13:33 (RSV)

> The kingdom of heaven is like treasure hidden in a field, which a man found and covered up; then in his joy

*he goes and sells all that he has and buys that field.*
*Matt 13:44*

*Again, the kingdom of heaven is like a merchant in*
*search of fine pearls, who, on finding one pearl of great*
*value, went and sold all that he had and bought it.*
*Matt 13:45-46*

*Again, the kingdom of heaven is like a net which was*
*thrown into the sea and gathered fish of every kind;*
*when it was full, men drew it ashore and sat down and*
*sorted the good into vessels but threw away the bad.*
*Matt 13:47-48*

What are a seed, a leaven, yeast, a treasure, a pearl, or a net?

These are small items but of great value. A seed can grow into a magnificent tree. With yeast, we can transform dough and bake it into bread. With a treasure or a pearl, we can acquire whatever we desire. With a net we can catch any fish in the sea.

Why are a seed, yeast, treasure, pearl or a net treasures beyond value? If we interpret Christ's parables from the physical perspective only, we will miss out on their inner, deeper, spiritual meaning. A seed, yeast, treasure, pearl or a net are transforming agents. Knowing how to use them effectively will help us get what we want and transform our lives.

The ultimate transforming agent is knowledge. It lies deep within us as our DNA. DNA is a treasure beyond value because it is compacted knowledge. We have two types of DNA, physical and spiritual. While the physical DNA is in every cell as our genetic blueprint, the spiritual DNA is in our spiritual body. Our spiritual body, when fully developed, is omniscient, hence all-powerful. While our physical DNA is on auto-pilot, we must cultivate, nurture and tend to our spiritual body so it grows and blossoms.

That is why Christ tells us to seek it ahead of everything else;

nothing else is as important.

> For what is a man profited, if he shall gain the whole
> world, and lose his own soul? or what shall a man give in
> exchange for his soul?      Matt 16:26

The spiritual body, once fully developed is a fountain of power
and miraculous capabilities. It is our spiritual DNA – pure
wisdom. It is the Holy Spirit incarnate.

> The LORD by wisdom founded the earth; by
> understanding he established the heavens; by his
> knowledge the deeps broke forth, and the clouds drop
> down the dew.      Prov 3:19-20

And that is why developing our spiritual body is so important.
It is where our true power resides. This is the seed buried
within us that we must seek and develop. This is the most
important task that we must undertake. Once developed into
a "tree", we will be not only mighty but transformed. Our eyes
will open, our ears will clear and our hearts will soften with
kindness and love. Our faith will be more than a mustard seed.
It will be a magnificent tree.

> And Jesus said unto them, Because of your unbelief: for
> verily I say unto you, If ye have faith as a grain of
> mustard seed, ye shall say unto this mountain, Remove
> hence to yonder place; and it shall remove; and nothing
> shall be impossible unto you. Matt 17:20

Faith is a component of the spiritual body based on
experiential knowledge. It is our responsibility to nurture the
seed of faith within us until it grows into a magnificent tree.

When the acorn becomes an oak tree;

When the mustard seed becomes a magnificent tree;

When we master being a net that attracts to itself all the

abundance we need;

When we value ourselves and others as pearls or treasures beyond value;

When we learn to leaven any situation into an opportunity for Love, Beauty and Joy;

When humanity comes together voluntarily, cooperatively and lovingly and functions as one harmonious body;

Then the kingdom of heaven would have been established on Earth and the prophecy of the Second Coming of Christ is fulfilled.

# SECRET OF PRAYER

*One single grateful thought raised to heaven is the
most perfect prayer.    −G. E. Lessing*

Prayer is communication with the deity. We pray to petition, for intercession and as an adoration. We pray alone or in a group. We pray in places of worship, at home or anywhere we happen to be. We pray on special occasions or we pray regularly as an expression of our faith.

We must believe that prayers get answered, otherwise we would not pray. It is Christ's promise.

*Ask, and it will be given to you; seek, and you will find; knock, and it will be opened to you. For everyone who asks receives, and the one who seeks finds, and to the one who knocks it will be opened.  Matt 7:7-8*

There are two types of prayer: outer and inner.

## Outer Prayer

To pray, we go to a house of worship. Places of worship have rituals that enhance our awareness of the presence of God. We prepare for prayer by either not doing anything special, or we cleanse ourselves, kneel down, and we put our hands together. We utter our prayers with or without much thought or feeling. Often, words flow out without emotion. Words without intent and feeling are powerless. Outer prayer can be habitual or out of necessity. Most outer prayers are scheduled, in public, with a group and often directed by the clergy.

## Inner Prayer

Inner prayer follows the teachings of Christ on how and where to pray.

> *But whenever you pray, go into your inner room, close the door, and pray to your Father in secret. And your Father, who sees in secret, will reward you. And when you pray, do not heap up empty phrases as the Gentiles do, for they think that they will be heard for their many words. Do not be like them, for your Father knows what you need before you ask him.*   *Matt 6:6-8*

In the King's James version of the Bible, the inner room is replaced by a closet.

> *But thou, when thou prayest, enter into thy closet, and when thou hast shut thy door, pray to thy Father which is in secret; and thy Father which seeth in secret shall reward thee openly. But when ye pray, use not vain repetitions, as the heathen do: for they think that they shall be heard for their much speaking. Be not ye therefore like unto them: for your Father knoweth what things ye have need of, before ye ask him. Matt 6:6-8 (KJV)*

The above quotes give us the formula for successful prayer:

1. Enter the closet or the inner room;
2. Shut the door;
3. Pray in secret;
4. Utter the word;
5. Seek, knock and ask;
6. No vain repetitions; and
7. Our needs are already known.

## 1. Entering The Closet

To pray, we enter our "closet."
A command by Christ to set aside a private, sacred space where we can be alone physically, mentally and spiritually. The closet is a metaphor for personal space. It could be a physical, mental or spiritual space.

**Physical space**: this can be a tiny space, a literal closet big enough for a small table. On this table we place a large mirror, a candle and incense. We retreat to this place, preferably on a regular basis to shut out the world and commune with deity through our inner self.

**Mental space**: we recollect and vividly imagine a beautiful garden, a sea-shore, a mountain resort or any gorgeous place we have seen or visited at some time.

**Spiritual space**: Any sacred place will do. This can be a church, cathedral, mosque, synagogue, or any place of worship. The best spiritual space is a heart full of love and devotion.

## 2. Shutting The Door

We isolate our minds by shutting the door on any intrusion. We leave behind all thoughts of the material world. Being in the presence of God with one and only one thought – we are in sacred space.

## Praying – Physical Space

Once we enter our physical sacred space, we close the door to the outer world. We light the candle, burn the incense and gaze into the mirror looking intently into our eyes. Alternatively, or additionally, we can read an inspirational message. Once finished, we put the book away and we reflect on the subject. We pray, meditate and radiate healing thoughts to anyone who is sick or needs help.

## Praying – Mental Space

Mentally, we detach from our surroundings. We recall the beautiful scenery. We take a deep breath, hold it for a few seconds, then we exhale. We repeat this a few times. With each inhalation, we draw in life energy. With each holding of the breath, we visualize an exchange taking place – vital life force for toxins. With each exhalation, we release the accumulated toxins from the body. The toxins are physical, emotional (negative emotions) and mental (negative thoughts).

## Praying – Spiritual Space

We enter the sacred space, the heart. We mentally detach from our surroundings. We close our eyes. We realize that we are in the presence of God. We vibrate with love and compassion. We commune with the spark of divinity within. We become still and we listen intently.

## 3. Praying In Secret

We do not pray to impress or show off. Praying in secret is praying in our hearts and with the full participation of our minds. Our thoughts are pure. Our feelings and emotions are of gratitude and love.

## 4. Uttering The Word

Uttering the word must be full of feeling, sincerity and intention. It should be clear and to the point. Uttering is expressing. It can be mental visualization or actual words. It is an emotional outpouring from our being.

## 5. Seeking, Knocking And Asking

We dive deep to connect with the spark of divinity within. Our seeking is in earnest. Our knocking is persistent and demanding. Our asking is a pleading. We flood ourselves with Love, Beauty and Joy. We are in the presence of God.

## 6. No Vain Repetitions

We plead our case, vividly, intensely and passionately.
Our communication is clear, direct and to the point. No need for empty repetitions. God is not deaf or hard of understanding. What we express is mostly gratitude.

## 7. Our Needs Are Already Known

We ask for guidance. We request a solution. We plead for the next step we need to take. Our prayer is a formality. God can read our hearts and minds. We pray to commune and to express gratitude, for our needs are already known.

## Expressing Gratitude

Once we express gratitude, we are done. We let go and revert back to our normal state. Gratitude, even though not required, goes a long way in keeping the lines of communication open. We should mostly pray to be thankful for our blessings. If we need something, we can pray and ask for it. Instead of asking for material things, we should ask for the wisdom to know what we need to do ourselves.

# Secret of Prayer

Christ promised us that:

> *If ye shall ask any thing in my name, I will do it.*     John
> *14:14*

Christ is life, love and the way. Asking in His name is assuming His qualities while communicating through prayer.

He also promised:

> *For where two or three are gathered together in my*
> *name, there am I in the midst of them. Matt 18:20*

What did He mean by two or three? Did He mean people? Do we enter the closet with another? Thousands of people have gathered together to pray over hundreds of years. Did their prayers get answered?

The above quote is a formula where numbers one, two and three have a spiritual significance.

Number one represents the supplicant with a need or a request.

Number two represents the object of the prayer, the purpose of the prayer.

If we follow the 7-steps of inner prayer, our prayer will be heard and answered. However, it is number three that guarantees the success of our prayer. Items one and two must unite, join together in a holy matrimony. This union however, often requires a catalyst before it can take place.

The third element, the catalyst, is the zeal, emotional intensity and the passion of the one in prayer. This catalyst is the spark needed to fuse the seeker with that which is sought, the supplicant with divinity. This catalyst is a fiery spark in the heart of the supplicant. It insures the union of the one in prayer with divinity. Once the seeker and that which is sought are united, the result follows automatically and our prayers are answered.

## How Prayers are Answered

There are three factors we need to keep in mind:

1.  First, there is a field that we exist in. It is like the ocean for the fish and the air for the birds. This field permeates all. It is within us and without us and is the medium that connects us all. It is into this medium that we pour out our hearts when we pray.

2.  Second, the language of communication in this field is clear intent with emotional energy and vibrant visualizations. This is the energy of our being. It is what we radiate. It is our magnetic field.

These two factors are based on laws of physics and spirituality.

**Fields of Force:**

*So far we have treated the gravitational attraction between masses as a direct interaction between the particles involved. Similarly, we have assumed that electric charges exert forces directly on each other. This kind of direct interaction between bodies is often called action at a distance. We shall now introduce a modification of this point of view that has proved to be enormously important in theory and very fruitful in application. In this modification we suppose that the space surrounding a mass (or charge) is somehow different from what it would be in the absence of the mass (or charge). In principle, this "distortion" extends throughout all space; in practice it often becomes quite negligible a short distance*

*from the source mass or source charge. We call the distortion associated with mass a gravitational field and that associated with charge an electric field. This distortion, or field, cannot be seen by the eye, but it is real nonetheless and can be measured.*
Borowitz and Bornstein, *A Contemporary View of Elementary Physics.*

Highlighting the important sections from above:

1. *The space surrounding a mass (or charge) is somehow different from what it would be in the absence of the mass (or charge);*

2. *This "distortion" extends throughout all space (becoming negligible the further from the source).*

In other words, whether we know it or not, the fact that we occupy space, we distort the energy field around us. How far our influence extends, depends on our charge, our magnetism, – how emotionally charged our visualizations are. By simply changing our charge through our emotions, we change the nature of the field. In other words, by simply changing ourselves, we impact the entire field.

There is a third aspect to this field that is not currently supported by conventional science.

3. This field is aware and intelligent and it responds in kind. It has no judgment and does not know good from evil. It is simply a mirror that reflects back to us what we project into it.

In other words, our attitudes, expectations, and beliefs play a major role in determining the type of distortion we cause in the field. If our charge is "good", or positive, then we affect this field in a good or positive way and the good or positive comes back to us. If, on the other hand, our charge is negative, then we affect the field in a bad or negative way and evil or negative comes back to us. For most, this field is neutral.

What is a field that is aware, intelligent and responds in kind? **It is consciousness**.

In summary:

1. There is an energy field that contains all;
2. We communicate with this field through our state of being;
3. This field responds in kind. What we send out comes back to us. What we sow, we reap.

Having this knowledge is powerful. We can use it to transform ourselves from helpless and weak beings – Children of Man, to beings of light, knowledge and wisdom – Children of God.

To connect to God or the spark of divinity within, we enter the field. We charge ourselves with the highest loving emotions we can muster. The nature of God is Love, Beauty and Joy. When we assume these qualities, we establish contact. We can then state our request with confidence, express gratitude and we let go. We revert back to our normal self.

A few things to keep in mind:

1. We can engage in prayers of adoration as often as we like. We cannot ask God for everything we need. God is not a genie;

2. We must work for, earn and mold our own lives;

3. There is one God and this God is **everyone's** God and not just ours. In other words, this God cannot and will not favor one child over another. Hence, we cannot ask for favors at the expense of others. There are no "chosen" groups in the eyes of God. All are equally loved. Instead of material things, we should ask for spiritual gifts – how to be compassionate, tolerant and forgiving;

4. We must be self-reliant. Often, not getting something is an incentive to try harder and be more determined. We are expected to do all we can for ourselves and only ask for help after we have exhausted all available options;

5. What we should ask for is the wisdom of what we need to do next;

6. We should always be thankful for what we already have. Gratitude and appreciation are essential for the enjoyment of what life has to offer;

7. Our state of being is a prayer. Let us endeavor to be our best at all times.

## Constant Prayer

We are always praying whether we know it or not. We are radiating our prayers as the state of our being. Our thoughts, coupled by our emotions, determine what we transmit. These are picked up by the "field". We attract to ourselves in accordance with the nature of our being. What we sow in thoughts and emotions, we reap in experiences.

Finally, when two or more individuals work together as one, they can achieve far more than any person can achieve alone. Working together is like the parts of a car assembled together. While separate, the parts are incapable of motion, but when put together a car can take us to places. The more individuals are united in purpose, harmoniously cooperating, the more benefits are derived for all to enjoy. This is clearly demonstrated in marriage, where 2 individuals working together harmoniously, build a life of comfort and joy that neither alone would be able to achieve separately.

Working together in the spirit of love is prayer.

# SECRET OF SLEEP AND DREAMS

*Each day is a little life: every waking and rising*
*a little birth, every fresh morning a little youth,*
*every going to rest and sleep a little death.*
*—Arthur Schopenhauer*

W e are most vulnerable when we are asleep. We are helpless at the mercy of anyone who could do us harm. Natural selection should have deselected sleep as part of our makeup. It did not. Why? Why must we sleep?

Sleep reveals a hidden aspect of our reality. We function in three bodies and in three worlds: physical, astral and spiritual. Each body must have its turn in being active and in the forefront. When we are awake, the physical body is active and the conscious mind is in the forefront. When we sleep and dream, the astral body is active, and the subconscious mind takes center stage. During deep and dreamless sleep, the spiritual body is active and the superconscious is in the forefront.

In our daily sleep, we dream. In dreaming, we experience the contents of our minds. Desires, memories and intentions are acted out. During deep, dreamless sleep we enter the spiritual world and are immersed in the superconscious where we receive answers to questions, find solutions to problems, attend classes and are in the presence of masters. Unless our spiritual faculties are developed, we do not remember our spiritual experiences. Upon awakening, the conscious mind takes over and we forget what we experienced during sleep.

Sleep reveals the nature of our reality. It is a reflection of the nature of life in general. We sleep and we wake up. Then we sleep again and again we wake up, repeatedly, until one day we do not wake up – we die. Sleep reveals three aspects about the nature of life.

First, life is cyclic. Our daily cycle of sleep and wakefulness is a micro-indicator of a macro cycle of living and dying. We are born, live and then we die repeating this cycle through reincarnation. We are eternal. Cyclic birth and death are how we manage our eternity. This is enacted daily by the cycles of wakefulness and sleep.

Second, we live as if we will never die. Sleep is a reminder that, in fact, we will die. Our nightly sleep is a mini-death, a reminder that one day we will transition to the longer sleep – death. Just as we cannot avoid sleep, we cannot escape death. Anyone who sleeps will eventually die. Death is not an enemy. It is not something that we should fear. It is a gateway that we go through as we transition from one reality to the next.

Third, life as a whole is a dream. We are asleep and dreaming and do not realize it. Just as we sleep and dream believing that to be real until we wake up, so it is with living. We live experiencing events and people as real until we die and wake up on the other side. Then we realize that this life was also a dream. It was a drama played on the larger stage of Earth.

## Life is a Dream

Where has the time gone?

We are born, and before we know it, we are going to school. And before we know it, we are grown up, married and have children.

And before we know it, if we are fortunate, we have grandchildren.

And before we know it, we look in the mirror and we see that we have aged.

Where has the time gone?

Looking back on the events of our lives, we realize that life is a dream.

## Secret of Dreams

*Life is a dream for the wise, a game for the fool, a comedy for the rich, a tragedy for the poor.*     *Sholom Aleichem*

1. It is frustrating to dream but not be able to remember it. This is because all dreams are mental creations. Unless our ability to mentally create is well-developed, the images created dissolve quickly and are no more. Individual creations are often feeble and do not endure. Just as we cannot hold onto our dreams, we cannot hold onto our daily events. Just as very few dreams are remembered, very few wakeful events are worth remembering. Nothing is real and lasting except for the dreamer and the witness – our I Am.

2. Dreams are real while we experience them. That is why we react to them. Upon awakening, we dismiss them as unreal and soon we forget them altogether. So it is with our lives. As we live, we give value and importance to the events of our lives. We react to them. We are happy when things go our way and we are miserable when they do not. Once we wake up to the true nature of reality, we realize that the events of our lives are fleeting mirages just as dreams

are. And just as dreams are an arena for dramas from which we can learn and benefit, so are the events of our lives. They too are dramas for our entertainment, education and an opportunity to learn and to contribute. We need to wake up from all dreams, night and day dreams.

3. Dreams just happen. We enter them and we leave them by "accident". So is our entry and exit from life. It seems to just happen "randomly" as well. Yet, nothing simply happens. Dreams and events are the results of our deep-seated conscious and subconscious desires and needs. There are always forces at play behind the scenes.

4. A dream is always a segment, a portion, an act, never a complete story with a meaningful beginning or an end. This is a reflection of our lives. It is difficult to make much sense of our lives because we are witnessing an isolated segment, one lifetime in an eternal chain of lifetimes.

## Lucid Dreams and Lucid Living

*Those who dream by day are cognizant of many things which escape those who dream only by night.*
*Edgar Allan Poe*

Lucid dreams are when we are awake while dreaming. This happens when we enter the borderline state and remain lucid. The difference between a normal dream and a lucid dream is the level of our awareness and the degree of control we have over the characters and the events. While we have no control in normal dreams, in lucid dreams, we direct the unfoldment of the events and the behavior of the characters.

Lucid dreams are visualizations with a purpose. It is to create the realities we want to experience at a later date. Keeping in mind that events and characters are ephemeral whether in dreams or daily life, we can mentally create anything we desire. Everything is like a dream – vaporous and transitory. There is no enduring reality other than the soul. Since all realities end up in the mind as mental images and memories, we can mentally create our chosen realities and release them in the cosmic mind. At the appropriate time, if unopposed, these visualizations will manifest as physical realities.

To master lucid dreaming, we must become adept at lucid visualization. To start, we must decide the type of life we want in the future. Next, we visualize that life in great detail. We imbue it with emotion, vivid colors, sounds and movement. We picture ourselves in the scene living our desired life. We repeat this exercise as often as we like. Releasing it at the end, we trust that the cosmic will fulfill our desires. We can use this exercise to create the relationships, finances and abundant health that we want. We can even use this visualization to attract friends, clients and a spouse. Mentally creating through visualization is one of the greatest powers we have. The secret of success lies in assuming and living the future we want, right now.

It is more important to be lucid while living than while dreaming. By acting instead of reacting, by choosing to not be drawn into ongoing dramas, and by detaching and seeing the larger picture, we can remain lucid. If we live without awareness and exercise no control over the events of our lives, we are asleep and dreaming regardless of whether we are in bed or up and about. Lucid living is the key. Living with lucidity, we are aware, awake and conscious. We remember that everything is impermanent. We detach, observe, evaluate and act only to make a positive contribution.

We are dreaming any time we are "asleep". This can happen in the daytime when we are so called wide-awake or when we are in bed at night. We are awake when we act with awareness, intelligence and intention. Otherwise, we are asleep. Being asleep, we react out of habit, get caught up in life's dramas and follow the crowd without questioning. Wakeful living entails being in charge of our lives, seeing dramas for what they are and not being pulled into them. We can guide our ship skillfully on the oceans of life without being influenced by the storms going on around us.

## Pleasant Dreams

Some dreams are pleasant while others are not.
Some dream figures are heroes, others villains, most are innocent bystanders.
We watch the drama unfold before our eyes as if we are in a theater.
At times we rejoice and at other times we dread. Mostly, we are indifferent.
We lose track of time. We are completely drawn into the ongoing drama.
Then it all ends and we wake up.
It was all a dream, a drama played out on the stage of our minds.
Nothing was real. Puff and everything is gone. Nothing endures.

What if our everyday dramas are like our dreams?
What if the people in life are actors just like in our dreams?
What if no one is good and no one is evil?
What if everyone is playing out their role to perfection?
What if our choice is to get pulled in and react, detach and observe, or act wisely when necessary?
What if this is the real purpose of our freedom of choice?
What if we train ourselves to view the events of our lives as short-lived dreams?
What if we force ourselves to be awake and remain lucid?

What if we realize that it is all for our entertainment, education and a means to observe, contribute and make a difference?

What if we understand that there have to be heroes and villains, but only as dream figures?

What if we live expecting surprises and unexpected turns of events as part of the drama?

Why do we have those in our lives who know how to push our buttons?

Are they our challenges, the obstacle in our path to grow and mature?

Is it possible they provide us the opportunity to practice detachment, a chance to simply observe and resist being pulled in?

Is it possible that those who know how to push our buttons are the "enemies" that we must love as Christ asked us to?

Is it possible that they are friends in disguise, acting as thorns in our side to give us the opportunity we need to practice detachment?

Mastering detachment requires practice, awareness and persistence.

It requires staying awake and lucid.

Detachment is a hard lesson to master, but well worth it.

Staying awake is not easy, but it can be done.

What if what is taking place is difficult to bear?

What if we say to ourselves, "This too shall pass"?

What power would that be?

What wisdom?

The veil would lift.

We would live life with eyes wide open.

We would see clearly, hear distinctly, feel genuinely and we would make a positive contribution.

# SECRET OF THE BREATH

*Breathe. Let go. And remind yourself that this very
moment is the only one you know you have for sure.*
*—Oprah Winfrey*

We can survive for a few weeks without food, a few
days without water and only a few minutes
without air. Why is breathing so critical to life? Is
it only because of the oxygen?

We live because we breathe. Without the breath, we resort back
to earth, dust to dust.

> *And the LORD God formed man of the dust of the
> ground, and breathed into his nostrils the breath of life;
> and man became a living soul. Gen 2:7*

The breath of God is life force. It is what animates us and
makes us living beings.

> *The Spirit of God hath made me, and the breath of the
> Almighty hath given me life. Job 33:4*

This breath is the same breath that is in all living beings,
especially the animals.

> *I said in my heart with regard to the children of man
> that God is testing them that they may see that they
> themselves are but beasts. For what happens to the
> children of man and what happens to the beasts is the
> same; as one dies, so dies the other. They all have the*

*same breath, and man has no advantage over the beasts,*
*for all is vanity. All go to one place. All are from the dust,*
*and to dust all return. Who knows whether the spirit of*
*man goes upward and the spirit of the beast goes down*
*into the earth?          Eccl 3: 18-21*

To be alive is to be aware, but not necessarily conscious. Consciousness is a higher faculty. While awareness is of the here and the now, consciousness can project into the past and the future. Living beings are aware because of the animating breath, the source of the life force. While our life comes from the breath, our consciousness is from our soul. Initially, humans had only life and awareness, but not consciousness. They lacked experience. They were innocent, pure, virginal, naïve, not knowing good from evil. Their eyes were "closed." They were naked and did not know it – naked in that they lacked a spiritual body.

There is an important distinction between humans and animals – we have consciousness and freedom of choice. The moment humans exercised their freedom, decided, acted and experienced, their spiritual bodies began to form and they had the beginnings of soul and consciousness. Awareness of the external became internalized into self-awareness. Their eyes opened and they could see, reason and decide. Slowly, over time, the spiritual body will grow and with it our soul will blossom into the Holy Spirit – our ultimate spiritual body bathed in the Christ Consciousness.

*And when he had said this, he breathed on them, and*
*saith unto them, Receive ye the Holy Ghost. John 20:22*

## Secret of the Breath

Breathing is the most obvious aspect of being in a physical body. Breathing is inhalation and exhalation. Inhalation is confinement, a gathering of what was dispersed. It is entrapment. Exhalation is the spreading out into space of what was confined. It is letting go. It is dispersion and freedom.

Breathing is not just inhalation and exhalation. It is also an exchange. It is receiving one thing and giving back something different in return. We inhale vitalizing life force, and in return, we exhale waste. When we inhale, we gather in and hold onto. When we exhale, we let go and we allow dispersion.

What is true about us, a microcosm, is true of the macrocosm as well. It is not only us that is breathing, so is the cosmos.

The explosion of the Big Bang into activity was an exhalation, a letting go, an expansion and a freedom. We are currently in the exchange mode. Nature is organizing, becoming more complex, efficient and aware. We are experiencing, learning, growing and maturing. At some point, the exhalation will come to an end and the inhalation will begin. This will be the beginning of an implosion, a contraction toward confinement and a gathering. The universes will revert back to a singularity. Then another exhalation will take place. These processes are ongoing, like the figure eight representing eternity. Inhalation, exchange, followed by exhalation, in us and in the cosmos. The simple act of breathing by a human is a reflection of what is going on in the cosmos.

First we inhale, then we exchange, and finally we exhale.

The cosmic, on the other hand, exhales first, then exchanges, and finally inhales.

We started our journey as an exhalation of Spirit or Pneuma. We left our source and are in the world. We are exchanging ignorance for wisdom, stagnation for growth, selfishness for altruism and childishness for maturity. At some point, it will be time for us to be inhaled back into our source. At that point, we will be on our way back home.

The story of the Prodigal Son is our story. While the Prodigal

Son, our lower self, separated and is in the physical world for exchange (learning, growing and contributing), the other son, our Higher Self, remains with the Father. While our lower self is having earthly experiences, our Higher Self is always with God.

These two sons are two aspects of the same person. Part of us is asleep, lost in the world, wasting our resources on trivia, while our Higher Self is awake with the Father looking after us. While physically we are searching and toiling to amass goods and wealth, our Higher Self is whispering to us: **Don't you know that all I have is yours?**

We have left home and the company of our Father. We are on our earthly journey. We have forgotten who we are. Once we remember, we will be on our way back home to our Father once more.

Leaving home as an exhalation, we separate and we fall asleep to our true nature. We are on our own. When we return home, we wake up. We remember. While asleep we dream of glory. We seek pleasures that we cannot hold onto. We waste our precious resources. Then, one day when we hit bottom, we wake up and our journey back home begins in earnest.

# SECRET OF THE ALCHEMISTS

*Alchemy is a kind of philosophy: a kind of thinking that leads to a way of understanding.*
*—Marcel Duchamp*

Alchemy is transmutation. The ultimate purpose of Alchemy is the creation of the philosopher's stone which is the agent of such transmutation. There are two forms of Alchemy – physical and spiritual. Physical Alchemy is the attempt to successfully transmute base matter such as tin into gold. Spiritual Alchemy is the transformation of our vices into virtues and the creation of our spiritual bodies.

In the Hermetic tradition, Alchemy has three stages:

## 1. Nigredo (blackening)

This is where we search for, isolate and work on our base or "black" matter.
In physical Alchemy, this is usually tin.
In spiritual Alchemy, these are our vices and our negative thoughts, feelings, and intentions.

## 2. Albedo (whitening)

In physical Alchemy, we expose tin to the intense heat of the sun to change its physical configuration.

In spiritual Alchemy, we spiritualize the material by transmuting our vices into virtues. By nurturing and progressively growing our spiritual body, we become white – enlightened.

## 3. Rubedo (reddening)

In physical Alchemy, the philosopher's stone and gold are created.
In spiritual Alchemy, the spiritual body is fashioned. We become golden like the sun. By radiating the magnetic power of the spiritual body, we function like the sun as enlightened beings.

### *Opus Magnum*

Our Opus Magnus is our greatest creation. It is what defines us. To create our Opus Magnus, we must first seek that which is precious. Our most precious aspect resides within us as a spark of divinity. This is our spiritual body in its infancy. We must set this spark ablaze. Discovering, nurturing and developing this spark is our utmost priority – our Opus Magnum. We must seek to develop our spiritual bodies above all else. Using spiritual Alchemy, we can spiritualize the physical, transmute our vices into virtues and use our senses to experience and express Love, Beauty and Joy. This transformation does not have to happen all at once. We can take small steps in the right direction. We can continue to practice until it is habitual and instinctive. With habit, everything is easy.

Alchemists hoped to create the philosopher's stone. With this stone, they believed they could transmute anything into gold. Gold is symbolic of what we deem precious. Our most precious aspect is our spiritual body.

The philosopher's stone is the toolset of our mind. The mind is the greatest transmuting agent. Using our mind, we can select our thoughts and decide how we feel. We can create habits that serve us, attitudes and expectations that keep us healthy and happy. We can change the nature of our experiences. This is our greatest endeavor – our Opus Magnum.

> The Great Work is, before all things, the creation of man by himself, that is to say, the full and entire conquest of his faculties and his future; it is especially the perfect emancipation of his will.          Eliphas Levi

The greatest work confronting us is to work on ourselves. By transmuting our base elements, our vices, into noble elements or virtues, we develop our spiritual bodies. We create our Opus Magnus – our pure, beautiful, shining spiritual self.

## The Alchemical Wedding of the King and Queen

The ancients symbolically alluded to the necessity of creating the spiritual body as the allegory of the Alchemical Wedding of the King and the Queen. The officiant at this wedding is the sun.

Alchemy: Transformation
Wedding: Union
King: Mind
Queen: Heart
Sun: Officiant, witness, agent of the transformation

When the king and the queen unite within us in the sacred rite of marriage, the spiritual union of the heart and the mind takes place. Officiated and witnessed by the Sun, which is pure love, both the king and the queen are transformed. The merging of the two gives birth to the infant spiritual body. In Alchemy, the spiritual body is symbolized as both male and female, a hermaphrodite.

## The Symbolic Meaning of the Rosy Cross

The Rosicrucian Order, AMORC is an ancient, non-sectarian, spiritual organization dedicated to the investigation, study and practical application of natural and spiritual laws. Its purpose is to further the evolution of humanity through the development of the full potential of each individual. The goal is to enable everyone to live in harmony with the creative, cosmic forces for the attainment of health, happiness and peace.[3] By understanding and mastering natural and spiritual laws, and by awakening and cultivating our spiritual faculties, individuals gain mastery of their circumstances. The most important symbol of the Rosicrucians is the Rosy Cross.

Cross: two bars, horizontal and vertical intersecting
    Horizontal bar: Heart, feminine qualities
    Vertical bar: Mind, masculine qualities
Point of Intersection: Union and the manifestation of the Rose
Rose: Christ Consciousness, spiritual body, soul

When the vertical "male" and the horizontal "female" within us unite in the sacred rite of marriage, the spiritual union of the heart and the mind takes place. Officiated and witnessed by the Light (Christ or the Sun), both are transformed through the agency of love. The merging of the two gives birth to the Rose, our spiritual body, a hermaphrodite, both male and female.

Initially, the rose is a rosebud. Through the trials and the tribulations of living and experiencing, our eyes open and with it the rosebud acquires more petals and begins to unfold and blossom. The wafting perfume of the Rose is an attribute of the developing spiritual body. It is our magnetic personality.

# SECRET OF THE MILLENNIUM

*You cannot have a positive life and a negative mind.*
*– Joyce Meyer*

There are many forms of power. Bodily might, wealth or position of authority are external, physical powers. They are used for work, to coerce or to influence. Love, compassion and knowledge are internal, spiritual powers. They are used to create, to heal and to transform. Will power is an internal power we can use to bring about desired changes in our lives. We have an inexhaustible supply of will power. We are powerful, but only if we know how to best use what powers we have. By merely intending and willing to change our mindset, we can shape our future.

*The greatest revolution in our time is the discovery that human beings, by changing the inner attitude of their minds, can change the outer aspects of their lives.*
*William James*

This is the secret of the millennium. **By changing our inner attitude, we can change the outer aspects of our lives.** We do this by willing to do so. Willing and acting in our best interests is the best use of our freedom of choice.

Accepting responsibility for our health and happiness is a first step. We must follow it with intelligent living. Using our mental tools to facilitate our lives is intelligent indeed. Even though we do not have complete control over all that we experience, we must manage what we can, especially the use of our time. Even though environment and genetics play major roles in our lives, we can influence our genetics by what we consume. By using positive emotions, employing visualization and by adapting our environment through the choices we make, we can modify outcomes.

> *"God made the world; but He does not make your world. He provides the raw materials, and out of them every man selects what he wants and builds an individual world for himself.*
>
> *The fool looks over the wealth of material provided, and selects a few plates of ham and eggs, a few pairs of trousers, a few dollar bills---and is satisfied.*
> *The wise man builds his world out of wonderful sunsets, and thrilling experiences, and the song of stars, and romance and miracles.*
> *Nothing wonderful ever happens in the life of the fool... an electric light is simply an electric light; a telephone is only a telephone---nothing unusual at all.*
>
> *But the wise man never ceases to wonder how a tiny speck of seed, apparently dead and buried, can produce a beautiful yellow flower. He never lifts a telephone receiver or switches on an electric light without a certain feeling of awe."* Bruce Barton

Attitudes are important. They are influenced by habits on one hand and expectations on the other. These we can control by choosing what we think and how we feel. Thoughts and feelings are the threads out of which we weave the tapestry of our lives.

Consider the following:

1. Every time we think, we are thinking in our minds – a

receptive, pliable field that is in contact with universal mind. Thinking and feeling influences the field in which all exist;

2. Conscious thoughts, through repetition, coalesce into habits;

3. Emotion-based thoughts set forces into motion which impact the body and affect our behavior;

4. Emotion-based thoughts are polarized. They attract and repel based on their nature. Positive thoughts attract the positive and negative thoughts attract the negative;

5. The mind is the internal soil where we drop our thoughts as seeds. The environment is the external soil where we scatter our spoken words as seeds. A thought and a word, once released into the proper environment, take root, associate, grow and attract into our life the experiences we go through.

We are not destined to know the far future. Our responsibility is knowing what the next step is for us to take. If we focus on what we can do right now, and do it well, everything else falls into place. We do not always get what we want. What we get is what we need based on who and what we are. If we guard our thoughts, watch how we feel, act intelligently and most importantly, clarify our intentions, then we are doing our part exceedingly well.

> *"..that the moment when one definitely commits oneself, then providence moves too. All sorts of things occur to help one that would have never otherwise occurred. A whole stream of events issue from the decision, raising in one's favor all manner of unforeseen incidents and meetings and material assistance which no man could have dreamt would have come his way."* The Scottish

*Himalayan Expediiton  W. H, Murry*

Our minds house the greatest arsenal of tools anyone can have. These are our thoughts, habits, attitudes, expectations, beliefs, will, intention and knowledge. Mastering the use of these tools is the secret to success and happiness. It is also the shortest path to any goal we set our hearts and minds on. Our minds can keep us healthy or make us sick, provide us with the energy we need or withhold it from us. Our minds can transform our earthly life into a garden of Eden or into a desert and a hell. What we focus on we empower. What we use, grows and multiplies. That which we ignore, withers away and atrophies. It is a valuable skill to know which tool to use and for what purpose. Mastering the use of our minds for specific, thought-out purposes is possessing the secret key of the millennium. Perhaps the first millennium was that of hard labor, the second millennium was that of industrialization, but the third millennium is the Millennium of the Mind.

# CONCLUSION

I love science and deeply appreciate all the wonderful discoveries and products that make our lives simple, enjoyable and healthy. Our living should be evidence-based. Science is a tool we should use to continuously improve our lives. Yet, science is not an exclusive tool. It is not the only source of knowledge. There is also personal experience.

My life is not what it is because of my DNA, environment, the microbes within me, my brain, hormones, abilities or my subconscious. These are critical, but are not the only forces that shaped me. Synchronicities and listening to The Voice Within played critical roles. These are external factors that I had no control over. We can influence and alter what aspects of our DNA get expressed through drugs and diet. We can alter our internal and external environments. We can change the microbes within us via diet and drugs. We can alter our brain and its neural connections through education, habits and activity. We can influence our hormones through drugs and diet. We can also add to our skills and abilities. What we cannot do is plan for synchronicities and cause The Voice Within to speak to us.

My life is evidence-based. I can never deny The Voice Within thundering within me during critical junctures in my life. I married my wife, not because of the image I had of what type of a wife I wanted, but because of The Voice Within. I did not join the US Army because I love being a soldier, quite the opposite. I had fear of the military. I joined the army because I listened to The Voice Within guiding me to do so. There are several other instances where I listened to and acted upon The Voice Within. These were the best decisions of my life.

Synchronicities play a major role in my life. A few could be explained away as random occurrences. I have too many of them to attribute to chance. Furthermore, how would I account for inspiration? This and my other books are not the product of my skills and labor alone. Inspiration plays a major part in my writings and presentations. Where do ideas and solutions totally unknown to me come from? My subconscious? How did novel ideas and solutions end up in my subconscious in the first place? Do my neurons have an autonomous ability to reason, analyze, recombine data and create new meanings on their own? Are they self-conscious? Can they see the future? I doubt it.

The Voice Within, synchronicities and novel ideas come from a realm beyond space and time. Their source must be able to see the future in order to guide me on the path to the best future outcome. My guide and my source is my Higher Self.

I was not always a believer in the existence of God, the spiritual or the soul. My personal experiences led me to change my mind. Having had several out-of-the-body experiences and a near-death experience (described in my book: A Passion for Living) altered what I accepted and believed. Defining God as Love, Beauty and Joy made me a believer in God.

In college, I learned that genes have an imperative to survive and to procreate. Where does this imperative come from? If survival is the name of the game, why do we die? Our cells replicate. Our bodies are renewed. Yet, we succumb to disease and we die. Why do some individuals sacrifice themselves to ensure the survival of others? Isn't their survival more important?

Why is procreation vital for our genes? Are we driven just to ensure the survival of our genes? If so, why do we not die after we procreate, like the salmon do? If survival and procreation are imperative, why has humanity been on a path of war and destruction for so long? Wouldn't cooperation make far more sense for survival and procreation?

There is a simpler way to survive and to procreate – the way of bacteria. They are better at survival and procreation. While we pass only 50% of our genes to the next generation, bacteria pass 100% of their genes. Even though mixing genes provides better survival for future generations, why care? Can genes foretell what the future holds?

Could it be that our imperative is not only to survive, but to experience; and the sex drive is not only to procreate, but to bring people together so they share, cooperate and commune? Is it possible that intimacy is more important than sex?

We do not get married for sex and procreation alone. These are the outer aspects. The inner aspects of sex and marriage are intimacy and the merging of two incomplete selves into a union of one whole being. In marriage, we shed our ego self and form a union, a more complete being. As we mature, we progress from the need for sex to the desire for intimacy. We value cuddling, hugging and being together. Our need for sex is for a relatively short duration compared to our desire to be together with our beloved. Perhaps the driving force of life is not survival and procreation, but rather love, belonging and intimacy.

And how do we settle on our mates? Is it due to pheromones secreted by our intestinal bacteria? Are we pairing with another of a complimentary immune system? Are our attractions based on subconscious desires? Are our inclinations and relationships governed by chemicals emitted by our bodies?

Perhaps. What I discovered is that we are attracted to mates who provide us the best opportunities to face our shortcomings so that we may grow and mature. Even our children expose us to what we need to work on in order to improve.

We are not mere biological machines. We are human beings who seek meaning to our lives and value from our activities. We abhor boredom and we crave social interactions. We have souls that soar with the sound of music, get intoxicated by love and transformed by beauty and joy. Because we recognize Love, Beauty and Joy externally, we must have these within us. These are elements of the divine within us – our soul.

We are human beings before we are Americans, Buddhists, male or female. We are not here to serve a system, be it religion, science, philosophy or even spirituality. They are here to serve us, not the other way around.

Our personal experiences are valuable. We must evaluate and use them as tools to discover ourselves. We are tool users. We should use science and our other tools to live healthy, happy and productive lives.

We are not here to abide by or defend religious dictates that do not measure up to our standards. Loving each other, especially our children, is more important than any tradition, custom or authority dictates. People are more important than systems. Other people's happiness should supersede our beliefs. We created systems to streamline our lives and have order and meaning, not to be enslaved by them.

It is about time we live our lives unencumbered by falsehoods such as sin or why we are here. We are here to develop our spiritual bodies and to help others do the same. We should review our beliefs and cull anything that is not in accordance with how we want our lives and the planet to be. We should discard any references in our holy books to violence, discrimination, favoritism and exceptionalism. Our religions should be based on love and the brotherhood of all. We should espouse forgiveness, tolerance, acceptance and appreciation of each other. We should not assume that our religious beliefs are superior. We should consider what others have to offer. There might be value in what they have discovered.

There is absolutely no real difference between people based on race, sex or nationality. The only differences are mental, emotional and spiritual values. Some people are more mature than others. That's it. We have been where others are. As children, we were immature. Just as we outgrew our childishness, so will everyone else. Give others a chance. Even better, lend them a helping hand. We received help when we needed it. It is our time to render service to others.

Our obligation is to ourselves, family, friends, society and the planet. We must continue to learn, to grow and to contribute. The more we give of ourselves, the better we will feel. We are not obligated to worship any deity or restrict ourselves to one method of discovering facts and truth. God does not need anything from us. Science is a tool to enrich our lives. We have what it takes to do what we are here for. All we need is courage and determination to be fearless. Knowing ourselves intimately, loving ourselves unconditionally and expressing ourselves fearlessly is the way to go. These three simple steps can change not only the trajectory of our lives, but the course of history as well. Having freedom of choice is useless unless we use it to serve our interests and to help others. Let us choose to live up to our potential and make a difference in our lives and in the world.

---

[1] For a detailed description of this and other incidents, please refer to my book: A Passion for Living and a path to meaning and joy.

[2] For a detailed description of the Higher Self, please refer to my book: Listening to the Voice Within.

[3] Paraphrased from The Mastery of Life booklet.

# ACKNOWLEDGEMENT

I am grateful to all those who helped make this book a reality. I would like to thank my wife Barbara for her review, editing and suggestions. I could not have written this book without her. Next, I would like to thank Joe Shammas for his suggestions and support. I would also like to acknowledge family and friends who supported me over the years, especially Leticia Aguilar, Vincent Eaglin, Mary Schaefer, Ann-Marie Johnson, Jeanette and Steve Pashigian, Peri, Serge and John Shammas.

# ABOUT THE AUTHOR

## Shahan Shammas

Shahan was born in Aleppo, Syria. At the age of 15, he went to Lebanon where he entered a monastery to study and prepare to be a monk. After two years in the monastery, he left to continue his education. Shahan graduated from the American University of Beirut with a Bachelor's degree in Biology. At the age of 24, Shahan left for the United States, became a US citizen after serving three years in the Army at the medical laboratory of Fort Meade, Md. After working as an Electron Microscopist at the Walter Reed Army Medical Center for 7 years, Shahan started a new career in Information Systems. He worked for the Treasury Department until he retired. After which, Shahan became a teacher at the Judy Hoyer Family Learning Center where he taught Life Skills to adults for ten years. Shahan's background is in the Sciences, Religion, Philosophy and Spirituality. Shahan has lectured extensively in the areas of acquiring knowledge, raising consciousness and actualizing the human potential.

# BOOKS BY THIS AUTHOR

## Mystery Solved! Human Immortality Revealed

What if suddenly we understood the mysteries of life and death? Why we were born? Why we age and die? Why we experience pain and suffer? Why does evil exist?

What if we knew that our birth was not an accident? That there is a plan for our lives and this plan is of our own choosing?

What if we knew why we are attracted to specific individuals, places and situations, but not by others?

What if we discovered that we have a soul and that this soul is of the nature of God? What if we had a better understanding of what this nature is?

Would any of this make a difference? How would having answers impact our lives?

The revelation I received can be yours. Peace, serenity and understanding await you. This book is based on personal experience and has the power to transform your life for the better.

# BOOKS BY THIS AUTHOR

## Listening To The Voice Within, Becoming Enlightened

What is one "gift" without which we cease to be human? Plants and animals do not have it. Only humans have it. Most do not appreciate this trademark of being human or use it effectively to advance their "Happiness Quotient." In fact, many use it to their detriment. We can learn to use this gift more effectively. It requires us to be fearless, open-minded and intent on improving our lot in life. This gift is Free Will and Freedom of Choice.

Listening to The Voice Within will show us how to best use our Free Will. It is a book that informs, empowers and liberates. It is a guide for transformation. It will help us become enlightened beings. It will push us to grow beyond our comfort zone. To grow, we must break loose of the tethers that constrict and stifle us. Life is a journey, not a destination. If we open our minds and hearts to reason and inspiration and listen to the promptings of The Voice Within, we can be transformed. We need to discover who we are spiritually, instead of what we are materially. Our journey of awakening starts when we let go of our fears and learn to exercise our freedom of choice. We are responsible for our lives and the decisions we make. This book is full of empowering and liberating insights any one of which has the potential to change lives. Here are some of the topics presented in this book: Who Am I? *Freedom of

Choice * Natural Enemies of Humanity * Aging * Life and Death * Raising Our Consciousness * What is Truth? * Journey to Enough * The Second Coming * Love is Power * In God's Image * Good, Bad and Evil * Good News and Sad News * Living in Truth * Self-Examination * The Path Less Travelled * The Transient and the Enduring * Life as an Experiment.
Available at Amazon

# BOOKS BY THIS AUTHOR

## A Passion For Living, A Path To Meaning And Joy

Why are we alive? What is the best way to live? Are we the result of an accident of nature? Were we created by God to be tested? Can we have real and satisfying answers to our fundamental questions? I believe so. The key is insistent desire, persistence and a demand to know. "Ask and it will be given to you; seek and you will find; knock and the door will be opened for you." Matt 7:7-8. This is what Christ promised us. These are active verbs. We must take the first steps. Our asking, seeking and knocking, however, must be loud, insistent and persistent until we experience an answer.

To live a life of meaning and joy, we must wake up to who we are. We must live for a purpose that embodies who we want to be. We can be victimized by our circumstances, or we can choose to create the life we want. This is a book about waking up, deciding on something worthwhile to live for, knowing ourselves, deciphering the meaning of life and mastering the art of living. This is a book that explains why we age and die, how to release our brakes, take it easy, do what we can and enjoy ourselves. If we apply the insights in this book, we will discover our passion for living and we will live a life of meaning and joy.

To order A Passion for Living, a path to meaning and joy,

for $19.95 plus $3.95 S/H. please email your request to: shahanshammas@gmail.com

Order 2 or more copies and the shipping is free.

For information about Shahan's workshops, seminars, and availability for speaking engagements, please email to: shahanshammas@gmail.com

www.ingramcontent.com/pod-product-compliance
Lightning Source LLC
Chambersburg PA
CBHW022114080426
42734CB00006B/123